The Complete Husband

a practical guide to biblical husbanding

Calvary Press Publishing
P.O. Box 805
Amityville, New York 11701
1-800-789-8175 / calvarypress.com

The Complete Husband

a practical guide to biblical husbanding

Lou Priolo

Calvary Press Publishing
P.O. Box 805
Amityville, NY 11701
U.S.A.
1 (800) 789-8175 / www.calvarypress.com
ISBN 1-879737-35-3

Unless otherwise noted, the Bible quotations contained in this manual are from the New American Standard Bible, © by the Lockman Foundation 1960, 1962, 1963, 1968, 1971, 1972, 1973, 1975, 1977. Used by permissionVerses marked CCNT are taken from the Christian Counselor's New Testament.
Verses marked KJV are taken from the King James Version of the Bible.
Verses marked NKJV are taken from the New King James Version of the Bible. Verses marked NIV are taken from the New International Version of the Bible.

Book & Cover Design: Anthony Rotolo

Priolo, Louis Paul, 1954-
    The Complete Husband
Recommended Dewey Decimal Classification: 234
Suggested Subject Headings:
1. Christian Living—Marriage—Husbanding
2. Religion—Men's Interest—Counseling
I. Title
Manufactured in the United States of America
8 9 10 11   06 05 04 03

Dedication

To Kimberly Diane:

Thank you sweetheart, for being the most wonderful "helper suitable" a man could ever hope to have, and for loving me in spite of my feeble attempts to be the husband you deserve:

"Like a lily among the thorns, so is my darling among the maidens" (Song 2:2).

Table of Contents

Acknowledgments

I would like to express my heartfelt gratitude to certain individuals whose assistance in various ways has made this publication possible.

To Jay Adams, Jay Younts, John McConahy, George Scipione, Bob Carroll and Milton Hodges for their counsel and assistance with content. To David & Linda Petro for their encouragement and generosity. To Patricia Kirkus and Ingrid Davis who assisted with typing. To my proofreaders Jack Stillman and "Fern". To Michael Rotolo who thought up the book's title. And to Kim Priolo who spent countless hours driving the family car here, there and yon so that her not-so-complete husband could spend his time working on *The Complete Husband* manuscript.

Introduction

The book you're holding in your hands is probably going to hit you right between the eyes! It may disturb you greatly. It will, no doubt, convict you of things you had no idea were wrong in your life. It may even make you angry —so angry that you may feel like throwing it against the wall or tearing it to shreds. Reading it, you might be tempted to say, "This is impossible! *Nobody* can consistently do the things written in this book!"

Let me be the first to sympathize with those sentiments. It *is* impossible for any man to consistently do what the Bible says without the assistance of the Holy Spirit's enabling power. So, if you're not a Christian (that is, if you've not put your trust in the Lord Jesus Christ alone for your eternal salvation), you'll not be able to apply the contents of this book. I say that because if you've not turned from your sin and trusted in Jesus Christ as your Lord and Savior, you don't have the Holy Spirit, whom God gives to those who, by His enabling grace, repent of their sins and believe in the Lord Jesus Christ (If this sounds like you, I suggest that you immediately go to the back of the book and read Appendix A: "How Can I be Saved?").

Chances are, if you're not a Christian, you'll not understand much of what's written in this book because it's based on the Bible. You may even find yourself scoffing at the very *idea* of some of what is written. The Bible actually explains why this is: *"But a natural man [a non-Christian] does not accept the things of the Spirit of God; for they are foolishness to him, and he cannot under-*

stand them, because they are spiritually appraised" (1 Cor. 2:14).

If, however, you *are* a Christian and believe that the Bible is the only complete and authoritative textbook which was written to provide both the answers to man's behavioral problems and the means for man's behavioral changes, then you'll probably not have difficulty understanding the things which are written in this book. You may resist the conviction that will come as you read what you know is biblical truth, but you'll at least *understand* what you're reading. Where you'll probably struggle most, however, is with the consistent application of the material contained in these pages. You'll have to change some of the ways you think and act, and develop new patterns of thinking and behavior in order to become the kind of husband the Bible says you should be.

God gives responsibilities to a Christian husband that are so great that they're impossible to accomplish apart from His grace. I believe the material in this volume is biblically accurate, and I, for one, desire to be the husband God wants me to be. Yet, in the process of writing this book, I have been terribly convicted about the inadequacies in my own life that need to be corrected. By God's grace, I'm working on them, and plan to spend the rest of my life learning how to consistently implement all of the truths contained in this book.

As you read *The Complete Husband*, remember that God never asks His children to do anything without giving them all of the resources necessary to obey Him. If you're a Christian, He has already given you the Spirit to teach (Jn. 16:13-15) and enable you (Jn. 14:16) to be a biblical husband. He also promises to give you the wisdom to do so:

> *But if any of you lacks wisdom, let him ask of God, who gives to all men generously and without reproach, and it will be given to him* (Jas. 1:5).

Furthermore, *"It is God who is producing in you the willingness and the ability to do the things that please Him"* (Phil. 2:13 CCNT).

Since one of the things that "pleases Him" is for you to be the kind of husband who will picture Christ's love for His church (Eph. 5:25-33), you can be confident that He will produce in you both the willingness and the ability to do the seemingly impossible: to love your wife as Christ loves the church.

So, don't get discouraged as you read. Don't expect to be able to change every area of your life at once. Little by little, God will give you the grace to be conformed to the image of Christ.

What I have attempted to do in this volume is to consider all of the New Testament commands that are addressed specifically to the husband. To my knowledge, there is not a work in print that has put them all in one volume.

Finally, let me point out that this is not a book you *read*; rather, it's the kind of book that you *study*. It's not a pop-psychology, self-help book based on the latest psychological fads. Rather, it's a reference book of practical theology that is designed to be used again and again; it's a workbook designed to train Christian husbands how to implement specific biblical commands. May God bless and enable you as you study how to become a more mature and *complete* husband.

> *And we proclaim Him, admonishing every man and teaching every man with all wisdom, that we may present every man complete in Christ* (Col.1:28).

Chapter 1

I Wish She Came with an Owner's Manual

Your car came with one. So did your television, your stereo, your camera and your computer. It's too bad your *wife* didn't come with an owner's manual as well.[1] Imagine how easy it would be to live with her if she came with a set of instructions—a book in which you could find everything you needed to know in order to keep her healthy, happy and humming at optimum capacity!

If you had a manual of this kind, it would provide you with current information about women in general. It would also furnish you with such valuable data as specific product information (information about your woman in particular), proper maintenance instructions, directions on how to read her various emotional meters and gauges, cleansing instructions, various warnings and hazards, and even a comprehensive section on "How to Trouble-Shoot When Difficulties Arise." But alas, your wife is a woman, and a woman simply doesn't come with an owner's manual—or does she?

Allow me to let you in on a little-known secret: Your wife *does* come with an owner's manual. The reason you've never seen it is because it's tucked away in her heart. Deep down in her heart is all the personal information you need to understand and nurture your wife according to the Bible.[2] There's just one catch: *You're* the one who's supposed to get it out of her. That's right, it's *your job* to get that valuable information out of her heart and, if necessary, transpose it onto a hard copy. ~~A plan (or~~

Typo

~~necessary, transpose it onto a hard copy.~~ "*A plan* (or "counsel"–KJV) *in the heart of a man is [like] deep water, but a man of understanding draws it out*" (Prov. 20:5). The responsibility for understanding your wife is given by God to you in First Peter, chapter three.

"First Peter, Chapter Three—I love that chapter! Isn't that the chapter that tells women to keep quiet?"

Well, yes, but I'm not referring to those verses (vv. 1 & 2). I want to talk to you about verse seven: "*You husbands likewise, live with [your wives] in an understanding way, as with a weaker vessel, since she is a woman; and grant her honor as a fellow heir of the grace of life, so that your prayers may not be hindered*" (1 Pet. 3:7). The Bible places the burden of understanding on you as the husband. You're the one who must take the initiative to draw out of your wife the information necessary to develop and maintain the one-flesh intimacy God intends you to have with her. Elisabeth Elliot, in her book *The Mark of a Man*, explains this concept of the man as the initiator:

> The important thing for you, as a man to remember... is that a woman cannot properly be the responder unless the man is properly the initiator. He must take the lead in order that she may follow, as in a dance. The willingness of each to perform the 'steps' that have been choreo-graphed gives the other freedom.[3]

"All right! Fine! You've convinced me! So, it's my job to understand her. But how do I get this information, this owner's manual, out of her heart?"

Well, to begin with, you'll need to understand both the *biblical view of marriage* and the *importance of communication in marriage.*

A Covenant of Companionship

Many believe that the propagation of the human race is the purpose of marriage. But marriage was designed by God to deal with the issue of *loneliness*:

> *Then the Lord God said, "It is not good for the man to be alone; I will make him a helper suitable for him"* (Gen. 2:18).

In his book, *Marriage Divorce and Remarriage in the Bible*, Jay Adams develops this concept:

> God made most of us so that we would be lonely without an intimate companion with whom to live. God provided Eve not only (or even primarily) as Adam's helper (though help is also one dimension of companionship), but as his companion. He too, as all other husbands since (we shall see), is to provide companionship for her. In the Bible, marriage is described in terms of *companionship*. In Proverbs 2:17, for example, we're told that *"the strange woman...forsakes the companion of her youth and forgets the covenant of her God."* The word translated "companion" in this verse has in it the idea of "one that is tamed" (it's used in speaking of tame animals), or "one that has a close, intimate relationship with another." It's obviously hard to establish a close relationship with a wild animal, but not nearly so with a domesticated (or "tame") animal. The core meaning has to do with a close, intimate relationship, and that is exactly what marriage companionship is—the close, intimate relationship of a husband and wife to one another. The concept of "marriage as companionship" also appears in Malachi 2:14, where a different, but very complementary, term is used: *"The Lord has been witness between you and the wife of your youth to whom you have been faithless, although she is your companion and your wife by covenant."* Now, the word here translated "companion" has as its kernel the idea of *union* or *association*. A companion, therefore, is that person with whom one enters into a close union or relationship. In putting the two terms together, we come to a full sense of the idea of companionship: A companion is one with whom you are intimately united in thoughts, goals, plans, efforts, and in the case of marriage—bodies. [4]

These two passages taken together make it clear, that for both husband and wife, *companionship* is the ideal. In Proverbs, the husband is called the companion (showing that he too, provides companionship for his wife); in Malachi, the wife is designated this way. For both, then, entrance into marriage should mean the desire to meet each other's need for companionship. Love in marriage focuses upon giving one's spouse the companionship he/she needs to eliminate loneliness.

In order to establish, maintain and mature this companionship, something of great significance is required, which we will now consider.

Revelation Is a Prerequisite to a Relationship

Have you ever seriously considered, that were it not for the Bible, you wouldn't be able to have a personal relationship with God through Jesus Christ? Think about it: If it weren't for God's written *revelation* of Himself to man, you simply wouldn't be able to *know enough* to become a Christian. To the extent that He revealed Himself to you through the Bible (and you understood that revelation), you could have an intimate relationship with Him; to the extent that He did not reveal Himself to you through the Bible (or to the extent that you did not understand that revelation), you would not be able to have a personal relationship with Him. *Revelation*, therefore, is a prerequisite for having a *relationship*. This is true not only of your relationship with God, but with *people* also.

To the extent that two people reveal themselves to each other, to that same degree they'll be able to have an intimate relationship with one another; to the extent that two people do *not* reveal themselves to each other, to that same degree they will *not* be able to have an intimate relationship with one another. Now, since marriage is the most intimate of interpersonal relationships, it stands to reason that a husband and wife, if they're to experience the "one flesh" intimacy intended by God, ought to reveal themselves more to each other than to anyone else. On every level (the physical, intellectual, emotional, etc.) they should be "naked and unashamed" (Gen. 2:25). Sadly, too often this is not the case. Indeed, because of sin, husbands and wives are ashamed and afraid to reveal themselves to one another. This lack of openness and honesty (this lack of revelation) keeps most couples (yes, even most *Christian* couples) from experiencing the security, refreshment and bliss that God intended for them within the oasis of marriage.

How about *you*? To what extent do *you* reveal yourself to your wife? Are you ashamed and afraid to do so? Do selfishness, pride, laziness or ignorance keep you from disclosing that information to your wife?

To what extent does your wife reveal herself to you? Is she ashamed or afraid to do so? What would you say prevents *her* from disclosing that information to you?

Hindrances to Revelation

1. Fear
Perhaps the greatest hindrance to revelation is *fear*.

> Then the eyes of both of them were opened, and they knew that they were naked; and they sewed fig leaves together and made themselves loin coverings. They heard the sound of the Lord God walking in the garden in the cool of the day, and the man and his wife hid themselves from the presence of the Lord God among the trees of the garden. Then the Lord God called to the man, and said to him, 'Where are you?' And he said, "I heard the sound of You in the garden, and I was afraid because I was naked; so I hid myself" (Gen. 3:7-10).

Adam and Eve were stricken with fear and hid themselves from God when they realized their own nakedness. So also, husbands and wives are often stricken with fear and hide their true selves from each other when they realize the sinfulness of their own hearts. Christian couples who are one flesh with each other, and who are committed to each other's mutual sanctification, ought not fear such embarrassment and rejection. Indeed, they should have realized long ago, that in the marriage of two sinners, both parties sin. Rather than being surprised when sin occurs, they ought to presuppose that it's inevitable (1 Jn. 2:1). Rather than concealing sin from one another, they ought to feel free to reveal to each other their struggles with indwelling sin in the hope of finding assistance to overcome it. The husband, as the one who is to *wash* (sanctify) his wife with the water of God's Word (Eph. 5:26), and the wife, as her husband's *helper*, are to participate actively in the sanctification process of one another.

2. Selfishness

There's a very real corollary in the Bible between sinful fear and *selfishness*. People who are selfish tend to be fearful. People who are fearful are necessarily selfish. Perhaps the best way to demonstrate this is by studying the antitheses of both sins. According to the Scriptures, the opposite of (and antidote for) sinful fear is *love*: *"There is no fear in love; but perfect love casts out fear, because fear involves punishment, and the one who fears is not perfected in love"* (I Jn. 4:18).

But, love is also the opposite of (and antidote for) the sin of selfishness. According to 1 Corinthians 13:5 love *"does not seek its own."* You may try looking at this as an equation:

$$\frac{\text{Fear}}{\text{Love}} \quad \text{is the opposite of} \quad \frac{\text{Love}}{\text{Selfishness}}$$

Now watch what happens when you factor out love from both sides of the equation.

$$\frac{\text{Fear}}{\text{\cancel{Love}}} \quad \text{is the opposite of} \quad \frac{\text{\cancel{Love}}}{\text{Selfishness}} \quad = \quad \frac{\text{Fear}}{\text{Selfishness}}$$

Yet another way to demonstrate the same relationship between fear and selfishness is by *definition*. Consider these definitions:

Love	is being more concerned with what I can *give* than with what I can *get*.
Selfishness	is being more concerned with what I can *get* than with what I can *give*.
Fear	is being more concerned with what I *might lose* than with what I can *give*.

When you allow the fear of your wife's rejection to keep you from loving her by not revealing to her what is biblically necessary for her to know about you, you're being *selfish*. You are, at that moment, more concerned about how such a revelation may hurt you than you are concerned about how it may help your wife. When you fail to love your wife (your closest neighbor) in this way, you simultaneously fail to love God, and you thus break the first and second greatest commandments (to love God and your neighbor—cf. Matt. 22:35-40).

3. Pride

The sin of *pride* carries with it God's swiftest and most severe judgment. It blinds you to other sins in your life and hinders you from repenting of them. Pride is the "Acquired Immune Deficiency Syndrome" (AIDS) of the soul. When a person dies as a result of acquiring AIDS, he does not really die of AIDS. Rather, he dies of an AIDS—complicated illness (pneumonia, tuberculosis, meningitis, etc.). Not unlike a cataract, the AIDS virus somehow blinds the eyes of its victim's bodily defense system. This prevents his auto immune system from seeing and consequently destroying those deadly viruses and bacteria that ultimately kill him.

Like AIDS, pride blinds you not only to itself, but to every other sin tucked away in the recesses of your heart and life. It causes you to *hate* correction and reproof. It *hides* your sin from you, it *justifies* your sin, it *excuses* your sin, and it *keeps you* from *repenting* of your sin. It *deceives* you into thinking that you're spiritually well when, in fact, you have a deadly cancer and are in desperate need of the Great Physician's balm.

Listen to Richard Baxter, the prolific Puritan writer, describe (in my updated English) the pathology of this horrible plague of the soul:

> Pride is a deep rooted and a self-preserving sin; and there-fore is harder to be killed and rooted up than other sins. It hinders the discovery of itself...It will not allow the sin-ner to see his pride when he is reproved; neither will it allow him to confess it if he sees it; nor...to loathe himself and forsake it...Even when he recognizes all of the evi-dences of pride in others, he will not see it in himself. When he feels himself despising reproof, and knows that this is a sign of pride in others, yet he will not know it in himself. If you would go about to cure him of this or any other fault, you shall feel that you are handling a wasp or an adder; yet when he is spitting the venom of pride against the reprover, he does not perceive that he is proud; this venom is a part of his nature and therefore is not felt as harmful or poisonous...[5]

Before the fall, Adam and Eve were both "naked" and "un-ashamed" (Gen. 2:25). These terms do not refer only to the fact that they weren't wearing any clothing. It primarily speaks of the total openness, honesty and frankness they enjoyed before their pride caused them to cover their sin. In the final analysis, what keeps a husband and wife from enjoying this "one flesh" intimacy that Adam and Eve knew in the Garden of Eden is *pride*. It's your pride that resists revealing those things to your wife about which you're ashamed. Because she's your wife, she has a biblical need to *know* certain things about your life that affect your relation-ship with her. Because she's your helper, she has a biblical need to know about certain things in your life that affect your relationship with God (remember: If God wants your believing wife to help you with anything, it's to help you to be a better Christian!). When you proudly resist revealing these things to her, you sin against God, against your wife, and against your marriage.

4. Laziness

If you're going to take God's commands to you as a husband seriously, you'll need to invest a considerable amount of time, effort and thought in studying and implementing the specific Scripture passages which I have tried to delineate in this book. It's likely that you'll have to change the way you think, act, and speak and also prioritize your other responsibilities. You may have to change from being a feelings-oriented[6] person (i.e., one who does what he feels like doing and not what he doesn't feel like doing), to an obedience-oriented person (i.e., one who does what's biblically required whether he feels like doing it or not). These changes will be difficult at first, but remember, there's something harder than changing—not changing: Proverbs 13:15 says, *"The way of the unfaithful is hard"* (NKJV). So, you have a choice: hard work now with the hope of God's blessing in the future, or an "easy" way now with the assurance of a hard road to travel under God's discipline in the future.

5. Ignorance

Have you ever stopped to consider that man was dependent upon God for counsel even *before* he fell into sin? Adam needed God's wisdom even in the Garden of Eden when he was still in his unfallen state. How much more do you need His wisdom as you attempt to love your wife and live with her in an understanding way!

Now, if you still believe that understanding your wife is an impossibility, it may be because you are ignorant not only of the Scriptures, but the power of God also. Jesus once addressed this kind of ignorance in another context:

> *Is this not the reason you are mistaken, that you do not understand the Scriptures, or the power of God?* (Mk. 12:24).

First, you may not realize that the Scriptures direct you to *understand* your wife. 1 Peter 3:7 is not a hint, a recommendation or a suggestion. It's a *command*. In other words, you *must learn* how to understand your wife!

Second, you may not understand the power of God. Whenever you see a biblical command which seems almost impossible to obey, you should remember that God never asks a Christian to obey Him without providing *three powerful resources.*

• God promises to give you the *wisdom* to obey Him:

> *But if any of you lacks wisdom, let him ask of God, who gives to all men generously and without reproach, and it will be given to him* (Jas.1:5).

If you don't know how to obey, ask God to teach you. This promise is first because it's usually necessary to know *how* to obey God before you are *able* to do so.

• God promises to give you the *ability* to change:

> *It is God who is at work in you, both to will and to work for [His] good pleasure* (Phil. 2:13).

As you step out in faith to *obey* what God has directed you to do in His Word, He provides the enabling power necessary *to do* even that which once may have seemed impossible. James said that the doer of the Word would be *"blessed in the process of doing"* (Jas. 1:25).

• God promises to give you the *desire* to change:

It is God who is at work in you, both to will and to work for [His] good pleasure (Phil.2:13).

It's after you've *obeyed* that directive (which you've *learned* how to do) that you will likely experience the *desire* to walk in obedience to Scripture.

All three of these promises are made only to Christians, who, in dependence upon God's Spirit and in conjunction with His Word, receive and implement them. As you continue reading this book, you'll learn *how* you can better understand your wife and how you can better fulfill your biblical responsibilities to her.

"Can I Keep a Hard Copy of the Owner's Manual?"

Yes, but only with your wife's approval.[7]

At the end of chapters two through thirteen, record on a separate piece of paper what you're learning about your wife. These pages will help you apply the biblical principles discussed in each chapter. Of course, you'll need input from your wife in order to fill in most of them. The pages should be photocopied before completion, whereupon they may be placed in a loose-leaf notebook for future perusal and revision. This "First Peter 3:7" notebook will become the "hard copy" of your wife's owner's manual.

Whether you choose to make a hard copy of the owner's manual or not, you'll benefit greatly by doing the exercises at the end of each chapter.

Notes

[1] It's important to recognize that the concept of bodily "ownership" is complementary and reciprocal in the Scriptures: *"The wife's body does not belong to her alone but also to her husband. In the same way, the husband's body does not belong to him alone but also to his wife"* (1 Cor. 7:4 NIV). Contrary to what feminists and others contend, the ownership of a wife by her *husband* is complemented and reciprocated by, the *wife's* ownership of her husband.

[2] Actually, the ultimate owner's manual is the Bible. All of the essential information that you and your wife need to understand and interpret life is found in its pages (cf. Psa. 19:7; 2 Pet. 1:3; 2 Tim. 3:16-17).

[3] Elisabeth Elliott, *The Mark of a Man* (Grand Rapids: Fleming H. Revell, 1991), p. 55. Used by permission.

[4] Jay E. Adams, *Marriage Divorce and Remarriage in the Bible* (Grand Rapids: Zondervan, 1980), pp. 11-12. Used by permission.

[5] Richard Baxter, *The Christian Directory* (Ligonier: Soli Dio Gloria, 1990 reprint), p. 207.

[6] Perhaps the greatest enemy of an undisciplined (or lazy) person is *his feelings.*

[7] Your wife may not be comfortable with the idea of your keeping a journal of what you're learning about her—especially if you've given her reason not to trust you in the past. If this is the case, simply do the best you can to remember and apply what you're learning about her as you read this book.

Chapter 2

Back to School for the Rest of My Life!

"Exactly what is it that I'm supposed to learn about my wife that I don't already know?"

The answer to that question is two-fold. *First*, you must learn a few things about women in general. *Second*, you must learn many things about your woman in particular.

You must learn about your wife's needs, her wants, her interests, her goals, her dreams, her joys, her sorrows, her fears, her problems, her thought processes, her desires (motivations), her feelings, her spiritual gifts and her temptations to sin.

To live with your wife in an "understanding" way ("according to knowledge"—KJV) means that you must become a *lifetime student* of your wife. You'll have to study and research your wife much the same way a salesman might study a prospective customer—except to a much greater and more intimate degree. You'll have to learn how to ask specific questions that will get you the precise information for which you're looking. You'll have to learn to be attentive to her (even during those times when she's seated next to you as you're driving down the road and you'd rather be solving some "more important" problem). You should learn to perceive what it is that pleases her if she happens not to mention it specifically—a service that your wife, by nature, probably provides quite adeptly for you. You should also study the various tones of her voice as well as her particular non-verbal forms of communication so you know when it's time to ask the appropriate "understanding" and "fine-tuning" kind of questions.

"But why," you may ask, "do I have to do this for my entire lifetime? How much about my wife could there possibly be to learn anyway? Once I learn what I need to learn, can't I stop studying her and go on to studying other things (like golf, or hunting, or fishing)?"

Yes and no. You probably will reach a point where you'll not have to invest quite as much time, effort and thought in studying your wife. I say this because the process of studying will become easier and you'll become increasingly more familiar with your subject as time goes by. However, because of the little thing commonly known as "a woman's prerogative" you'll never be able to throw the books away for good.

A Woman's Prerogative

Men and women regularly change their minds on all kinds of issues—from the choice of their daily clothing to their theological views. When my wife Kim and I were on a trip in our first year of marriage, I stopped to fill the car with gasoline at a local convenience store. She asked me if I would please get her something to drink. I remembered she had told me several times previously that her favorite soft drink was Diet Pepsi™. As I opened the glass door to the refrigerator, I spied a Tab™ and remembered her telling me that she hated Tab™. "I've got to find a Diet Pepsi™," I thought to myself. "She hates Tab™." After locating the Diet Pepsi™ and paying for it along with the gas, I confidently walked up to her side of the car with "her favorite soft drink" in my hand, expecting her to be so pleased that I had remembered.

"Diet Pepsi™," she said, with disappointment in her voice. "I really wanted a Tab™".

"But you told me that you *absolutely hated* Tab™," I said with profound incredulity!

"I know, but today I want a Tab™ and I think I'm starting to prefer Tab™ to Diet Pepsi™."

You see, it's because your wife has the prerogative (if not the penchant) to change her mind that you must, to some extent, *continue to study her.* It's much like a software upgrade. I'm typing the manuscript for this book on my laptop computer, using the most popular word processing software. There have been, to date, two additional upgrades for this program. In a few years, the programmers will update the program again. If, at that time, someone were to secretly install the latest version in my computer, it would cause all kinds of difficulty and confusion until I read the newly updated owner's manual.

Understanding Women in General

The first thing you must realize is, that there are some *significant* differences between men and women. Biologically, for example, every cell in your body differs slightly from the cells in your female counterpart. Your cells contain a set of 'x' and 'y' chromosomes, while your wife's cells possess a pair of 'xx' chromosomes. It's the distinct combination of these chromosomes which genetically determines the other "feminine" and "masculine" physiological differences between the sexes. Here are a few more examples of the biological differences between men and women.

Women have a subcutaneous (below the skin) layer of fat which we don't have. As a woman goes through puberty, she experiences a thickening of this fatty tissue, which produces a more rounded body shape as well as skin that feels softer to the touch than that of a man. No doubt God designed this feminine feature of your wife to work in conjunction with your sight—oriented sexual response (which is different from a woman's touch-oriented sexual response).

The posterior end of the corpus collosum, an elongated fibrous part of the brain which connects its two hemispheres (and which presently is thought to serve as the communication link between them), is noticeably smaller in men than in women.

Women have smaller lungs than we do. Their stomach, kidney, liver and appendix, however, are proportionately larger than ours. They have a faster heart rate, a smaller percentage of water in their bodies, less red cells in their blood, and lower blood pressure than we do. From head to toe, a woman's muscles and skeletal structure differs noticeably from ours in a variety of ways.

> Women are generally smaller than men...Men are likely to be 40 percent muscle and 15 percent fat; women tend to be 23 percent muscle and 25 percent fat. Men's arms are longer and their shoulders wider...Their upper body is two to three times more powerful than women's pound for pound, which gives men an enormous advantage in any activity or sport that requires power, muscle strength (and...visual-spatial coordination).[1]

These inherent physiological differences between men and women demonstrate how the Creator and Sustainer of the universe designed a man and a woman to complement (rather than compete with) one another. However, the gender differences between you and your wife go well beyond anatomy.

Another, perhaps even more important, area of understanding with which you must acquaint yourself is the *biblical roles and responsibilities given by God to the woman*. As you study these specific functions of the Christian woman, you will gain new insight and understanding into the feminine nature of your woman in particular. Understanding the extent to which God has given different duties to your wife than He has to you will help you appreciate the nuances of difference between masculinity and femininity.

Woman's Role / Responsibility:	Scripture Reference:
To be a suitable helper	Gen. 2:18—Then the Lord God said, "It is not good for the man to be alone; I will make him a helper suitable for him."
To be submissive to her husband	Eph. 5:22—Wives, [be subject] to your own husbands, as to the Lord.
To glorify her husband	1 Cor. 11:7-9—For a man ought not to have his head covered, since he is the image and glory of

God; but the woman is the glory of man. For man does not originate from woman, but woman from man; for indeed man was not created for the woman's sake, but woman for the man's sake.

To reverence her husband

Eph. 5:33—Nevertheless, let each individual among you also love his own wife even as himself; and [let] the wife [see to it] that she respect her husband.

To adorn herself with a meek and quiet spirit

1 Pet. 3:3-4—And let not your adornment be [merely] external—braiding the hair, and wearing gold jewelry, or putting on dresses; but [let it be] the hidden person of the heart, with the imperishable quality of a gentle and quiet spirit, which is precious in the sight of God.

To be pure and respectful in her conduct

1 Pet. 3:2—...as they observe your chaste and respectful behavior.

To be wise and kind in word (and heart)

Prov. 31:26—She opens her mouth in wisdom, And the teaching of kindness is on her tongue.

An older woman is:
  To be reverent in behavior
  To not be enslaved to wine
  To not be a malicious gossip
  To teach what is good
  To teach younger women
A younger woman is:
  To be loving to her husband and children
  To be discreet
  To be pure
  To be a keeper of the home
  To be kind
  To be subject to her husband

Tt. 2:3-4—Older women likewise are to be reverent in their behavior, not malicious gossips, nor enslaved to much wine, teaching what is good, that they may encourage the young women to...

Tt. 2:5—Older women are to encourage the younger women] to love their husbands, to love their children, to be sensible, [to be] pure, workers at home, kind, being subject to their own husbands, that the word of God may not be dishonored.

Characterological Make-up	Scripture Reference
She was made out of man	1 Cor. 11:8—For man does not originate from woman, but woman from man.
She was made for man	1 Cor. 11:9—For indeed man was not created for the woman's sake, but woman for the man's sake.
She was made after man	1 Tim. 2:13—For it was Adam who was first created, [and] then Eve.
She has a penchant to control her husband[2]	Gen. 3:16—To the woman He said, "I will greatly multiply your pain in childbirth, In pain you shall bring forth children; Yet your desire shall be for your husband, And he shall rule over you."
She is more easily deceived	1 Tim. 2:14—And [it was] not Adam [who] was deceived, but the woman being quite deceived, fell into transgression.
She is to view herself as a bodily member and her husband as her head[3]	Eph. 5:23—For the husband is the head of the wife, as Christ also is the head of the church, He Himself [being] the Savior of the body.

Understanding Your Woman in Particular

Not all women are alike. While your wife, no doubt, has certain feminine characteristics which are consistent with others of her sex, she also has many more distinctive characteristics which make her a unique individual. As I've already explained, you must learn about her needs, her wants, her interests, her goals, her dreams, her joys, her sorrows, her fears, her problems, her thought processes, her desires (motivations), her feelings, her spiritual gifts and her temptations to sin. Your job is to understand those distinctive and idiosyncratic qualities that form her personality and to live with her accordingly. Those "personality flaws" which are inconsistent with the character of Christ, you'll need to patiently and lovingly cleanse by washing her "with the water of the Word" (Eph. 5:26). Those characteristics irksome to you, but not inconsistent with Scripture, you may have to learn to put up with (showing forbearance to her in love, according to Eph. 4:2). Those Christ-like character qualities which she possesses you'll need to commend (Prov. 31:28-29).

"OK, I'm convinced. I've not been living with my wife according to knowledge. I've got to start doing so but this is a big task, and I don't know where to begin."

Where Do I Begin?

Perhaps the best starting point is to learn how to *ask the right questions.* It's been said that "questions are to communication as food is to eating." You need one in order to effectively have the other. The ability to ask the appropriate questions is a skill at which you must become adept if you're going to "draw out" of your wife the information you need in order to live with her in an understanding way and experience the "one flesh" intimacy that God intended for your marriage. Remember: *Revelation is a prerequisite for any relationship.* The more you reveal yourself to your wife, and the more you can encourage your wife to reveal herself to you (by asking the right questions), the greater will be the intimacy you'll achieve. Here are a few basic questions with which you may begin interviewing your wife.

Suggested Questions to Build Intimacy

1. If you could change three things about me that would make me more Christ-like, what would you change? This one question will likely generate hours of conversation. By focusing first on your own weaknesses and taking the beam out of your own eye (cf. Matt. 7:1-5), you'll not only demonstrate humility, but also make it easier for your wife to reveal herself to you later on. Your wife is probably quite aware of those character flaws in you that are in need of change. She may even be more aware of them than you are. Your sin will need to be discussed in answering this question. Personality traits (character flaws) you possess that are inconsistent with the character of Christ must be corrected by God's grace. That's non-negotiable and non-optional. If she can present evidence to convict you of your sin (cf. 2 Tim. 3:16-17), you ought to acknowledge your transgression to her, and with God's help (as well as your wife's), begin to replace the sinful pattern with its biblical alternative.[4]

2. Do I have any other annoying mannerisms or irritating idiosyncrasies that you would like to see me change? In addition to pointing out those character deficiencies that the Bible says you must change, your wife also may have some suggestions for you to consider concerning other issues. There are probably certain other annoying personal mannerisms and habits you've developed, that, although not necessarily sinful, tend to irritate her. These would include such things as wearing certain items of clothing, personal grooming habits, and/or a lack of certain social graces. While your wife should forbear with you, because of your desire to please her (1 Cor. 7:33), you ought to consider working on these habits as well. Your willingness to discuss these matters with her will demonstrate your love for her and likely give her hope.

3. How does it make you feel when I…(name something that you know displeases her)? Once you've discovered exactly what it is that she wants you to change, you can begin encouraging her to reveal herself to you. I suggest you begin by asking about her *feelings*. We men tend not to place as much emphasis on the emotions that God has given us as do our wives. Of course, as Christians, we ought not to make decisions primarily based on our feelings, but rather on the biblical principles that apply to each situation. To do otherwise is dangerous because it leads to a feelings-oriented lifestyle rather than an obedience-oriented lifestyle. Our feelings can lead us astray and tempt us to respond unbiblically to the problems and pressures of life.

"Well, I could've told you that. Women are just more emotional than men and are misled by their emotions, so why bother talking about them? By asking her how *she feels*, won't I be encouraging her to emote rather than think logically?"

You will if you simply listen to her feelings without also helping her relate those feelings to her thoughts, her actions and the Bible. The point here is that you must not ignore the place of your wife's feelings, since they've been given to her by God.

Have you ever considered the fact that emotionally-caused pain can be a *good* thing?[5] Just like physical pain can be a good thing because it lets you know when something is wrong with your body, emotionally-caused pain can be a good thing because it lets you know when there's something wrong with your thinking. Anxiety, fear, anger, loneliness, depression and despair all may indicate that there's a bigger problem in one's life that needs to be addressed. This kind of pain is often a symptom for a deeper problem. That's why drug therapy is largely ineffective for the long-term treatment of so-called "emotional disorders"—it treats only the *symptoms* rather than what's often the *cause* of the problem: sinful thoughts and actions.

It's 3:30 in the morning and you're sound asleep. The smoke detector in your bedroom startles you from the depths of slumber as it pierces your tranquillity with 103 decibels of pulsating cacophony. Your heart is pounding; you're breathing rapidly as the adrenaline in your body activates almost every nerve in your being. "Now what do I do," you think to yourself as you scramble for some solution to the alarm. "I've got it," you say to yourself, "I'll pull the pillow around my head, stick my fingers in my ears, and try to get back to sleep!" A few seconds go by. You realize that your solution isn't going to work. You think again as the smoke detector provokes you to more and more anger. Finally, in desperation you reach under the bed, quickly grasp the largest shoe you can find, make a beeline for the smoke detector and smash the alarm to smithereens. "Finally, I can get back to sleep," you say to yourself as you drop the shoe, head back to your bed and totally forget about the fire in the hall that triggered the smoke detector in the first place.

To tranquilize these so-called "emotional pains" with psychotropic medications (or electro-shock therapy, or binge eating or shopping) without trying to discover what caused the pain is as foolish as smashing the smoke detector without trying to put out the fire. Usually, when you locate and extinguish the fire in your life (i.e., wrong thinking and behavior) the cacophony of discomforting emotions will eventually cease. As you encourage your wife to discuss her feelings with you in this way (with the aim of helping her identify and extinguish any potential fires in her life), you'll not only be "living with her in an understanding way," but will also be preparing the way to "wash her with the water of the Word" (see Chapter Nine). It may be helpful at this point to express back to her in your own words the feelings she's relating to you. It may take more than one attempt before you can express it in such a way as to convince her that you truly understand.

"Now let me see if I have this right, when I don't pay attention to you in public you feel ABCDWXYZ."

"No," she says, "When you don't pay attention to me in public

I feel ABCDEFG."

"OH! ABCDEFG! That's how you feel when I don't pay attention to you in public?"

"Exactly!"

Another reason why it's so important for you to understand her feelings is because her pain may be, in part, the result of your sin. If you understand the extent to which your rudeness has hurt her, it may motivate you to stop being so rude to her in the future. Of course, in order for your repentance to be genuine, you must also understand that your sin has offended God and not just your wife (cf. Ps. 51:4).

4. What goes through your mind when I...(name something that you know displeases her)? Having first asked her to reveal her emotions to you, you're now ready to inquire about her *thoughts*. Encourage her to be totally candid and frank with you. Ask her to give you a verbatim account of her thoughts. You should again be looking to see the impact that your behavior has had on your wife. As her spiritual leader, you ought to be concerned about any sinful thought patterns she reveals to you in this process. First, however, you must be willing to get the beam out of your own eye—confessing and forsaking the sin in your life that she's disclosing to you.

Did you know that you have the ability to talk to yourself at the rate of over 1,300 words per minute? Think about that. In 10 seconds you can tell yourself at least *a dozen lies.* The problem with most of us is that we *listen* rather than *talk* to ourselves. That's right—rather than *"speaking the truth in our hearts"* (Ps. 15:2), and being *"transformed by the renewing of our minds"* (Rom. 12:2), and *"bringing into captivity every thought to the obedience of Christ"* (2 Cor. 10:5), we preach to ourselves at the rate of 1,300 words per minute the fibs, falsehoods and fabrications of our deceitful hearts. Rather than passively *listening* to ourselves say something like, "I can't do anything right," we should actively *exhort* ourselves in this manner: "No, I can't say 'can't' when God says I must! I *can* do all things through Him who strengthens me!" Here are a few more common examples of such unbiblical self-talk:

- "I'll probably make a fool of myself."
- "If people don't love me, I'll be miserable."
- "Making mistakes is terrible."
- "I can't control my emotions."
- "I must strive to be better than others."
- "It is wrong to show weakness."
- "I should never hurt anyone."
- "I can't do something unless I feel up to it."
- "I'll never change."
- "I'll never get the victory over that habit."
- "I'm a failure."
- "I'll never forgive him."
- "My marriage will never work out."
- "I may say something that would embarrass me."

When your wife reveals these kinds of sinful thought patterns to you, you must help her learn how to think biblically: *"whatever is true, whatever is honorable, whatever is right, whatever is pure, whatever is lovely, whatever is of good repute, if there is any excellence and if anything worthy of praise, let your mind dwell on these things"* (Phil. 4:8). At the same time, however, don't minimize her negative evaluations of herself. Explore and deal with them.

5. What do you want from me that I'm not giving you at the moment I...(name something that you know displeases her)? This question goes beyond feelings and thoughts and helps you obtain information about her *motives*. The Bible has much to say about our motives. Consider this verse in Hebrews 4:12, *"For the word of God is living and active and sharper than any two-edged sword, and piercing as far as the division of soul and spirit, of both* *joints and marrow, and able to judge the thoughts and intentions of the heart.*" The Bible is necessary to accurately diagnose not only our thoughts, but also our *motives*.

Living with your wife in "an understanding way" involves understanding those desires which generate her thoughts, words and actions. Her desires may be righteous or unrighteous. She may, for example, have a righteous desire for more intimacy with you and therefore is disappointed when you don't communicate enough with her (of course, if her disappointment turns into unrighteous anger or anxiety, it may be because she desires that good thing inordinately). On the other hand, if she is pressuring you to get a better-paying job because she wants you to buy her that new Jaguar sports coupe, most likely her desire is unrighteous.

An understanding husband is one who will make every reasonable effort to give his wife not only what she needs, but also what she lawfully desires, provided he can do so without sinning (cf. Rom. 8:32 in light of Eph. 5:25).

6. What specifically would you like to see me do to change in this area (name something that you know displeases her)? *Warning: Do not ask this question unless you're committed to making every reasonable effort to change (either by implementing her suggestions or by coming up with your own, biblically-based ones).* In most cases, your wife will have already thought through some specific changes she'd like to see you implement. In fact, it's likely that she has already made these suggestions in various ways to you in the past (though you may not have been paying attention to her at the time). If her answer to this question is general and abstract (e.g.,"You need to be more considerate of me.") rather than specific and concrete (e.g.,"Don't throw your socks on the floor and expect me to pick them up for you."), ask her to be more specific. Being "inconsiderate" is *abstract*. "Socks on the floor instead of in the hamper" is *concrete. One* requires you to guess what would please her, while the *other* gives you the exact information you are looking for. *One* misses the target, while the *other* hits the bull's-eye.

7. On a scale of one to ten, how would you rate our marriage? This question is designed to give you some idea of how well you're doing at fulfilling your responsibilities as a husband. It may also indicate how content your wife is with you. Don't be surprised if your wife rates your relationship significantly lower than you do. The reason for her lower score is probably due to the fact that she's doing a better job of meeting your needs than you are of meeting hers. God made your wife to be your suitable helper. Because she's a woman, she's probably more aware of how to help (Gen. 2:18) and please (1 Cor. 7:34) you than you are of her. After her relationship with God, you're her first priority in life (or at least you should be). She, by the same token, should be yours. However, many men, after successfully accomplishing the challenge of securing themselves a wife, have often gone on to other challenges, such as being successful in their vocations or avocations. As a Christian husband you must not do so. You must not allow *anything* short of your relationship with Christ to become more of a priority than ministering to your wife.[6]

8. What would it take to make our marriage a ten? Once again you should encourage your wife to be *as specific as possible*. Again you ought not to ask this question if you're not serious about implementing her ideas. Be sure to ask her how she believes each suggestion will benefit the marriage if it's not *extremely* apparent to you. She may have some insights that you've overlooked. It might also be helpful for her to prioritize the suggestions, from "most important" to "least important." Remember, as your helper she has vital information that you need to make your marriage a ten.

9. What is your opinion about…? It's a little question but it's loaded. Let me explain how your wife might be tempted to think if you don't regularly ask this question.

"My heart is filled with all kinds of interesting things. I have many good ideas, beliefs, convictions, plans, hopes and dreams. Who I am as a person is related to what I think in my heart. What is in my heart is who I am as a person before God. My husband doesn't seem to care about what's in my heart. I guess that means he doesn't care about me. Maybe it's because he doesn't like what he's heard me tell him from my heart. If he doesn't like what's in my heart, then he doesn't like me. If he rejects what's in my heart, then he rejects me. I feel so rejected and hurt because I realize that my husband doesn't love me."

Before you scoff at this "feminine logic," remember that it's just as possible for you to think logically to a wrong conclusion if your presuppositions are not biblical. Furthermore, if you're not interested in your wife's opinion, then according to the Bible, her conclusion is partially right: *you really don't love her*. 1 Corinthians 13 is clear: Biblical love is not *proud* (it doesn't think that it can make every decision without input from others), it's not *selfish* (it doesn't only care about how a decision will affect itself), and it *rejoices in the truth* (it actively seeks the truth and is happy when it discovers truth, even if discovered in the heart of another rather than its own).

In addition to getting her opinion in reference to your decisions, you should also learn to get her input concerning such things as judgments you make, her perceptions, insights and intuition about people you both know (especially your children), your strengths and weaknesses as a Christian, husband, father, businessman, etc., and how you may apply specific portions of Scripture to your life and family.

10. What personal goals do you have for your life? How may I help you achieve them? "The two shall become one and *I'm the one*, and don't you forget it!" That's the attitude with which many men enter marriage. Your wife has goals of her own, most of which benefit you and your children directly, some of which benefit you indirectly, if at all. Being an understanding husband (a loving servant-leader) involves following Phil. 2:3-4 (two of the most difficult verses in the entire Bible for many).

> *Do nothing from selfishness or empty conceit, but with humility of mind let each of you regard one another as more important than himself; do not [merely] look out for your own personal interests, but also for the interests of others.*

Your wife has interests that you need to "look out for." She has objectives she would like to reach that would enable her to be a more godly and satisfied Christian woman (cf. Prov. 12:14; 14:14). Such goals might include losing weight, memorizing Scripture, changing a bad habit, being a better parent, learning to paint or play golf, taking some college courses, starting a home business or reading a particular book. When you invest the time to talk to her about how she can achieve these objectives (and are willing to sacrifice some of your resources to help her do so), you are regarding your wife as more important than yourself.

A husband sometimes makes the mistake of selfishly expecting his wife not to do anything except that which relates to being his wife and the mother of his children. Yes, these are her primary God-given responsibilities. However, if she does them satisfactorily, what biblical basis do you have to keep her from involving herself in other scripturally-lawful pursuits? If her desires are in keeping with the Scriptures, and if she can pursue them without violating biblical priorities, one of the most loving and unselfish things that you can do is to help her in reaching those personal goals that have little or nothing to do with her being married to you.

11. Do you have any needs or desires that you believe I ought to be meeting or fulfilling better than I do? What are they? Do you know the difference between a *need* and a *desire*? You should. Today's Christian literature is filled with references to man's (and woman's) "needs." Be careful! There aren't nearly as many truly biblical needs as many Christian authors suppose. In fact, with rare exception, you could (and should) substitute the word "desire" for the word "need" in your reading, and you would be more theologically accurate.

"So what's the difference?"

The difference between a "need" and a "desire" is whether or not the Bible identifies it as a "need." As Jesus put it to Martha "only a few things are necessary, really only one." What's most necessary for us is to sit at the feet of Christ and to hear his Word: *"Man shall not live on bread alone, but on every word that proceeds out of the mouth of God"* (Matt. 4:4). Whatever is not identified in Scripture as a *need* (e.g., 1 Tim. 6:8, *"if we have food and covering, with these we shall be content."*) should more properly be called a *desire*. If your wife is confused as to the difference between them, you must help her distinguish between the two.

As your wife's provider (cf. Eph. 5:23), you should consider it your responsibility to see to it that her true needs are being met. Actually, it's God who is using you to provide for these needs. Of course, she must ultimately rely on God to meet them, since you can't meet all of them. You may even have to help her depend on God to do those things for her which you're not totally able to do. As her loving leader, however, you ought to make every effort to meet as many of her needs and lawful desires as you can without sinning in the process.

These eleven questions should help get you started. Remember, this is only a suggested list. Some of the questions should serve to get you started in developing your own personalized catalogue of questions to ask your wife. You'll need to add to the list until you become proficient at asking questions that produce intimacy-building communication. After you read each chapter of this book, why not take a few moments to develop your own additional questions (based on the content of that unit) and add them to your list?

Questions I Would Like to Ask Her

1. If you could change three things about me that would make me more Christ-like, what would you change?

2. Do I have any other annoying mannerisms or irritating idio-syncrasies that you would like to see me change?

3. How does it make you feel when I...(name something that you know displeases her)?

4. What goes through your mind when I...(name something that you know displeases her)?

5. What do you want from me that I'm not giving you at the moment I...(name something that you know displeases her)?

6. What specifically would you like to see me do to change in this area (name something that you know displeases her)?

7. On a scale of one to ten, how would you rate our marriage?

8. What would it take to make our marriage a ten?

9. What is your opinion about?

10. What personal goals do you have for your life? How may I help you achieve them?

11. Do you have any needs or desires that you believe I ought to be meeting or fulfilling better than I do? What are they?

Add further questions of your own...

Notes

[1]Dianne Desimone and Joe Durden Smith, *Sex and the Brain* (New York: Arbor House, 1983), p 93.

[2]c.f. Gen. 4:7: *God said to Cain, "If you do well, will not [your countenance] be lifted up? And if you do not do well, sin is crouching at the door; and its desire is for you"* (that is, 'its desire is to control you'), *"but you must master it."* The grammatical construction of the Hebrew is identical in this verse with the construction of Gen. 3:16. See Chapter 13 for a fuller explanation.

[3]The wife is to view her husband the way an arm, leg, or foot would view the head. She is to follow the leading, direction and advice of her spiritual head— her husband.

[4]Christians don't *break* bad habits—they *replace them* with the appropriate *biblical* habits. That is, they "put off the old man" and "put on the new man" (cf. Eph. 4:22-24). Rather than simply committing to not lying any more, a Christian makes it his goal to become proficient at telling the truth. "*Therefore, laying aside falsehood, speak truth, each one [of you] with his neighbor, for we are members of one another*" (Eph. 4:25).

[5]Since all pain is physical, it is probably more accurate to say "emotionally caused pain" than the common phrase "emotional pain."

[6]The outline of Ephesians 5:18-6:9 provides the biblical priorities for fulfilling responsibilities: 1. Your relationship with God (being controlled by the Spirit) 2. Your relationship with your spouse 3. Your relationship with your children and, 4. Your relationship with your employer and employees (your job).

Chapter 3

So, What's There to Talk About?

Have you ever had a rather obscure conversation with someone, only to walk away deeply moved by something he or she said? I have. Years ago the music minister at the church I was attending engaged me in a discussion (actually it was more like a lecture) about why the church needed a new public address system. I never understood why he was trying to persuade me since I had neither the authority nor the ability to help him. Nevertheless, during the course of his pitch he said something that has made a profound impact on my life.

His exact words were, "If we Christians are in any business at all, it's the *communication* business." As he spoke, I knew that he was right. When the conversation was over, I couldn't get his thesis out of my mind. The more I thought about it and studied my Bible, the more I realized how true his expression was. As I meditated on some of the many passages of Scripture supporting his statement, I was amazed to discover how many ways Christians are to effectively use communication.

Consider, for instance, the great commission: *"Go into all the world and preach the gospel to every creature"* (Mk. 16:15). "Preach" is a communication word. Or, consider Matthew 28:19: *"Go therefore and make disciples of all the nations, baptizing them in the name of the Father and the Son and the Holy Spirit, teaching them to observe all that I commanded you."* "Teaching" is a form of communication that is essential to making disciples. Then there is

Ephesians 4:15: *"but speaking the truth in love, we are to grow up in all [aspects] into Him, who is the head, [even] Christ."* When "the truth" is communicated in love, it enables the believer to grow and mature in Christ.

Solomon wrote many proverbs about communication. Perhaps his most comprehensive statement is in Proverbs 18:21: *"Death and life are in the power of the tongue..."* The potency of your words is tremendous. They are far more powerful than you probably realize. With your tongue you can kill or you can heal, you can save or you can destroy.[1] Solomon continues, (18:21b) *"...And those who love it will eat its fruit."* That is, if you make use of (love) the power of the tongue, you will see its results (eat its fruit). If you use your tongue for your own selfish purposes, you'll end up hurting people. If, on the other hand, you use your tongue to build people up, you can influence them greatly, and you'll experience tremendous satisfaction. Proverbs 18:20 states: *"With the fruit of a man's mouth his stomach will be satisfied; He will be satisfied [with] the product of his lips."*

Take my job for example: I'm a counselor. As a biblical counselor, I have the joy of regularly seeing people's lives radically transformed. People are changed in very significant ways as a result of the counseling I do. Of course, I'm not the one who changes them—God's Spirit does that. There is, however, something I do from the human perspective to facilitate these changes. What is it? I ask questions, I listen, and I talk. I *communicate*. I explain to people what the Bible has to say about their problems. I use the Scriptures to teach, to convict, to correct and to instruct in righteousness (2 Tim. 3:16), and somehow the Spirit of God uses His Word to change lives, transforming them and conforming them to the image of Christ. Teaching, convicting, correcting and instructing in righteousness all involve communication. Yes, words are powerful—especially God's words spoken by His ministers for His purposes.

Did you know that you, as a Christian, are given over forty communication commands in the New Testament epistles? Think about that. Not including the Gospels, the book of Acts, the Book of Revelation or the entire Old Testament, you are given *more than forty* communication imperatives. When I use the word "imperatives," I'm excluding all the good and bad examples of communication, all the principles and teaching on communication not directly commanded, and all the ancillary insights that might be acquired through diligent study of the Bible. Rather, I'm including only the New Testament imperative directives which require you to communicate or not communicate in specific ways. I've not been able to do it, but if they could be counted, there would be *hundreds* of Bible verses that deal with communication in some form.

It's true! If you're in any business at all, my Christian friend, you're in the communication business.

Revelation and Intimacy

Do you remember in Chapter One how we saw the relationship that exists between revelation and intimacy? Let's briefly review and expand upon it. If it weren't for the Bible (God's revelation of Himself to man), you wouldn't know enough about Him to be saved—let alone to have an intimate relationship with Him. You might know through *general revelation*[2] that God exists, but it takes *special revelation*[3] for you to know how to be saved, how to glorify Him, and how to enjoy intimate fellowship with Him. To the extent that God reveals Himself to you, you may have a relationship with Him. To the extent that you don't comprehend His revelation, your intimacy with Him will be adversely affected. *Revelation is a prerequisite to having a relationship.*

The same principle holds true in all relationships (cf. Jn. 15:15). As I mentioned earlier, to the degree that two people reveal themselves to one another, *to that same degree* they will or will not experience relational intimacy. Since marriage (becoming one flesh) is the most intimate of personal relationships, the revelation of yourself to your spouse should exceed the revelation of yourself to any other person (except the Lord, who knows you more intimately than you know yourself; cf. Psa. 139:1-6). Practically speaking, that means you should be more intimate with, and reveal more of yourself to, your spouse than your closest friend, your parents or your children.

We read in Genesis 2:24-25: *"For this cause a man shall leave his father and his mother, and shall cleave to his wife; and they shall become one flesh. And the man and his wife were both naked and were not ashamed."* Adam and Eve's "nakedness" speaks not primarily of their lack of clothing, but rather of the total openness and frankness which they enjoyed with one another before sin entered into their lives. It's our *sin* (especially the sin of pride) that keeps us from being as candid and straightforward as were Adam and Eve before the fall. It's God's intention for Christian husbands and wives to increasingly become more and more "naked and unashamed" with each other, as were our first parents in the Garden of Eden.

Creating a Comfortable Environment

While it's necessary for you to become comfortable revealing yourself to your wife, it's also important for you to create an environment in which she can be comfortable revealing herself to you. One of the best ways for you to make her comfortable is for you to demonstrate to her that you not only communicate effectively with her, but that you actually *enjoy* doing so. It's something like sex. Sexual relations in marriage are usually more enjoyable to a husband when he senses that his wife is not only *capable* of pleasing him, but when she's obviously *enjoying* the sexual experience. Your wife will probably enjoy revealing herself to you more when she senses that you enjoy the process of verbal intercourse.

"But the truth is, I don't really enjoy talking to my wife, especially at night when I'm tired after having talked all day! I usually talk for one reason—*because* I *have to.* Communication is a means to an end for me: the means of accomplishing some task. For my wife, communication seems to be a means *in and of itself*. I don't get it, and I certainly don't enjoy it!"

As someone who has to talk all day long, I can appreciate those sentiments, but you can learn to enjoy the process of communicating with your wife much like you can learn to enjoy other biblical responsibilities. The trick is to begin doing it *whether you enjoy doing it or not.*

As I began to write this segment of *The Complete Husband*, I did so in the midst of one of the most difficult trials of my life. I really didn't feel like sitting down 90 minutes ago to work on this project. What I felt like doing was putting my mind in neutral. Moreover, moments before I began, Kim and I had a conflict in which I violated some of the very biblical principles I intend to explain in this chapter and the next. I had to ask her forgiveness for these things before I began to write. But at this moment, I'm actually enjoying the opportunity to minister to you through these pages. My feelings, in other words, changed a few moments after I began writing. The more you and your wife practice biblical communication, the more you'll become proficient in communication, and the more you'll learn to enjoy those moments of intimate communication with her.

Asking questions (which we looked at in the last chapter) is not the only way to "draw out" of your wife those things that are deep inside her heart. Another option is for you to engage her in conversation concerning those things that interest her. You've probably heard it said in some form or fashion that one of the best ways to "win friends and influence people" is to talk in terms of another man's interest.[4] Consider Philippians 2:4, *"do not [merely] look out for your own personal interests, but also for the interests of others."* Your motive for obeying this verse, of course, should not be for the purpose of winning friends and influencing people, but rather for the purpose of glorifying God and ministering to others. Nevertheless, people are drawn to those who selflessly and sacrificially are willing to invest time and effort discussing topics not of interest to themselves.

I once sat next to a meteorologist at a college banquet. For two hours I picked his brain about weather forecasting. I probably asked him every question I ever had about the weather. When the evening was over, he shook my hand and said, "I can't remember the last time I enjoyed talking to someone as interesting as you." Me, interesting? We spent five percent of the time talking about me and ninety-five percent of the time talking about the weather. Yet I was perceived as interesting.

When you're willing to talk to your wife about the things that interest her (no matter how trivial or uninteresting they may be to you), you'll be demonstrating a Christ-like, sacrificial love that makes it easier for her to open up to you. Here is a suggested list of possible topics of interest to get you started.

1. Bible doctrine. How comfortable does your wife feel when asking questions about the Bible? It's your responsibility to help her find the answers to those questions she has about the Scriptures and their application to her life. Referring to this, Paul writes: *"And if they desire to learn anything, let them ask their own husbands at home"* (1 Cor. 14:35a). Even if your wife has more Bible knowledge than you do, you must be willing to help her with any questions she may have. You may even have to spend some extra time in the Bible or ask your spiritual leaders for assistance. In other words, when she asks you a question for which you have no answer, don't just say, "I don't know." Instead, tell her that you'll take the time and effort to find the answer for her.

2. Your home. Do you realize that your home is the "base of operations" for your wife's ministry? *"Older women likewise are to...encourage the young women...[to be]...workers at home...that the word of God may not be dishonored"* (Tt. 2:3-5). Think about it: From your home your wife fulfills her two most important ministries—being your helper (Gen. 2:18) and your children's mother (1 Tim. 2:15). From your home, she also extends hospitality to family and friends and prepares food and other gifts to meet the needs of others. The condition and appearance of your home is probably more important to her than you realize. Just as the environment of your workplace can positively or negatively affect your job performance and attitude, so the environment of your home can significantly influence her attitude and the effectiveness of your wife's ministry.

3. The children. The instructions in the New Testament referring to parental responsibilities are often given with reference to the father (cf. Gal. 4:2; Eph. 6:4; Col. 3:21; 1Thess. 2:11; Heb. 12:7). That's not to imply the mother isn't an integral part of the discipline process, but rather that the father, as the manager of the family, is to see to it that the instruction and discipline given the children is truly "in the Lord." Your children (their strengths, weaknesses, needs, desires, responsibilities, instruction and disciplinary options) ought to be a frequent topic of discussion between you and your wife.[5] It's one which she'll almost invariably find of interest. How much does this topic interest you?

4. Your job. The routine activities and events that occur throughout your workday may have more interest to your wife than you realize. Since she's your helper (Gen. 2:18), she may be better able to help you if she knows exactly what it is you do and precisely what you are going through each day.

"But when I come home from work, the last thing I want to talk about is all the stressful stuff that happened at work."

Although I can very much identify with such thoughts, I must remind you that she is your helper, and as such, the Lord may be wanting to use her to minister to your needs somehow. She, however, can't minister to you effectively if you won't tell her what's happening in your life. If you really are too weary to discuss your day when you first come home from work, you may want to consider saying to you wife what I've said to Kim many times, "Sweetheart, I really am not in the mood to rehash that scenario again right now, but if it's that important to you, perhaps we can talk about it after supper."

5. Her family (your in-laws). The Bible has more to say about in-law relationships than you might realize. There have been a few notable contests mentioned in the Scripture. First, there's Esau and his wives vs. Isaac and Rebekah: *"And when Esau was forty years old he married Judith the daughter of Beeri the Hittite, and Basemath the daughter of Elon the Hittite; and they brought grief to Isaac and Rebekah"* (Gen. 26:34,35). We can read next of the conflict between Jacob and Laban in Genesis Chapter 29. Then there is the fiery dispute between Samson and his father-in-law, who gave his wife to someone else (Judg. 15). And, of course, don't forget that David and Saul were in-laws, as well.

More importantly, the most foundational verse in the Bible dealing with marriage (to which all marital conflicts can be traced) is Gen. 2:24: *"For this cause a man shall leave his father and his mother, and shall cleave to his wife; and they shall become one flesh."* Marriage problems ultimately come from a failure to *leave* (in-law problems), failure to *cleave*, and failure to *become one flesh*. If you want to avoid serious trouble in your marriage, don't avoid biblical discussions about your in-laws. Also, don't forget that your wife's *siblings* are your in-laws as well.

6. Her friends. Do you care about who your wife chooses as her friends? Do you know who her friends are? Or, like many men, do you tune out when she begins talking about them? Chapters could be written about the benefits and dangers of developing friendships in the context of marriage. Here I can do little more than whet your appetite in the hope you may do more thorough scriptural study on this fascinating subject.

Your wife's friends can influence her for good or for evil. I've been a full-time biblical counselor for thirteen years. In all of my counseling experience, I can't recall ever having observed a Christian couple go through an unbiblical (i.e., sinful) divorce without the initiating party being heavily influenced by an outside "third" party.[6] Sometimes the influence is from family, sometimes it's from the workplace, but very often it's from a friend (of either the same or the opposite sex). Over and over again, the Bible speaks about the power of *influence* (i.e., 1 Kings 11:3-4; 21:25; Prov. 22:24-25; 29:12; 1 Cor. 5:6-8; 15:33; Gal. 3:1; Heb. 12:5). People can influence our thoughts, our values, our motives, our desires, our moods, our decisions, our language, and even our appearance. Do you know the extent to which your wife is being influenced by those closest to her? You'd *better* if you want to help protect her! But you may never know how she's being influenced if you're unwilling to talk to her about her friends.

Perhaps one of the most often misquoted Bible verses on the power of influence is 1 Corinthians 15:33, *"Bad company corrupts good morals."* I say "misquoted" because the first half of the verse is usually omitted from the quotation. Can you recall the first four words of this verse? They are, "Do not be deceived." *"Do not be deceived: Bad company corrupts good morals."* This little four word preface is significant because it's a warning. Paul is saying in effect, "Watch out! Don't be misled! Wrong friends can influence you to sin so subtly that if you don't have your guard up, you'll not even realize that you're being influenced." The rule of thumb I give my counselees when they're developing friendships with individuals whose character is questionable is this: If there is no evidence that you're influencing that person for good (for Christ), you ought to assume that you're being influenced for evil (by the world, the flesh and/or the Devil).

On what basis do you and your wife develop friendships with others? Is it on the basis of how they can minister *to you*, or rather, on the basis of how you can minister *to them*? While it's wonderful to have those special friends who minister to us, we should also be willing to develop friendships based on how we can minister to others (cf. Phil. 2:3-4).

Another reason for you to invest the time discussing your wife's friendships with her is so you can encourage her to minister to those friends (especially non-believers) and influence them for Christ. As your wife continues to minister to her friends, one of two responses will likely occur: Either she will be a positive influence on her friends and they will be drawn closer to Christ, or her witness will prove to be an affront to them and they will separate themselves from her, thus eliminating the danger of a negative influence (cf. Lk. 6:22-23).

I'll be addressing the matter of influence in greater detail in Chapter Eleven, but for now, let me give you a final thought to contemplate: Since you and your wife are one flesh, you should be her most intimate friend. If you're not interested or available to talk to her about the concerns in her heart, she'll most likely turn to others for counsel and advice.

7. Her ministries (inside and outside of the home). "Life is ministry." Is that your philosophy? It should be because it's biblical (Gal. 5:13; 1 Thess. 1:9). We were created to glorify God by worshipping Him and ministering to others (1 Cor. 10:31). Your ministry involves being your wife's leader, bringing up your children in the discipline and instruction of the Lord, and serving in and through your local church. The same is true for your believing wife. Her first priority, after her fellowship with the Lord through the Word of God and prayer, is to be your helper.[7] Then, she is to minister to any children with which the Lord has blessed you. Her next important area of ministry is to others in the church and outside the church. God has blessed her with various spiritual gifts and abilities which she is to use for His glory (cf. Matt. 25:14-30; Rom. 12:6-8; 1 Cor. 12:4-6; Eph. 4:7-12). Part of your job is to help her discover and effectively use those gifts in practical ways. This, of course, requires *communication*. Don't be selfish with your wife's time. If she's faithfully fulfilling all of her domestic biblical responsibilities, be careful not to hinder her from the blessings of Christian service. Remember, she'll be rewarded both in this life and in the next for service done for Christ with a pure motive (cf. Matt. 10:41,42; 1 Cor. 3:8; 4:5). Time, effort, thought and money that you invest helping her identify and implement possible ministry opportunities will compound into temporal and eternal rewards for you both.

8. Her goals for the future. Your wife, like every wife and mother, has various goals (hopes, dreams, desires and expectations) for herself, her marriage, and her children. She probably derives great joy and satisfaction not only in anticipating them, but also from enthusiastically discussing them with someone who is interested in sharing them. Her goals may be personal (to lose 20 lbs., to learn to ride a horse, or to commit a certain passage of Scripture to memory). Her goals may involve you, the children or others (to go on vacation to some romantic city in Europe; to develop a mutual interest in a particular recreational activity; to cut down the amount of time the family spends watching television and spend more time together around the Word, or to open the house more often to minister to others through hospitality). One of the ways you can please your wife (1 Cor. 7:32) and *"enjoy life with the woman whom you love all the days of your fleeting life"* (Eccl. 9:9), is to become excited with her about building and fulfilling some of those special dreams.

9. Specific ways you can be a better husband and father. When was the last time you took a personal inventory of how you're doing as a husband and a father? When was the last time you asked your wife for her evaluation of how you're doing in these areas? God requires us to regularly take inventory of our Christian walk (1 Cor. 11:27-31; 2 Cor. 13:5; Gal. 6:3-5). I'd like to suggest a project for you to try when you believe your communication skills are advanced enough to accomplish it successfully. Why not begin (after you've finished reading the entire book) by making a list of some ways you can remember where you've failed in these areas. You may want to pause right now and look at Appendix B, "Common Ways in which Husbands Sin against Their Wives." When you write your list, don't be vague and abstract, but rather, be *concrete* and *specific*. Don't simply say, "I've been inconsiderate of you." Say rather, "I've been inconsiderate of you in that I routinely leave my clothes all over the bedroom and expect you to pick up after me," or, "I've been inconsiderate of you in that when I shave every morning, I leave my whiskers in the sink where they dry and get stuck to the porcelain, and then expect you to clean up after I'm through."

Next, make an appointment with your wife, explaining to her that you'll need about 90 minutes of her undivided attention so she can help you be a better husband and father. Begin that meeting with prayer and Scripture reading. Then begin confessing your sins to your wife. When you're finished reading the list to her, ask her to forgive you (Now the fun begins!). Once you've been granted forgiveness, give the list to her and ask her to add to the list any additional ways in which you've sinned against her. Finally, ask her to prioritize the entire list numerically (both the items you've identified and the ones she's added), making one master list in order of priority. This list should provide you with hours of stimulating conversation!

10. Things you do which bother her. If you're ever at a loss for a topic that will pique your wife's interest, try this one. It is *guaranteed* to provide you with hours of fascinating discussion! In fact, you'll be happy to know that she'll probably make it easy for you by carrying on most of the conversation herself.

"This is all fine and good, but aren't you assuming that my wife and I are already good communicators? Frankly, with our communication skills, I'd be scared to death to attempt discussing some of these issues with my spouse!"

Well then, we'll just have to give you a crash course in the basics of biblical communication. Class will begin as soon as you're ready to turn the page to the next chapter.

Topics for Discussion

1. Bible doctrine

2. Our home

3. The children

4. My job

5. Her family (your in-laws)

6. Her friends

7. Her ministries (inside and outside the home)

8. Her goals for the future

9. Specific ways I can be a better husband and father

10. Things I do which bother her

Add to this list any further topics which may come up...

Notes

[1]cf. Prov. 12:18: *"There is one who speaks rashly like the thrusts of a sword, but the tongue of the wise brings healing."*

[2]*General revelation* is that which may be generally known about God (such as His eternal power and Godhead; cf. Rom. 1:20) through His creation.

[3]*Special revelation* (the Bible) is necessary because of the limitations of general revelation to fallen man. General revelation is incapable of describing the many perfections of God which are necessary for man to know in order to glorify and enjoy Him. Also, man's sinfulness distorts his ability to perceive God through general revelation. Additionally, God's transcendence, makes it impossible for man to comprehend Him apart from special revelation.

[4]This idea of course, was highly popularized by Dale Carnegie in book form.

[5]For an excellent resource to facilitate such discussion, see Wayne Mack's *Stengthening Your Marriage*, (Phillipsburg: Presbyterian and Reformed, 1977), and in particular, Chapter Seven entitled "Unity Through a Common Philosophy of Raising Children."

[6]By "unbiblical" divorce, I mean a divorce where neither sexual immorality (Matt. 19: 1-12) nor desertion by an unbelieving spouse (1 Cor. 7:15-16) were present. See *Marriage Divorce and Remarriage in the Bible* by Jay E. Adams (Zondervan: 1980) for an excellent treatment of this subject.

[7]Again, I know of no better priority list in the Bible than the outline of Ephesians 5:18 through 6:7. After being filled with the Spirit (our ultimate priority of worshipping God), the text moves to the husband-wife relationship, then to the parent-child relationship, and then to the employer-employee relationship.

Chapter 4

A Crash Course in Biblical Communication

Volumes could and should be written to explain the many Bible references that address communication. The five principles contained in this chapter, although not exhaustive, can help you to become a more effective communicator and conflict-resolver. Some of these principles may be difficult for you to practice consistently at first. Being an effective communicator is not only a *biblical responsibility*, it's also a *skill* that takes time to develop. The more you practice the truths you're about to learn (or review), the more proficient you'll become in using them effectively.

LESSON ONE:
You can't fake it (if it's not in there).

Harvey and Priscilla were seated facing each other in my office, and attempting to resolve a conflict. Soon after they began speaking, Priscilla made a very sarcastic and vitriolic comment to Harvey.

"Whoa!" I said. "Priscilla, those words were not honoring to your husband. Would you please try saying that again."

At that point, I took the essence of what she was apparently trying to say to Harvey and reworded it in a much more gracious fashion than her original version.

"Try it this way," I said. "ABCDEFG," attempting to put into her mouth an amended version of her thoughts.

I'll never forget what happened next. Looking Harvey straight in the eyes, she opened her mouth trying to form the words, but nothing came out. She just sat there with her mouth open and her tongue sort of dangling in mid-air between her upper and lower sets of teeth.

"Go on. You can do it," I said encouragingly.

After momentarily closing her mouth (for a rest), she tried it again. When she did, a rather raspy, guttural, and choking kind of sound came out, but nothing else.

"It's really hard for me to say those words," she said to me with a troubled look on her face.

After reflecting momentarily, I asked, "Would you like to know why?"

"Tell me please!"

"What I asked you to say to Harvey was quite gracious and humble. The reason you're so speechless, Priscilla, is because there's not enough grace and humility in your heart for you to utter those words without choking on them."

She finally understood that she could not truly sweeten her speech without first changing her *heart*. By God's grace, she eventually learned how to "put on" more humility and grace.

But no one can tame the tongue (Jas. 3:8a).

Have you ever wondered why James said that "no man" can tame the *tongue*? Perhaps it's because the tongue is only a muscle that doesn't have a mind of its own—it simply does what it's told to do by the heart.

The Bible speaks often of the connection between the heart and the mouth (and lips and tongue—cf. 1 Sam. 1:13; Job 33:3; Psa. 12:2; 17:10; 19:14; Prov. 15:2,28; 16:23; 26:23-25; Matt. 15:8). The two verses in Proverbs Chapter 15 use the words *spout* (v. 2) and *pour* (v. 28) to describe the tongue and mouth respectively. The picture that comes to mind is that of a pitcher:

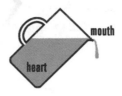

*The **tongue** of the wise makes knowledge acceptable, But the **mouth** of fools **spouts** folly* (Prov.15:2).

*The **heart** of the righteous ponders how to answer, But the **mouth** of the wicked **pours out** evil things* (Prov. 15:28).

In this analogy, the *reservoir* of the pitcher (which contains the liquid) corresponds to your heart. The *spout* of the pitcher corresponds to your mouth (or lips or tongue). Whatever is in the reservoir will "pour out" of the spout when the pitcher is appropriately tilted. If the reservoir contains milk, *milk* will pour out of the spout. If it contains coffee, *coffee* will pour out. If gasoline is put in, then *gasoline* will flow out. And so it is with whatever fluid (whether it be palatable or poisonous) is contained in the pitcher. It's just as Jesus said: *"The mouth speaks out of that which fills the heart. The good man out of [his] good treasure brings forth what is good; and the evil man out of [his] evil treasure brings forth what is evil"* (Matt. 12:34b-35).

The first lesson in the school of biblical communication is: You can't expect to speak that which is good if there's evil in your heart. Jesus asked the question, *"How can you, being evil, speak what is good?"* (Matt. 12:34a). The only way to have your heart truly cleansed is through the regenerating work of the Holy Spirit who indwells only those who have put their faith in the Lord Jesus Christ. This must be followed by His sanctifying work.

LESSON TWO:
Your words aren't enough!

The next lesson in biblical communication has to do with something I call the "communication pie." Communication involves more than just *words* (cf. Prov. 16:24). It also involves our *tone of voice* (cf. Prov. 16:21) and our *non-verbal communication* (cf. Acts 12:17). If you're going to learn how to communicate properly, you must learn how to do so in all three areas.

The Communication Pie

Choose the right words

Of the three slices, the Bible places the greatest emphasis on *words*.

> *And I say to you, that every careless word that men shall speak, they shall render account for it in the day of judgment. For by your words you shall be justified, and by your words you shall be condemned* (Matt. 12:36-37).

Your words, even the careless ones, will be examined on the Day of Judgment. They will *justify* you or *condemn* you. Other people also judge us by our words. So do our wives. Do your words justify you in your wife's mind or do they condemn you?

With your words, you can harm her or heal her: "*There is one who speaks rashly like the thrusts of a sword, but the tongue of the wise brings healing*" (Prov. 12:18). You can build her up or tear her down. "*Let no unwholesome word proceed from your mouth, but only such [a word] as is good for edification according to the need [of the moment,] that it may give grace to those who hear*" (Eph. 4:29). Your words can encourage her or discourage her (cf. Deut. 1:28; 1 Thess. 4:18; 5:11; Heb. 3:13).

Which of these two approaches is better? "How many times

do I have to tell you not to overcook the chicken?" or, "Sweet-heart, you've obviously spent a lot of time preparing this meal. Thank you. It's quite good. Have you been able to figure out how to keep the chicken moist and juicy?"

Use the appropriate tone of voice

The Bible also addresses the importance of using the proper tone of voice in Proverbs 15:1: *"A gentle answer turns away wrath, but a harsh word stirs up anger"* (cf. Judg. 1:8; Prov. 16:21,24; 18:22; Col. 4:6). Some communication professionals believe that, in the English language, the tone of one's *voice* may communicate up to seven times more of the message than one's *words*.

For example, suppose your wife asks you, "Would you like some more meatloaf?" Your "No thank you" could be interpreted in two very different ways, depending on your tone of voice.

"No (that was so good I've already had three helpings), thank you (but, I couldn't eat another bite)," you say with a pleasant inflection in your voice. Or, you gruffly bark out, "No, thank you (I almost gagged forcing myself to swallow this slop)!"

Think about the many bad attitudes your voice inflection is capable of communicating. There is disrespect, anger, hatred, bitterness, contempt, vengeance, fear, anxiety, pride, condescension, harshness, superiority, self-righteousness, sarcasm, criticism, callousness, impatience and indifference, to name a few. On the other hand, with the tone of your voice you can also communicate such righteous attitudes as love, acceptance, compassion, forgiveness, patience, submissiveness, forbearance, humility, and gentleness.

Use the appropriate forms of non-verbal communication

The Bible has much to say about non-verbal forms of communication. Non-verbal communication encompasses such things as your facial expressions, eye contact, gestures, posture, and touch.

Many in our day believe this to carry even more of the total communication message than words and tone of voice *put together.*[1]

Let's begin with your *face.* Anger is one of several sins that
the Bible specifically indicates can show up on your face. *"Why
are you angry?"* the Lord asked Cain (Gen. 4:6), *"and why has
your countenance fallen?"*[2] Do you remember the pitcher illustration? Well, not only is the spout analogous to your lips, tongue
and mouth, but it's also analogous to your *face.* What's in your
heart also bleeds through your countenance (cf. Neh. 2:2; Prov.
15:13; Eccl. 7:3). In the Bible, the word "heart" represents the
"inner man" and it's invariably held over against the "outer man"
(mouth, tongue, lips, eyes, countenance, hands, feet, etc.). Isaiah
put it this way, *"The expression of their faces bears witness against
them. And they display their sin like Sodom"* (Isa. 3:9a).

Have you ever wondered why David refers to God as *"the help
of my countenance"* (Psa. 42:11; 43:5)? It's because he realized that
only *God* can remove from our hearts the sin that mars our countenance. Solomon also understood the connection between man's
heart (the reservoir of wisdom; cf. Prov. 2:10; 14:33; 17:16) and
his *face*: *"A man's wisdom illumines him and causes his stern face to
beam"* (Eccl. 8:1).

Now, since you can neither hear nor see the look on your
own face, detecting inappropriate facial expressions is much more
difficult than detecting wrong words or voice inflections. You'll
need the assistance of your wife (and perhaps your children) to
correct any inappropriate facial casts. Ask her to let you know
when your face is saying something wrong. The single best
correction you can make is to smile. One smile can often cover
a multitude of sins. At the very least, smiling lets people know
that you're *trying to* communicate in a warm, friendly, pleasant,
kind, and pro-active manner. Remember though, the long-term
solution to improving your looks is to do it from the inside-out
by cooperating with the Spirit of God as He develops in you the
character of the Lord Jesus Christ.

In some cultures of the world, it's considered rude to look

people in the eyes. In our culture, it's generally considered rude *not* to look at people when talking to them. The Bible says in 1 Corinthians 13:5 that love is not "rude." When God counsels us, He is said to do so with His "eye" upon us (Psa. 32:8). Job said to one of his counselors, *"And now please look at me, And [see] if I lie to your face"* (Job. 6:28). One of the clues that may indicate a potential lie (or at least some kind of fearful emotion) is the dilation of the speaker's eyes. Look at your wife when she's talking to you. As much as possible, make it a habit to practice "Stop, Look, and Listen" when your wife is addressing you. *Stop* what you're doing when she begins talking to you (i.e., put down the newspaper or magazine, turn off the television set, etc.), *look* her directly in the eyes, and *listen* intently to what she's saying to you.

A final element of non-verbal communication I'd like to address is *touch*. John, the disciple whom Jesus "loved," was "reclining on Jesus' breast" (Jn. 13:23; 21:20). The Song of Solomon is replete with references to various forms of affection between Solomon and the Shulamite woman. Jesus showed His compassion on numerous people as He touched them in the process of healing their infirmities. In the context of marriage and the family, certain forms of (non-sexual) touching are used to communicate feelings such as love, compassion, comfort and sympathy. How often do you touch your wife (when you're not interested in having sexual relations with her)? Another question you may want to add to the list at the end of Chapter Two is, "How (in what specific ways) would you like for me to express my love for you through touch?"

LESSON THREE:
You must learn how to control your anger.

It's Saturday morning. You went to sleep very late last night and had to get up early this morning to go on an errand you're not particularly looking forward to. You're running late. You convince yourself that your wife hasn't been doing enough to help you get out of the house on time. Little by little you begin to get on each other's nerves. You start fussing at her. She retaliates in kind. The conflict grows worse as you grow more and more impatient. The battle escalates to a full-fledged war, the likes of which neither of you has known for many years. Both of you are violating a dozen Scriptures. As the battle rages, the telephone rings. You prepare to answer it, thinking it's your appointment wanting to know where you are. You pick up the receiver and in a very calm and controlled tone of voice you pleasantly say, "Good Morning!...Oh, hello Mrs. Neighborhood Gossip. How are you today?"

We *nouthetic* counselors like to relate this story when our counselees tell us that they can't control their tempers.[2] Actually, you control your temper more than you realize. The reason you control it with some and not with others is because you know you *can't* get away with losing your temper with some, and you know you *can* get away with it with others (especially those in your immediate family).

Nothing will foul up your ability to communicate effectively with your wife (or anyone else for that matter) more than sinful anger. Of course, not all anger is sinful. Ephesians 4:26 is actually a command to be angry: *"Be angry and do not sin"* (cf. Psa. 17:11; Mk. 3:5).[3] But remember: Even righteous anger can be expressed sinfully when principles of biblical communication are not followed.

Whenever we are faced with a problem, the potential for us to become unrighteously angry (or to communicate righteous anger sinfully) increases. There are two extremes these corrupt expressions of anger usually take. You've probably heard the expression "fight or flight syndrome." This describes what happens physiologically when the adrenal glands pump extra adrenaline into the blood stream at the moment people experience stress. Jay Adams' popular diagram is a helpful tool in understanding this dynamic in the context of interpersonal relationships.[4]

The Two Extremes of Sinful Anger

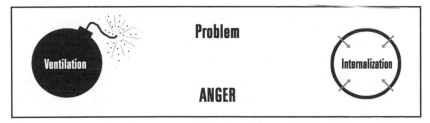

Sinful expressions of anger: Ventilation and Internalization

At one end of the spectrum is *ventilation* ("blowing up"). The anger which resides in the human heart (with a little help from our adrenal glands) manifests itself in various forms of unbiblical communication. Sinful expressions of anger include such things as yelling, name-calling, profanity, malicious words, disrespect, false accusations, throwing, hitting and kicking things and people.

At the other end of the spectrum is *internalization* ("clamming up"). Many who "clam up" thinks that it's a good thing to do. They cite verses like Proverbs 17:17a, *"He who restrains his words has knowledge,"* not realizing that to refrain from speaking can also be *evil* (cf. Prov. 6:1-5; 24:11-12; Eccl. 3:7; Eph. 6:19-20). Moreover, they often fail to consider the many physiological and spiritual effects of internalizing their anger.

When there's a problem (especially in marriage), in all likelihood it's not going to be solved effectively without someone doing some talking. Bear in mind that God has made *you* the initiator and spiritual leader (the chief problem solver, if you please) of the family. Sinful "clam up" techniques include such things as sulking, pouting, walking away (or "going for a drive") with no explanation. Other techniques are refusing to "discuss it any further," and retreating to your favorite pastime (television, golf, fishing, work, etc.) rather than addressing the problem.

Now, sometimes people don't just blow up or clam up; they mix and match these sinful responses. That is, they either blow up first and then clam up, or they clam up until they "can't take it anymore," and then they blow up.

Anger is an emotion God designed to *destroy something*. Who are you destroying with your anger when you blow up?

"I'm destroying the person on whom I vent my anger."

That's right. Of course you're also destroying your own self —physically as well as spiritually. When you clam up, who then are you destroying with your anger?

"I'm destroying myself as well as the other person."

Exactly. Now look back at our diagram again. If God built into your body this "fight or flight syndrome" for the purpose of destroying something (and He does not want you to destroy yourself or the person with whom you're angry) what do you suppose He desires to destroy with your anger?

"God wants me to destroy *the problem*."

You've got it!

"But how do I destroy the problem with my anger?"

You do it through *biblical communication*. Communication is almost always necessary to solve problems with people. When was the last time you got angry at something other than a person? Do you remember your most recent episode of getting angry while driving your car? Think about it: Were you actually angry at the *automobile* that cut you off (or made some other dangerous or inconsiderate move), or did you get angry at the *driver* of that car? You got angry at the driver. Granted, there's little you can do to solve such a problem through communication if you and the other driver are in different cars going 65 miles per hour—unless, of course, you happen to have his cellular telephone number. Perhaps that's why such incidents are so frustrating. But people usually have problems with *people*. That's why communication is necessary to solve them. That's also why people who are habitually angry will find it almost impossible to control their tempers until they learn how to communicate biblically.

The key to communicating biblically when you're angry is twofold. First, as you've already realized, you must direct your anger toward the problem. Rather than throwing that dart at the person who made you angry by "blowing up," and rather than swallowing that dart yourself by "clamming up," you must remember to *throw that dart at the real problem.* Secondly, under the control of the Holy Spirit, you must *release your anger.* You must depend upon the Spirit of God to help you obey those Scriptures that are to govern your speech. To put it in biblical language, you are to *"speak as it were, the utterances of God"* (1 Pet. 4:11).

The Two Extremes of Sinful Anger

Under the control of the Holy Spirit, release the anger toward the problem.

Communication can be likened to the circuit-breakers in your home. When you and your wife are communicating without anger, the circuits are open and the electricity is flowing. However, when one of you "blows up," it breaks the circuits and the power is cut off. It has the same effect when one of you "clams up." It's as if someone secretly breaks into the fuse box and silently throws the switch, interrupting the flow of current. Keep the connection intact. Don't let anger short-circuit your communication. I've included in Appendix G, "Things to Say to Defuse an Argument with Your Wife," some helpful transition statements that may make it easier for you and your wife to keep from blowing a fuse in this way.

LESSON FOUR:
You may not use unbiblical forms of communication.

The following list, although certainly not exhaustive, identifies eleven of the most common forms of unbiblical communication.

Common Violations of Biblical Communication in Marriage

1. Interruption: Whether it's in the middle of a sentence or a paragraph, when you interrupt your wife before she finishes her thoughts, you violate several scriptural principles. First, you show yourself to be quick to speak and slow to hear: *"But let everyone be quick to hear, slow to speak [and] slow to anger"* (Jas. 1:19). You also err by answering a matter before you hear it. *"He who gives an answer before he hears, it is folly and shame to him"* (Prov. 18:13). Don't be inconsiderate. Let your wife finish before you end up playing the fool and being embarrassed by your own hastiness.

2. Inattentiveness: One of my female counselees coined a phrase years ago that accurately describes a problem truly common to most men. "Man fog" is the term she used to describe her husband and several other men she observed who often were preoccupied and distracted as she was trying to talk with them. Like the cartoon character "Pig-Pen" in Charles Schultz's comic strip *Peanuts*, many men seem to have a cloud around their heads that keeps them from hearing what their wives are saying; they are too preoccupied and distracted by "more important things." Some of them are quite good at camouflaging their secret cogitations. They nod and smile and use a variety of verbal affirmations as their wives wax eloquent about some important matter, but their minds are light-years away. Others, like me, give off certain idiosyncratic clues (staring, hand and head movements, etc.) that tip off their wives to the fact they're oblivious to the conversation in which they only appear to be participating.[5]

Another version of inattentiveness occurs when a husband

hears the first part of what his wife is saying but quickly "tunes her out" as he begins to mentally formulate his response: "*A fool finds no pleasure in understanding, but delights in airing his own opinions*" (Prov. 18:2 NIV). Like Elihu, who paid close attention to Job (Job. 32:11; 33:1,33) and his other counselors (who themselves answered a matter before they heard it, and were reproved for their folly and shame), you should pay close attention to what your wife is saying. If you truly can't be attentive the moment she wants to talk, then at least explain why you're not able to do so, and offer her a rain check for your undivided attention later that day (if at all possible).

3. Judging Motives: Notice what's wrong with the following statements:
- "You only said that because you want me to feel guilty."
- "The reason you're being nice to me is so I'll buy you that dress."
- "You only married me for my money."

The problem with each of these judgments is that they presuppose an *evil motive*. Unless your wife specifically tells you exactly what her motives are (i.e., what she wants or why she does something) you may not take it upon yourself to presume or deduce what they are. You may rightfully judge her words and actions (and perhaps her attitudes), but you may not judge her motives. That is, you may not, as her judge, slam the gavel down in your mind or with your mouth and pronounce her guilty of having evil motives:

> *Therefore do not go on passing judgment before the time, [but wait] until the Lord comes who will both bring to light the things hidden in the darkness and disclose the motives of [men's] hearts; and then each man's praise will come to him from God* (1 Cor. 4:5).

Now, if you have a suspicion about her motives, you may ask her to judge them for herself and tell you what they are (e.g., "Honey, what motivated you to say that?"). If she admits to having a wrong motive, you may then discuss with her what is wrong about it and what might be done to change it. If, however, she tells you that her motives are good, then based on 1 Corinthians 13:7 ("love believes all things"— i.e., it believes the best), you must believe her. Love, in the absence of real evidence, puts the best possible interpretation on the facts.

4. Not Communicating Willingly: One of the most common communication difficulties for husbands is being *passive* rather than *active* in the communication process. This reluctance to communicate is not in keeping with God's design for man to be the leader (and initiator) of the marital relationship. You simply don't have the right to *not* engage your wife in the communication that is so essential to a one-flesh relationship. There are many things which you have a biblical responsibility to discuss with your wife (i.e., problems she perceives in your relationship, her personal problems, certain issues concerning the children, family finances, etc.). Unwillingness to discuss these things is usually sin.

5. Sweeping Generalizations: Notice again what's wrong with statements such as the following:
- "You *never* listen to me"
- "You're *always* dissatisfied with *everything* I do"
- "The *only time* you're nice to me is when *you want something.*"
- "You're *the worst* housekeeper I've ever known"

In addition to being harsh and unloving, these statements are *dishonest*. In fact, they are lies! *"Laying aside falsehood,"* the Bible says, *"speak truth, each one [of you] with his neighbor, for we are members of one another"* (Eph. 4:25). It's almost certainly *not* true that your wife (your closest neighbor and a personal member of your body) is *always* or *never* or *only* as bad as you make her out to be when you use such inaccurate language. If you truly believe there's some sinful snare into which she regularly falls, try using such phrases as "you *tend* to," or "I think I've observed a *pattern*," or "you seem to *habitually* struggle." Failure to use such terminology can lead to arguing over the frequency of the problem and side-stepping the real issue (e.g., "That's not true! Two years ago I initiated sexual relations without any prompting from you!").

6. Blame-Shifting: This is literally the oldest trick in the Book: "*The woman whom Thou gavest [to be] with me, she gave me from the tree, and I ate*" (Gen. 3:12 KJV). Pride not only blinds us to our own sin, it also looks for someone other than ourselves to blame. You must "*first take the log out of your own eye, and then you will see clearly to take the speck out of your brother's eye*" (Matt. 7:5). You ought to assume one hundred percent of the responsibility for your own sin, even if you believe you're only five percent wrong and your wife is ninety-five percent wrong.

The next time you and she begin to blame each other for something, why not offer to be the first one to lay your head on the chopping block? Perhaps you might say words to this effect, "Honey, look, you think I'm to blame and I think you are. Why don't you tell me exactly what you think I've done wrong. When you do, I promise to be attentive, to acknowledge where I've sinned, to ask your forgiveness, and by God's grace to repent of my sin. The only thing I ask is that, after we've dealt with my sin, you let me talk to you about how I believe you've sinned."

Such a response not only sets a good example of humility, it also makes it easier for your wife to lower her resistance and humble herself. Don't be surprised if, after you've finished acknowledging and repenting of your faults, she voluntarily acknowledges her faults even before you've had a chance to point them out to her.

7. Apologizing (rather than asking for forgiveness):
"Why do you say that apologizing is not biblical?"
Because it does not thoroughly deal with the offense.

You say, "Honey, I'm sorry for not listening to you when you were talking to me."

She says, "You *sure are* sorry! You're one of the sorriest men I've ever met!"

The ball is still up in the air when you simply say, "I'm sorry." The loose ends are not tied up biblically. You both may walk away not knowing if the issue is resolved, never to be brought up again. By asking your wife to forgive you, you're securing a certain commitment from her that will truly put the offense behind you both and tie up any loose ends.

What Does it Mean to Forgive?

You are commanded to forgive, *"just as God in Christ also has forgiven you"* (Eph. 4:32). What does that mean? God says, *"I, even I, am the one who wipes out your transgressions for My own sake; And I will not remember your sins"* and *"I will forgive their iniquity, and their sin I will remember no more"* (Isa. 43:25; Jer. 31:34).

So, does God have amnesia? Certainly not! God is *omniscient* ("all- knowing") and knew about your sins even before you committed them. When the Bible speaks of God "forgetting" our sins, it refers to the fact that when a person has truly been forgiven by God, God does not hold them against the sinner. He doesn't charge or impute them to our account. Rather, God charges them to the account of the Lord Jesus Christ, who died on the cross to pay the penalty for guilty sinners like you and me. Christ's death was a substitution. He died in our place to take the punishment for our sin so that we, as saved individuals, might be credited with His righteousness. When we truly believe the gospel, God *promises* to not hold our sins against us. Instead, He imputes the perfect righteousness of His Son to our account.

What is the gospel, or good news? The gospel is simply this: If we repent and place our faith in what Christ has done by substituting Himself for us on the cross and rising from the dead in our place, God forgives all our sins and gives us eternal life.

Forgiveness, therefore, is first and foremost, a *promise*. As God promises not to hold the sins of repentant and believing sinners against them, so we also must promise not to hold the sins of those we've forgiven against them. You may demonstrate this promise by *not* doing at least *three things* to the person you've forgiven. *First*, you may not bring up the forgiven offense to the forgiven person so as to use it against him/her. *Second*, you may not discuss the forgiven offense with others. *Finally*, you may not dwell on the forgiven offense yourself but rather remind yourself that you have forgiven your offender, "just as God in Christ also has forgiven you."[6]

When you ask for forgiveness, rather than simply apologizing, you secure for yourself those three promises. Isn't that much better than leaving the ball up in the air? Wouldn't you rather tie up those loose ends by having your wife commit to not holding your offense against you ever again? In light of this, I'd like to suggest a very effective approach for a husband to use when seeking forgiveness from his wife. The approach usually has five steps.[7]

Step 1. Acknowledge you've sinned against her. Let her know that you realize what you did was wrong. *Example*: "I was wrong for not listening to you when you were talking to me."

Step 2. Identify your specific sin by its biblical name. Using biblical terminology, let her know that you realize your sin was also a violation of God's Word and therefore a sin against Him. *Example*: "That was selfish and inconsiderate of me."

Step 3. Acknowledge the harm your offense caused her. Show remorse for the hurt your sin has caused. *Example*: "I really am sorry I hurt and rejected you."

Step 4. Identify an alternative biblical behavior to demonstrate repentance. One of the best ways to demonstrate to your wife that you have repented (changed your mind) is by letting her know you have thought through a more biblical option than the one for which you are about to ask her forgiveness. *Example*: "I should've turned off the television when you first told me that you thought you were having a "nervous breakdown."

Step 5. Ask her for forgiveness. This step puts the ball in her court (It's as if you're saying, "Are you going to obey God and forgive me or aren't you?"). *Example*: "Will you forgive me?"

8. Exhumation: One of my pastor friends tells a story about a woman he met in counseling. In response to his question, "What is your problem?," she proceeded to toss onto his desk a bounded book of notes she had been keeping for years. "This is our problem," she said confidently. My friend picked up the tome (which was typed single-space on both sides of the paper) and began to peruse it. He soon discovered this woman had kept a thirteen-year account of the various ways her husband had failed her. My friend looked the woman in her eyes and said, "It's been a long time since I've met someone as bitter as you."

If your wife sins against you, you must either "overlook the transgression" and "cover" it in love (cf. Prov. 19:11; 1 Pet. 4:8), or you must pursue (confront) her with the intent of granting forgiveness (Lk. 17:3) once she acknowledges her sin. If you've granted forgiveness for her sins against you, you ought not to exhume them (dig them up). If you've truly forgiven her, you may not use those offenses in a pejorative way against her. Love "does not take into account a wrong suffered" ("it keeps no record of wrongs" 1 Cor. 13:5 NIV).

9. Scolding:

> *And while He was in Bethany at the home of Simon the leper, and reclining [at the table,] there came a woman with an alabaster vial of very costly perfume of pure nard; [and] she broke the vial and poured it over His head. But some*

> *were indignantly [remarking] to one another, "Why has this*
> *perfume been wasted? For this perfume might have been sold*
> *for over three hundred denarii, and [the money] given to the*
> *poor?" And they were scolding her* (Mk. 14:3-5).

One of the Greek words from which the word *scolding* in this
text is derived means "to snort with anger."

> To "scold" is to assail or revile with boisterous speech. The
> word itself seems to have a primary meaning akin to that
> of barking or howling. Scolding is always an expression
> of a bad spirit and of a loss of temper…the essence of the
> scolding is in the multiplication of hot words in expres-
> sion of strong feelings that, while eminently natural, ought
> to be held in better control.[8]

Do you snort at your wife? The manner in which you speak
to her should be gentle, not harsh: *"A gentle answer turns away*
wrath, But a harsh word stirs up anger" (Prov. 15:1). Your communication with her is to *"always be with grace, seasoned, [as it were]*
with salt" (Col. 4:6).

10. Using Put-Downs:

- "Can't you do anything right?"
- "I see you've prepared another burnt offering for my supper
  tonight."
- "Why don't you ask your mother how to fix this meal the
  right way?"
- "My mother never left the dishes in the sink overnight."
- "You have to be the most ungrateful woman I ever met!"
- "I don't see how you can call yourself a 'suitable helper' to me."

> *Do not speak against [lit. "speak down" towards] one an-*
> *other, brethren. He who speaks against a brother, or judges*
> *his brother, speaks against the law, and judges the law;*
> *but if you judge the law, you are not a doer of the law, but*
> *a judge [of it.]* (Jas. 4:11).

> *Let no unwholesome word proceed from your mouth, but*
> *only such [a word] as is good for edification according to*
> *the need [of the moment,] that it may give grace to those*
> *who hear* (Eph. 4:29).

Putting your wife down (whether through such things as name-calling, condescending or contemptuous speech, innuendo, derogatory comments, belittling questions, unfair comparisons, biting sarcasm, or the use of profanity) falls under the prohibitions of these two verses. You're to treat her as a weaker vessel (a fragile vase), not a garbage can (1 Pet. 3:7).

11. Harshness: The Bible says of Nabal that he was a "harsh" and "evil" man: *"Now the man's name was Nabal, and his wife's name was Abigail. And the woman was intelligent and beautiful in appearance, but the man was harsh and evil in [his] dealings, and he was a Calebite"* (1 Sam. 25:3). Listen to what he said when David requested provisions for himself and his men.

> *But Nabal answered David's servants, and said, "Who is*
> *David? And who is the son of Jesse? There are many ser-*
> *vants today who are each breaking away from his master.*
> *Shall I then take my bread and my water and my meat that*
> *I have slaughtered for my shearers, and give it to men whose*
> *origin I do not know?"* (1 Sam. 25:10-11)

Some men speak to their wives and treat them with a severity that might cause even a Nabal to blush. Listed below are some common ways husbands are harsh in dealing with their wives. Even though some of the items on the list may not directly involve speech, the harshness of these attitudes is usually communicated very clearly. As you read over the list, ask yourself, "How might I be communicating these attitudes of harshness to my wife?" (Incidentally, this list could also be entitled: "Specific Ways Husbands Abuse Authority Over their Wives.")

Common Manifestations of Harshness in Husbands

- Unwillingness to grant requests made by their wives.
- Granting those requests begrudgingly and with complaint.
- Refusing to allow their wives to appeal (or question) their decisions.
- Being discontent with their wives' performance of their duties.
- Fussing about their wives' neglect of domestic responsibilities without sincerely offering assistance.
- Responding to their wives in a discourteous or condescending way.
- Having a critical, condemnatory, judgmental attitude toward them.
- Having unrealistic expectations of them and/or exacting too many demands from them.
- Being intolerant of their (non-sinful) idiosyncratic behaviors.
- Prohibiting their wives from doing anything without their express knowledge or consent.
- Micro-managing every aspect of their wives' responsibilities.
- Being unjustly suspicious of their wives (rather than trusting them).

What is the antidote to harshness? It's *mildness* (or meekness). I've taken some poetic license to modernize the words of William Gouge as we conclude this lesson.

> Mildness is a special fruit, and evidence of love. It is a notable means to remove offenses that might otherwise be taken from the many hurtful things which a husband does to his wife. Sugar and honey are not more pleasant to the tongue than mildness is to the heart. It causes those things which are otherwise irksome to the soul, to be well received and applied—even as bitter pills dipped in sweet syrup, or rolled up in the soft pulp of an apple are soon swallowed down and digested. If a husband desires to be

considered "a servant of the Lord," he must learn this lesson. For, *the servant of the Lord must be gentle to all men.* If any other servant of the Lord [is to be gentle,] much more should husbands. If to *all men* [they are to be gentle] much more their wives.[9]

LESSON FIVE:
You must make every effort to maintain the unity of the Spirit.

"Make every effort to keep the unity of the Spirit through the bond of peace" (Eph. 4:3 NIV).

God does not want conflicts between His children to go unresolved. He places the responsibility squarely on the shoulders of each Christian to be at peace with each other. If you have offended someone, *you* are to go to that person and be reconciled to him.

> *If therefore you are presenting your offering at the altar, and there remember that your brother has something against you, leave your offering there before the altar, and go your way; first be reconciled to your brother, and then come and present your offering* (Matt. 5:23-24).

If you've been offended by someone, *you* are to go to him with the intent of granting him forgiveness (thus restoring your relationship with him) once you've convinced him he's sinned.

> *Be on your guard! If your brother sins, rebuke him; and if he repents, forgive him* (Lk. 17:3).

If you're not able to get the issues resolved between you, *you* must seek the assistance of other Christians.

> *And if your brother sins, go and reprove him in private; if he listens to you, you have won your brother. But if he does not listen [to you,] take one or two more with you, so that by the mouth of two or three witnesses every fact may be confirmed* (Matt. 18:15-16).

> *I urge Euodia and I urge Syntyche to live in harmony in the Lord. Indeed, true comrade, I ask you also to help these women, who have shared my struggle in [the cause of] the gospel, together with Clement also, and the rest of my fellow workers, whose names are in the book of life* (Phil. 4:2-3).

Now, if these rules are binding on you as a Christian who's having conflict with another Christian in your church, how much more binding are they on you as a covenantal member of a *Christian marriage*! You must use all the resources God has given you to maintain the unity between you and your wife. You must *"not let the sun go down on your anger"* toward her (Eph. 4:26), but instead you should *"pursue peace"* with her (Heb. 12:14; cf. Rom. 14:19). If, after doing everything within your power *"so far as it depends on you"* to *"be at peace with"* her (Rom. 12:18), you're unable to resolve your conflict with her biblically, you'll need to enlist the help of another Christian. I recommend that you and she find some mutually agreeable person(s) whose biblical wisdom you trust (preferably a church leader), and agree beforehand that at least one of you will contact that person(s) the next time you're unable to resolve a conflict biblically in a reasonable amount of time.

Biblical Communication Inventory

The following evaluation should give you some idea of how biblically you communicate with your wife. Take the test the first time by yourself. Then ask your wife to evaluate you in each category. When you're finished with the evaluations, ask her to prioritize your areas of greatest weakness (i.e., the areas she would like to see you change first, second, third, etc.). Ask her to give you examples of both how you've miscommunicated in the past and how she would like to see you improve your communication in the future. Do this for at least the first five prioritized items. When you're through, ask her to help you in the future by graciously bringing to your attention those specific violations of biblical communication which she's prioritized. Ask her also to be prepared to suggest a more biblical alternative in case you can't figure out how to make the improvement yourself.

Rating Scale:	Points:
Hardly ever	5
Seldom	4
Sometimes	3
Frequently	2
Almost always	1

Evaluation of Self by Self:

1.___	6.___	11.___	16.___
2.___	7.___	12.___	17.___
3.___	8.___	13.___	18.___
4.___	9.___	14.___	19.___
5.___	10.__	15.___	20.___

Evaluation of Self by Wife:

1.___	6.___	11.___	16.___
2.___	7.___	12.___	17.___
3.___	8.___	13.___	18.___
4.___	9.___	14.___	19.___
5.___	10.__	15.___	20.___

Biblical Communication Inventory:

1. I use *words* that are inappropriate when I talk with you.

2. I use *inflections* that are inappropriate when I talk to you.

3. I use inappropriate *facial expressions* when I talk to you.

4. I do not *look at you* when I talk to you.

5. I do not *touch* you enough when I talk to you.

6. I *blow-up* (ventilate my anger) when I talk to you.

7. I *clam-up* (internalize my anger) instead of talking to you.

8. I *interrupt* you when you're talking to me.

9. I'm *inattentive* when you're talking to me.

10. I *judge* your *motives*.

11. I seem *uninterested* or *unwilling* to talk to you.

12. I use *sweeping generalizations* when I talk to you.

13. I *blameshift* my responsibilities, to you.

14. I do not *ask for your forgiveness.*

15. I *exhume* from you past things I've promised to forgive.

16. I *scold* you.

17. I *put you down* when I talk to you.

18. I use *harshness* when I talk to you.

19. I *do not* make every effort to *resolve conflicts* with you.

20. I've *not sought help* from other Christians as I should have.

Notes

[1]This is probably not as it should be. Although the Bible addresses all three forms of communication, the preponderance of references argues that our *words* should be given most significant attention.

[2] "Nouthetic" counseling is a form of counseling which is based solely on Scripture, without reference to modern psychology.

[3] I've included in Appendix I, "Righteous Anger vs. Sinful Anger," some information from my book *The Heart of Anger* that will help you distinguish between the two.

[4]For a more complete explanation of the this diagram see *What to Do When Anger Gets the Upper Hand* by Jay E. Adams, which is currently available from Presbyterian and Reformed Publishing.

[5]I have a penchant for holding conversations in my mind with various people I know. I may be debating a point of theology, or attempting to persuade one of my counselees to obey the Bible, or defending myself against some unscrupulous lawyer who is cross-examining me on the witness stand. The problem is I move my lips and gesture slightly with my right hand as I'm talking to myself. It's so bad that both my wife and daughter frequently ask me, "Who are you talking to *now*?" Both of them have also asked me when they perceived I was not paying attention to them, "Did you hear what I just said to you?"

[6] From *The Heart of Anger* pp.179-180. For information on how to obtain a copy of this book, please contact Calvary Press, Amityville, New York, Tel. 1-800-789-8175. For a thorough treatment of biblical forgiveness see: *From Forgiven to Forgiving* by Jay E. Adams also available through Calvary Press.

[7]The third step may not always be appropriate.

[8]H. Clay Trumbull, *Hints on Child Training*, (Brentwood, Tennessee: Wolgemuth & Hyatt, 1993), pp. 129-131.

[9]William Gouge, *Of Domestic Duties* (London: W. Bladen, 1622), pp. 370-371 [paraphrased].

Chapter 5

How to Love Your Wife (part one)

The story is told of a man who sought out his pastor for counsel.

The pastor asked the man, "What can I do for you?"

"Pastor, I think I have a problem."

"What's your problem?"

"Well, I think I love my wife too much!"

"I see. Tell me, do you love her as much as Christ loves the church?"

"No, I don't love her that much!"

"Then your problem is not that you love her too much. Your problem is you still don't love her enough!"

The real problem with many men who are "in love" with their wives is they think of love as a *feeling*. As one person put it, "Love is a feeling you feel when you feel like your going to get a feeling that you never felt before." To the extent that love is a feeling (and, to a limited extent it *is* an emotion), it's possible to love someone too much. You can actually love someone (or something) to the point of idolizing him or her (or it). When a man desires and dotes over his wife inordinately (i.e., to the point of expecting her to do for him those things only God can do for him) he has, in this sinful sense, loved her "too much."

Biblical love, however, is not primarily a feeling. In fact, such love isn't even an emotion primarily. What part of speech is the word "love?"

"Why, love is a noun."

No, love is fundamentally a *verb*.

"A verb?"

Yes, that's right! Do you remember what the classic passage in the Bible is that defines what biblical love is all about?

"Sure, It's 1 Corinthians 13."

Right again. Let's take a closer look at this well-known passage of Scripture which even in the eyes of many pagans is unsurpassed for its accuracy and literary genius.

> *Love is patient, love is kind, [and] is not jealous; love does not brag [and] is not arrogant, does not act unbecomingly; it does not seek its own, is not provoked, does not take into account a wrong suffered, does not rejoice in unrighteousness, but rejoices with the truth; bears all things, believes all things, hopes all things, endures all things* (1 Cor. 13:5-7).

Now let me break this passage down into its component parts of speech so you can see for yourself what I'm talking about. "Love is *patient*." "Is patient" in the original Greek New Testament is one participle, and thus, verbal in nature. "Love is *kind*"—"is kind" is likewise a participle. "Love is *not jealous*" is a *verb*. And so it is for all the rest:

Love does not brag [and]	Verb
Is not arrogant	Verb
Does not act unbecomingly	Verb
It does not seek its own	Verb
Is not provoked	Verb
Does not take into account a wrong [suffered]	Verb
Does not rejoice in unrighteousness	Verb
But rejoices with the truth	Verb
Bears all things	Verb
Believes all things	Verb
Hopes all things	Verb
Endures all things	Verb

Do you see the picture? When God wanted to define love, He used *verbs* because love is something you *do* much more than something you *feel*. It involves *motion* much more than it does fleeting *emotion*!

Since love is something you *do*, is it really possible to love someone too much? You can be thinking about that for a moment. I'll give you the answer before you finish this chapter.

The real problem most of us face is not that we love our wives too much; the real problem is, like the man in the opening story, we don't love our wives *enough*.

> *Husbands, love your wives, just as Christ also loved the church and gave Himself up for her* (Eph. 5:25).

Do you love your wife as much as Christ loves the church?

"I'm not sure if I even know what love *is* anymore. I now know that it's more a verb than a noun, but how do I define it? Maybe when I understand what real love is, I can answer your question."

That's fair enough. Let's begin our attempt to define love by finding an accurate, equivalent term, or a one-word synonym for it. Here are some references that may shed light on the subject:

> *Husbands, love your wives, just as Christ also loved the church and gave Himself up for her* (Eph. 5:25).

> *For God so loved the world, that He gave His only begotten Son, that whoever believes in Him should not perish, but have eternal life* (Jn. 3:16).

> *Walk in love, just as Christ also loved you, and gave Himself up for us, an offering and a sacrifice to God as a fragrant aroma* (Eph. 5:2).

> *I have been crucified with Christ; it is no longer I who live, but Christ lives in me; and the [life] which I now live in the*

flesh I live by faith in the Son of God, who loved me and gave Himself for me (Gal. 2:20 NKJV).

Jesus tells us to love our enemies:

You have heard that it was said, "You shall love your neighbor, and hate your enemy." But I say to you, "love your enemies, and pray for those who persecute you" (Matt. 5:43-44).

Solomon tells us how to do it:

If your enemy is hungry, give him food to eat; And if he is thirsty, give him water to drink (Prov. 25:21).

"I see it—Love is *giving*."

That's a good start, but we can't stop there. Biblical love requires more. Let's take another look at 1 Corinthians 13.

If I speak with the tongues of men and of angels, but do not have love, I have become a noisy gong or a clanging cymbal. And if I have [the gift of] prophecy, and know all mysteries and all knowledge; and if I have all faith, so as to remove mountains, but do not have love, I am nothing. And if I give all my possessions to feed [the poor,] and if I deliver [give] my body to be burned, but do not have love, it profits me nothing (1 Cor. 13:1-3).

"Wait a minute! Now I'm really confused! If love is *giving*, how could a person give away all his possessions to feed the poor and then make the ultimate sacrifice and give up his *life*—and yet still not have love? "

Good question! A lot of people *give*—even sinners give to sinners (cf. Matt. 5:44-47). What's missing from the "love is giving" definition is your *motive*. If you give away all your possessions (or even your life) in order to get something in return, you don't really qualify as having biblical love and you'll lose your eternal reward. (cf. Acts 8:18-20; Matt. 6:2). Real love gives without expecting anything in return. Real love does not need to be requited to keep on loving.

"OK, I've got it. Love is giving without having some temporal reward as the primary motive."

Very good, but there's still one thing missing from our definition. To whom or to what are you going to give? If someone says to you, "If you love me you should give me anything I want," would you do it?

"Of course not! It would depend first of all on what it is he needed."

Exactly right. You wouldn't necessarily give him what he *wanted* but, if you could, you would give him what he *needed*. In our day, the line separating needs from wants has been severely blurred—even in the Christian community which should know better. We have been told over and over again that our two basic needs are security and significance, that we have a need for unconditional love and acceptance; a need for positive self esteem, and a need to love ourselves before we can truly love God and others. These "needs" simply are not identified as such in the Bible. In fact, if you change the word "need" to the word "want" whenever you read it in today's Christian literature, you'll be more theologically accurate.

Martha thought she had a need for something—help in the kitchen.

> Now as they were traveling along, He entered a certain village; and a woman named Martha welcomed Him into her home. And she had a sister called Mary, who moreover was listening to the Lord's word, seated at His feet. But Martha was distracted with all her preparations; and she came up [to Him] and said, "Lord, do You not care that my sister has left me to do all the serving alone? Then tell her to help me." But the Lord answered and said to her, "Martha, Martha, you are worried and bothered about so many things; but [only] a few things are necessary, really [only] one, for Mary has chosen the good part, which shall not be taken away from her" (Lk. 10:38-42).

What Martha *wanted* was for her sister to help her. What she *needed* was to sit at the feet of Christ and hear His Word.

I believe that man's two greatest needs are not for security and significance but rather, (1) to *love God* with all of his heart, mind, soul and strength, and, (2) to *love his neighbor* as (with the same intensity that he loves) himself (cf. Matt. 22:36-40). Beyond these, man has other valid needs, such as counsel from God through His Word, and food and shelter (cf. Matt. 4:4; 1 Tim. 6:8).

Here then, is our new working definition of love: *Love is giving others what they need without having some temporal reward as the primary motive.* Love in the context of marriage is giving to your wife that which the Bible says she needs without having some temporal reward as your primary motive. Of course, as we will see later, you may also (and in some cases, *should* also) give her what she wants when that's biblically appropriate.

Is it really possible, in light of this definition, to love someone too much? Probably not. If you're giving with the right motive and giving to the needs (rather than wants) of the person you love, it would be very difficult to inordinately love someone (unless you're giving to that person that which more rightly belongs to someone else).

Now, according to this definition, what would you say is the antithesis or opposite of love?

"I always thought the opposite of love is *hate*, but now I'm not so sure."

To the extent that love is a noun, "hate" is a good antithetical construct for it. But to the extent that love is a verb, it's probably more accurate to identify its antonym as *selfishness*. I say this, not primarily because one of the characteristics of love identified in 1 Corinthians 13 is that it "is not selfish," but rather because *taking* is the opposite of *giving*. Giving, as we have seen, is at the heart of love. Love is giving. Selfishness is *taking*. "Am I a giver or a taker?" That is the question you must ask yourself as you evaluate your love for your wife.

The Root Cause of All Marriage Problems

I can tell you without any fear of contradiction or oversimplification that the root cause of all marriage conflicts is *selfishness*. I can say that because there's probably no better practical synonym for the concept of sin than selfishness. Sin (i.e., selfishness) is at the heart of all marriage problems. Now obviously, just as our "love is giving" definition was deficient because it was too limited in scope, so "sin is selfishness" is too narrow to be theologically accurate. Any complete definition of sin must make reference to the fact that the sin is committed against a holy and just God. But for our practical purposes, I would like to develop this concept of "sin as selfishness" a little further.

As the prolific Puritan Richard Baxter wrote, selfishness "... is the radical, positive sin of the soul, comprehending seminally [or in seed form] and causally all the rest."[1] That is to say, our greatest sin of *commission* out of which all others flow is selfishness. Practically speaking, it's the selfishness in our hearts that generates all our other sins.

Your heart is like a two-sided coin. On one side the coin reads "selfishness," while on the other side the coin reads "lack of love for God and neighbor." This two-sided coin (or shall we say "two-headed monster?") is our greatest sin of *omission*. Here's the way Baxter put it:

> Man's fall was his turning from God to himself; and his regeneration consisteth in the turning of him from himself to God...and the mortifying of self love. Selfishness therefore is all positive sin in one, as want of the love of God is all privative sin in one.[2]

Because man is sinful (i.e., selfish), God's practical remedy is for him to learn how to love God and love his neighbor.

And one of them, a lawyer, asked Him [a question] testing

Him, "Teacher, which is the great commandment in the Law?" And He said to him, "You shall love the Lord your God with all your heart, and with all your soul, and with all your mind. This is the great and foremost commandment. The second is like it, You shall love your neighbor as yourself. On these two commandments depend the whole Law and the Prophets" (Matt. 22:36-40).

These two great commandments, on which all the others depend, are the two greatest practical antidotes for indwelling sin. The more you love God and your neighbor, the less selfish (sinful) you will be.

Now, who is your closest neighbor? Who shares your house, your food, your bed? With whom are you one flesh? You're not one flesh with your parents, nor are you one flesh with your children, but rather you're one flesh with *your wife*. She is your closest neighbor and, as such, you should love (unselfishly give to) her the most.

You're commanded to love her not only in a general way as your neighbor but in a very specific way as your wife.

Husbands, love your wives, just as Christ also loved the church and gave Himself up for her; that He might sanctify her, having cleansed her by the washing of water with the word; that He might present to Himself the church in all her glory, having no spot or wrinkle or any such thing; but that she should be holy and blameless. So husbands ought also to love their own wives as their own bodies. He who loves his own wife loves himself; for no one ever hated his own flesh, but nourishes and cherishes it, just as Christ also [does] the church, because we are members of His body. "For this cause a man shall leave his father and mother, and shall cleave to his wife; and the two shall become one flesh." This mystery is great; but I am speaking with reference to Christ and the church. Nevertheless let each individual among you also love his own wife even as himself; and [let] the wife [see to it] that she respect her husband (Eph. 5:25-33).

This passage is pregnant with instruction which I'll expound and apply in various ways throughout this book. But for now, I'd like you to see that the specific instruction for initiating love in the context of marriage has been clearly given to the husband. In fact, the Bible really doesn't specifically command your wife to love you the way it commands you to love her.

"Really? But isn't there a verse somewhere in the book of Titus that tells her to love me?"

Not exactly. The passage you may be thinking of is Titus 2:3-4.

> *Older women likewise are to be reverent in their behavior,*
> *not malicious gossips, nor enslaved to much wine, teaching*
> *what is good, that they may encourage the young women*
> *to love their husbands, to love their children...*

The phrase "to love their husbands" is one compound word in the Greek New Testament that is different in meaning from the love we've been focusing on in this chapter. The meaning of "love" in the Titus verse wherein younger women are to be taught by the older (or more mature) women, is probably more in line with the concept of "affection." The older women are to teach the younger women how to be affectionate to their husbands. The kind of love you are to show your wife is a much more powerful kind of love.

"Well, that doesn't seem very fair to me."

Keep in mind that God made man to be the *initiator* and woman the *responder*. Remember also that you are commanded to love your wife "as Christ loved the church." Who took the initiative in that relationship? Was the church of Jesus Christ pleading with Him for thousands of years to be His Bride, as if to say, "O Lord Jesus, I love you so much, please come and love me!"? No! Christ *initiated* the love and the church *responded*. As 1 John 4:19 affirms, the reason we love, is because He first loved us. Even though your wife is not commanded to love you in the same way you're to love her, if she loves God it will be difficult for her not to warmly respond to your love, if you're increasingly loving her as

Christ loved the church.[1]

"So, in addition to unselfishly giving myself to her, and taking the initiative to love her, what else is involved in loving my wife as 'Christ loved the church'?"

Plenty! But for now let me mention only one more thing. The church for whom Christ died is a church that contains *sinners*. Consider the following passage:

> *For while we were still helpless, at the right time, Christ died for the ungodly. For one will hardly die for a righteous man; though perhaps for the good man someone would dare even to die. But God demonstrates His own love toward us, in that while we were yet sinners, Christ died for us* (Rom. 5:6-8).

How do you respond to your wife when she sins? Is it *in love*, with forgiveness, or with anger and bitterness? Do you keep an account of her sins (love "keeps no record of wrongs" 1 Cor. 13:5) or do you cover them in love? *"Above all, keep fervent in your love for one another, because love covers a multitude of sins"* (1 Pet. 4:8). Are you mindful that you've married a sinner who will often need to be forgiven, or do you expect her to be perfect? Are you patient with her while she's trying to change, or do you expect her to change overnight? Do you love the sinner you married *even as* Christ loves His sinful bride, the church?

How Do I Love Thee? Let Me Count the Ways

There's much more that can be said about loving your wife as Christ loves the church. I've put all that I can justify in this chapter. You, however, can continue to study and meditate on the various ways Christ demonstrates His love to the church. At the end of this chapter, you will find a worksheet to assist you in your study. As you read through the New Testament, see how many examples of Christ's love for the church you can discover. Record these in the first column ("Scripture Reference"). In the second

[1] Not that Christ's love is increasing, but that you're increasing your love to meet the level of love Christ has for the church.

column ("How Christ Loves the Church"), you may record the interpretation or explanation of exactly how Christ demonstrated His love for His bride. In the third column (Application: "How I Can Show Love to My Wife"), record how many personal applications of the passage you can make in your marriage (how you can similarly demonstrate your love to your wife). Remember, although there may be very many ways to apply a passage of Scripture (column three), there is only one interpretation (column two) of Scripture—that interpretation intended by the Holy Spirit: *"But know this first of all, that no prophecy of Scripture is [a matter] of one's own interpretation"* (2 Pet. 1:20).

Another element of biblical love mentioned in the Ephesians 5 passage has to do not with the way Christ loves the church, but with the way you love yourself:

> *So husbands ought also to love their own wives as their own bodies. He who loves his own wife loves himself; for no one ever hated his own flesh, but nourishes and cherishes it, just as Christ also [does] the church, because we are members of His body. "For this cause a man shall leave his father and mother, and shall cleave to his wife; and the two shall become one flesh." This mystery is great; but I am speaking with reference to Christ and the church. Nevertheless let each individual among you also love his own wife even as himself* (Eph. 5:28-33).

The advent of the modern self-esteem movement has brought about much confusion in the church about self-love.[3] Many well-meaning authors and Bible teachers distort the teachings of Christ in their attempts to make the Scriptures compatible with pop-psychology.[4] Perhaps the greatest of these distortions is the mishandling of a passage we've already mentioned, Matthew 22:36-40.

> *And one of them, a lawyer, asked Him [a question,] testing Him, "Teacher, which is the great commandment in the Law?" And He said to him, "You shall love the Lord your*

God with all your heart, and with all your soul, and with
all your mind.' This is the great and foremost command-
ment. The second is like it, 'You shall love your neighbor as
yourself.' On these two commandments depend the whole
Law and the Prophets."

The gist of this incorrect doctrine goes like this: "You cannot really love God and your neighbor unless and until you first learn to love yourself." This teaching turns the two greatest commandments into three and makes the original two dependent on the third.

Commandment Number One: *Love Yourself*
Commandment Number Two: *Love your neighbor*
Commandment Number Three: *Love God*

At first glance, this may *sound* plausible. However, nowhere does the Bible instruct you to love yourself. The Bible teaches in many places the very opposite: You are to *deny yourself* (cf. Matt. 10:39; 16:24; Mk. 8:34; Lk. 9:23; Jn. 12:25-26; Rom. 8:13; Col. 3:5; Tt. 2:12). When Jesus says, "love your neighbor as yourself," He does not mean that you should necessarily love your neighbor *in the same ways* you love yourself, but rather *with the same intensity* with which you naturally love yourself. He is not giving a third commandment as some have supposed, but is simply acknowledging that we all naturally love ourselves with a certain zeal and ardency—and He is commanding us to love others to that degree.

That is what Paul is reiterating to husbands in our passage. Read it again with this in mind.

So husbands ought also to love their own wives as their own
bodies. He who loves his own wife loves himself; for no one
ever hated his own flesh, but nourishes and cherishes it,
just as Christ also [does] the church, because we are mem-
bers of His body. "For this cause a man shall leave his

father and mother, and shall cleave to his wife; and the two
shall become one flesh." This mystery is great; but I am
speaking with reference to Christ and the church. Never-
theless let each individual among you also love his own wife
even as himself.

"Christian husband," he says, "you need to love and care for
your wife just as intensely as you naturally love and care for your
own body. When you love your wife, *you are loving yourself.* After
all, she is one flesh (one person) with you. You don't hate your
body or harm it, do you? You feed it and clothe it. You make sure
it has all it needs to function properly and grow. This is what
Christ does for the church, and this is the way God directs us to
think about and treat your wife. You've left Mom and Dad and
have become one body (one person) with her. You need to take
care of that new part of your body. I know this concept is hard to
fully comprehend, but think about the way Christ loves the church
and make it your goal to love your wife the same way. You must
love and care for your wife with the same intense fervor and ve-
hemence with which you already love and care for your own body."

How does your love for your wife compare with your love for
yourself? Do you provide for her needs as readily as you do your
own? If you don't love and care for her as intently as you love and
care for yourself, you don't love her enough.

"Lou, what about this 'cherish' word? I'm a man, and men
don't go around cherishing themselves. That terminology isn't
even in my vocabulary! How am I to cherish my wife when I'm
not even sure I know what 'cherish' means ?"

Do you remember what you did the last time you acciden-
tally cut your finger at home? Chances are you ran to the nearest
sink and began to run some cold water over the wound. Then,
you inspected the cut to determine just how deep it was. Next,
you put pressure on or around the wound to stop or slow the
bleeding. Then, you darted off to the nearest medicine cabinet to
find some disinfecting dressing and a bandage. With care, you
again cleansed the wound with the anti-infection spray, being

careful not to apply so much that it stung. At that point, you tore open the bandage, peeled off the protective covering, and carefully wrapped the wound—with just the right amount of pressure to inhibit the bleeding—without cutting off the circulation from the capillaries in your little finger. The point in this illustration, is that you *do*, in fact, know quite a lot about "cherishing."

Dr. Wayne Mack, in his excellent workbook of Bible studies for couples, *Strengthening Your Marriage*, gives additional insight into this passage.

> Normally, a man uses a lot of time and gives a great deal of thought, effort, and money to take care of himself... His needs, his desires, his aspirations, his hopes, his body, his comfort are very important to him. He nourishes and cherishes himself. He carefully protects and provides for the needs of his body. He does not deliberately do that which would bring harm to himself. When he is hungry, he eats. When he is thirsty, he drinks. When he is tired, he sleeps. When he is in pain, he goes to the doctor. When he cuts himself, he washes the wound and binds it up. When he sees an object coming toward him, he puts up his hands for protection. He very naturally and carefully and fervently nourishes and cherishes himself.[5]

These are the kinds of things you must do to your wife since she's now *"bone of your bone and flesh of your flesh"* (cf. Gen. 2:23).

"Well then, to what extent am I to give my wife what she *wants*?"

The answer to this question is a bit more difficult. In Chapter Eight, I will address this matter more fully. The short answer, however, is that you should try to give her as many of her wants as you can without sinning yourself, or tempting her to sin.

> But this I say, brethren, the time has been shortened, so that from now on those who have wives should be as though they had none; and those who weep, as though they did not weep; and those who rejoice, as though they did not rejoice;

and those who buy, as though they did not possess; and those
who use the world, as though they did not make full use of
it; for the form of this world is passing away. But I want
you to be free from concern. One who is unmarried is con-
cerned about the things of the Lord, how he may please the
Lord; but one who is married is concerned about the things
of the world, how he may please his wife, and [his inter-
ests] are divided. And the woman who is unmarried, and
the virgin, is concerned about the things of the Lord, that
she may be holy both in body and spirit; but one who is
married is concerned about the things of the world, how
she may please her husband (1 Cor. 7:29-34).

The principle (which again is assumed by Paul) is that a married person is naturally concerned about pleasing his or her spouse. This implies not only meeting a spouse's needs, but also to a certain extent, fulfilling his or her desires. The Bible assumes that you'll spend a certain amount of time, effort and thought pleasing your wife. However, moderation (and self-control) is to be shown in all things: "and those who use the world, as though they did not make full use of it" (v. 31; see also 1 Cor. 9:25). Other issues to consider include stewardship of time and money (Lk. 16:1-8; 19:12-27; Eph. 5:16), and whether or not the fulfilling of a particular desire might place a stumbling block before your wife (Lk. 17: 1-2; Rom. 14; 1 Cor. 8).

At the end of this chapter, you'll find an exercise to assist you in evaluating your wife's needs as well as your own resources. On the left-hand side of the page, begin to list those items you believe constitute her valid biblical needs as well as her desires. On the right-hand side of the page, start listing the resources God has given you to meet her needs and desires. When you're done, ask your wife to help you complete and prioritize both lists.

There's one more very important point that must be made before we end this chapter: *No husband can love his wife as Christ loves the church unless and until he is himself a Christian.* The love described in 1 Corinthians 13 cannot be consistently generated in the heart of a man who does not know Christ. A non-believer may be able to produce a few of the elements of true love for brief periods of time, but only a Christian (one who has the Holy Spirit residing within) can, day-in and day-out, love his wife with the kind of supernatural, sacrificial love which God requires. Only a real Christian has the ability to bear all things, believe all things, hope all things, and endure all things.

Again, if you have any questions about how to become a Christian, or about your relationship with Christ, take a moment right now to read Appendix A, "How Can I Be Saved?"

My Wife's Needs:	My Resources:
1. Time in the Word	1. (fill in.)
2. Time with you	2.
3. Food and shelter	3.
4. Sufficient sleep	4.

Add further information…

My Wife's Desires:	My Resources:
1. To go on dates/trips together.	1. (fill in.)
2.	
3.	
4.	

Add any further material at this point….

Specific Ways Christ Loves the Church

As you read through the New Testament, see how many examples of Christ's love for the church you can discover. Record these in the first column ("Scripture Reference"). In the second column ("How Christ Loves the Church") you may record the interpretation or explanation of exactly how Christ demonstrated His love for His bride. In the third column (Application: "How I Can Love My Wife?") record how many personal applications of the passage you can make in your marriage (i.e., how you can similarly demonstrate your love to your wife). Remember again that though there might be many ways to apply a passage of Scripture (column three), there is only one interpretation (column two) of Scripture (cf. 2 Pet. 1:20).

Scripture Reference	How Christ Loves the Church	Application: How can I love my wife?
1. Romans 5: 6-8	1. He loves sinners.	1. By quickly forgiving her.
2. 1 John 4:19	2. He initiated love.	2. By taking the initiative to...
3. John 3:16	3.	3.
4. Ephesians 5:2	4.	4.
5. Matthew 20:8	5.	5.
6. John 15:13	6.	6.

Notes

[1]Richard Baxter, *The Practical Works of Richard Baxter Volume One: A Christian Directory* (Ligonier: Soli Deo Gloria, 1990), p. 868.

[2]Ibid., pp. 868-869.

[3]For an excellent treatment of this subject see *The Biblical View of Self-Esteem, Self-Love, Self-Image* by Jay E. Adams (Eugene, Oregon: Harvest House Publishers, 1986).

[4]For a concise treatment of the sufficiency of the Scriptures in counseling, see my booklet *Is the Bible a Textbook for Counseling?* (Lindenhurst, NY: Reformation Press, 1999).

[5]Wayne Mack, *Strengthening Your Marriage* (Phillipsburg, NJ: Presbyterian and Reformed Publishing Company, 1977), pg. 31.

Chapter 6

How to Love Your Wife (part two)

Husbands, love your wives, and do not be embittered against them (Col. 3:19).

Witness one, "Frank." Frank came home from a late night at the office. After scarfing down his re-heated supper, he went upstairs to brush his teeth. The moment he opened the vanity drawer and spied the tube of toothpaste, which his wife had once again squashed in the middle, he flew into a rage. Slamming the drawer closed and flailing his arms he began to verbalize his anger in a very loud and irritated tone of voice.

"That woman! She's always squeezing the toothpaste tube in the middle. I've asked her a thousand times to roll it up from the end, but does she listen to me? Never! I might as well talk to the toothpaste tube itself than to try to ask her to do something for me. She's the most selfish and inconsiderate woman I've ever met. How would she like it if I ignored her incessant requests? She wouldn't like it one bit."

At this point, Frank stops speaking out loud but continues to muse over the toothpaste tube as he plots his revenge.

"I'll teach her a lesson. She hates it when anyone forgets to replace the cap on the toothpaste tube. I'm going to *leave it off*. Tomorrow morning when she comes in here to brush her teeth, she'll be furious that I forgot to replace the cap and that'll ruin her whole morning. And maybe, if I'm lucky, overnight the tooth-paste will harden in the neck of the tube and when she goes to squeeze out some toothpaste she wont be able to. And if I'm re-ally lucky, maybe she'll look into the neck of the tube as she tries to firmly squeeze it and that little pellet of hardened toothpaste will pop out of the tube and hit her in the eye!"

Now I ask you, is a squashed tube of toothpaste worth ex-pending all of that emotional energy? Hardly! What kind of re-sponse does a tube of toothpaste that has been repeatedly squashed in the middle deserve? If the toothpaste incident could not be overlooked altogether, then at the very most, here is about all the time, effort and thought that should be devoted to it:

"Oh, look at that! She squashed the toothpaste tube in the middle again. I'll have to keep on reminding her until she learns how to roll the tube up from the end."

When you exert inordinate amounts of emotional energy over such trivial disappointments, it's a good indication that you may be bitter.

"What is bitterness and how does a person become bitter?"

Bitterness is the result of *responding improperly to a hurt*. Take a look at Hebrews 12:15:

> See to it that no one comes short of the grace of God; that no
> root of bitterness springing up causes trouble, and by it many
> be defiled.

The Scripture likens bitterness to a *root*. Roots have to be planted. So, what's the seed that sprouts into a root of bitterness when planted? It's a *hurt*. When someone hurts you it's as if a seed has been dropped onto the soil of your heart.[1] You can choose to respond in two ways: You can either reach down and pluck up the seed by forgiving your offender, or you can begin to cultivate the seed by reviewing the hurt over and over again in your mind. Bitterness is the result of *dwelling too long on a hurt*; it's the result of not truly forgiving an offender (cf. Matt. 18:34-35).

Sam went into marriage assuming that his wife Laura would

be as interested in having sexual relations as frequently as he desired. At first she seemed to be, but soon after the honeymoon, things began to change. Her desire for sexual relations seemed to be diminishing. Laura would often be "too tired" for sex, or have some other reason for not participating. She hardly ever initiated relations, and when she did participate, she was very passive. Days without sex would turn into weeks. One Saturday morning, as they were lying in bed, Sam attempted to initiate a time of intimacy. As he did, Laura was unresponsive. She didn't verbally refuse to participate, she just didn't seem interested. Sam felt angry and rejected. She just dropped that proverbial seed of hurt onto his heart as she had done on many occasions in the past. Sam bolted out of the bed, threw on his clothes and stomped downstairs fuming over his profound disappointment.

As we take a peek into his secret thoughts, notice the cultivation process that transformed Sam's hurt into a root of bitterness.

Sam's Internal Monologue (Cultivation of Sam's Bitterness):

- "I can't believe she turned me down again." *Sam pokes the seed an inch into the soil of his heart with his finger.*
- "She never wants to have sex." *Sam covers the seed with more soil.*
- "She's as frigid as an ice cube." *Sam is aerating the soil.*
- "Doesn't she realize how selfish she's being?" *Sam is watering the seed.*
- "She's defrauding me. I never should have married her." *Sam is fertilizing his hurt (it's now starting to sprout).*
- "I have needs too and she's tempting me to lust after other women." *Sam is weeding his little sprout (as its roots grow deeper into his heart).*
- "She can't do this to me. I'll teach her not to reject me. I'm not going to talk to her for a few days. Let's see how she likes to face rejection." *Sam has built a greenhouse around his stink weed and is now charging people admission to see it.*

Sam should've removed the seed by explaining his disappointment to his wife, forgiving her when she repented, and working with her on a biblical solution to the problem. Instead, he allowed his hurt to paralyze him from taking the appropriate action, he replayed her offense over and over again in his mind, and he consequently became embittered against her. Have you ever done that with your wife? *Of course* you have, and so have I. The Bible calls this *sin*.

What are the evidences that a husband has become embittered towards his wife?[2] Here are a few I've come across in my twelve plus years of marriage counseling. How many can you personally identify in your own marriage?

- Frequent arguments (inability to resolve conflicts)
- Outbursts of anger (raising of the voice, throwing, hitting, etc.)
- Withdrawal (giving her the silent treatment or the cold shoulder)
- Diminished affection and sexual activity
- Sarcasm (mocking, ridiculing, mean-spirited joking, etc.)
- Acts of vengeance (getting even or trying to hurt her back)
- Condescending communication (speaking to her as though she were a child or an inferior person)
- Criticism (a critical, condemnatory, judgmental attitude)
- Suspicion and distrust
- Hypersensitivity (treating a pin prick as though it were a knife in the heart)
- Intolerance (not overlooking little offenses that once went unnoticed)
- Impatience
- Misuse of authority (domineering, dictatorial, or tyrannical attitudes which require needless exactions of obedience)
- Lack of social interaction with others as a couple
- Loss of companionship (the intimacy of the one flesh relationship is damaged and communication becomes superficial)
- Lack of respect (dishonoring her to her face and in the presence of others)

- Lack of kindness and sympathy
- Angry children (who have been greatly provoked by their parents)[3]

"I've tried to forgive my wife for the hurts she has caused me, but it's so hard to do—especially when she does the same hurtful things over and over again."

Perhaps that's because you've never understood what it really means to forgive someone *biblically*. You may, like so many, have a feelings-oriented view of forgiveness. Notice though, what God's Word says about forgiveness:

> For I will be merciful to their iniquities, And I will remember their sins [against them] no more (Heb. 8:12).

What is forgiveness? Forgiveness is not a feeling. Forgiveness, first and fundamentally, is a *promise*. Jay Adams has put it this way:

> Obviously, when God forgives us, He does not simply sit in the heavens and emote. So forgiveness isn't a feeling. If it were, we would never know that we have been forgiven. No, when God forgives, He goes on record. He says so. He declares, "I will not remember your sins" (Is. 43:25; see also Jer. 31:34). Isn't that wonderful? When He forgives, God lets us know that He will no longer hold our sins against us. If forgiveness were merely an emotional experience, we would not know that we were forgiven. But praise God, we do, because forgiveness is a process at the end of which God declares that the matter of sin has been dealt with once for all. Now what is that declaration? What does God do when He goes on record saying that our sins are forgiven? God makes a promise. Forgiveness is not a feeling; forgiveness is a *promise*![4]

When you grant forgiveness to someone, you're making a promise to that person which involves the following three things:

1. You're promising not to bring up the offense again to the forgiven person in the future. You will not use the offense "against him" in any kind of pejorative way.

2. You're promising not to speak to others about the offense. That is, you will cover the sin in love, not revealing to others that which has been covered.

3. You're promising not to dwell on the offense yourself. This is perhaps the most important of the three steps involved in forgiveness. By promising not to dwell on the offense, you're promising that you'll not "cultivate" the hurt by replaying it over and over again in your mind. Rather than seeing the face of your offender on a dart board ready to receive a dart right between the eyes (or on a golf ball which you intend to drive three hundred yards down the fairway), you will see him/her with the words "I Have Forgiven You" written in big bold letters across his/her face.

"But I still don't understand how I can forgive until I can *forget*."

Forgetting is not the same thing as not remembering. When you forgive, you will not remember your offender's sins *against him*, just like God does not remember your sins *against you* as a forgiven sinner. Does God have amnesia? No, God is omniscient and therefore knew about your sins even before you were born. When the Bible speaks of God "forgetting" our sins, it does not mean that He ceases to be omniscient. God's forgetting amounts to His *not reviewing our sins in His mind and not holding our sins against us*. God "remembers" the righteousness of His Son and imputes that righteousness to our account when we place our trust in the merit and mediation of Christ.[1] Similarly, *you* are required to "impute" your forgiveness to those who ask you to forgive them. Forgiveness is an act of the will, not an act of the emotions. Forgetting is not the *means* of forgiving, but the *result* of forgiving. It is the last step, not the first.

"I've been hurt so often by my wife, I just can't forgive her."

[1] Amen!

If you're a Christian, you *can* and you *must*. You can't say "can't" as a Christian. No, the Christian will say with Paul, *"I can do all things through Him who strengthens me"* (Phil. 4:13). When God tells you to do something, you must believe that He will enable you to obey Him. That is, you must believe that He will give you all the resources to do what He has commanded you to do. He promises to give you the wisdom to obey him: *"But if any of you lacks wisdom, let him ask of God, who gives to all men generously and without reproach, and it will be given to him"* (Jas. 1:5). He also promises to give you the ability and desire to obey Him: *"It is God who is producing in you both the willingness and the ability to do the things that please Him"* (Phil.. 2:13 CCNT).

The disciples had a hard time accepting Christ's command that they forgive an offender seven times in one day if he claimed that he was repentant.

> Be on your guard! If your brother sins, rebuke him; and if
> he repents, forgive him. And if he sins against you seven
> times a day, and returns to you seven times, saying, "I re-
> pent," forgive him (Lk. 17:3-4).

Think about that for a moment. Your wife rejects you seven times in one day, and seven times returns to you asking your forgiveness and you've got to forgive her. Now after the second or third time, you're going to have some serious doubts as to the sincerity of her repentance, aren't you? Yet Jesus says if she returns to you seven times a day saying "I repent," you must take her at her word and forgive her. That's kind of hard to believe, right?

The disciples were also incredulous when they heard this, and exclaimed: "Increase our faith!" (v. 5)

Well, did Jesus accept their incredulity? Not for a moment!

> And the Lord said, "If you had faith like a mustard seed,
> you would say to this mulberry tree, 'Be uprooted and be

planted in the sea'; and it would obey you. But which of you, having a slave plowing or tending sheep, will say to him when he has come in from the field, 'Come immediately and sit down to eat?' But will he not say to him, 'Prepare something for me to eat, and [properly] clothe yourself and serve me until I have eaten and drunk; and afterward you will eat and drink'? He does not thank the slave because he did the things which were commanded, does he? So you too, when you do all the things which are commanded you, say, 'We are unworthy slaves; we have done [only] that which we ought to have done'" (Lk. 17: 6-10).

Jesus says in effect, "Look guys, what I'm asking you to do is not optional. Don't be so incredulous. You don't need more faith, what you need is to be more obedient. You knew it would be tough when I signed you up for this job. All I'm asking you to do is what your job description calls for."

Perhaps the most convicting words Jesus ever spoke about forgiveness are found in Matthew 18: 21-35:

Then Peter came and said to Him, "Lord, how often shall my brother sin against me and I forgive him? Up to seven times?" Jesus said to him, "I do not say to you, up to seven times, but up to seventy times seven. For this reason the kingdom of heaven may be compared to a certain king who wished to settle accounts with his slaves. And when he had begun to settle [them,] there was brought to him one who owed him ten thousand talents. But since he did not have [the means] to repay, his lord commanded him to be sold, along with his wife and children and all that he had, and repayment to be made. The slave therefore falling down, prostrated himself before him, saying, 'Have patience with me, and I will repay you everything.' And the lord of that slave felt compassion and released him and forgave him the debt. But that slave went out and found one of his fellow slaves who owed him a hundred denarii; and he seized him and [began] to choke [him,] saying, 'Pay back what you owe.' His fellow slave fell down and [began] to entreat

him, saying, 'Have patience with me and I will repay you.'
He was unwilling however, but went and threw him in
prison until he should pay back what was owed. So when
his fellow slaves saw what had happened, they were deeply
grieved and came and reported to their lord all that had
happened. Then summoning him, his lord said to him, 'You
wicked slave, I forgave you all that debt because you en-
treated me. Should you not also have had mercy on your
fellow slave, even as I had mercy on you?' And his lord,
moved with anger, handed him over to the torturers until
he should repay all that was owed him. So shall My heav-
enly Father also do to you, if each of you does not forgive
his brother from your heart."

The king in the parable (God the Father), has forgiven his servant (the Christian) of a debt that was so great it could never be repaid. This debt is representative of the incalculable and incomprehensible debt of sin which we owe God and which we could never repay. When the servant was unwilling to forgive his fellow servant (probably another Christian), the king became angry, calling the unforgiving servant "wicked."

The point here is that it's nothing but sheer wickedness for you not to forgive your offender (wife) for what she's done, in light of all that you've been forgiven. When you compare the trivial offenses which you must forgive, with the enormous, eternal offenses you've committed against a holy God, the point is uncontestable.

"What about those torturers that God says He will hand me over to if I don't forgive from my heart?"

I personally believe those torturers are the mental, emotional, physiological and relational consequences associated with bitterness.¹ In other words, I believe that God chastises (cf. 1 Cor. 5:5, 11:30; Heb. 12:5-8; 1 Jn. 5:6) unforgiving Christians for their sin of not forgiving others. Insomnia, fear, anxiety, depression, broken fellowship with God and man, unanswered prayer, as well as dozens of psychosomatically-induced illnesses have been

¹ Not a bad point, but remember: not every single detail of a parable has direct application.

associated with bitterness. Perhaps one of the most devastating consequences of bitterness in marriage is the defilement of the children who become angry and bitter (and often rebellious) as a result of being exposed to their parents malignant relationship:[1]

> See to it that no one comes short of the grace of God; that no root of bitterness springing up causes trouble, and by it many be defiled (Heb. 12:15).

"How can I overcome my feelings of bitterness toward my wife?"

The practical answer to that question will be thoroughly explained in the next chapter, "How to Fight Back Without Getting Even." The short answer is, that having granted her forgiveness as an act of your will (inwardly), you'll now have to respond to her hurts with various acts of love and kindness (outwardly). As you overcome evil with good (Rom. 12:21), your feelings of bitterness will be replaced with the loving feelings that are in accordance with kindness, tenderheartedness and forgiveness (Eph. 4:31-32).

Before we go there, however, I must talk to you about bitterness' cousin, commonly known as *anger*. What is sinful anger? Simply put, sinful anger is God's built-in "alarm system" to let you know that you desire something too much. I've written elsewhere on this subject in my book, *The Heart of Anger*. The following is an extended excerpt from the book:

> The book of James was possibly the first New Testament book that was written. The Christians to whom the Lord's brother was writing were having such conflicts with each other that James used the words *wars* and *fightings* to describe the outward manifestation of their anger. In the beginning of Chapter Four, the question he asks cuts right through such outward manifestations and focuses on the internal causes or motives of the anger. "What is the *source* of quarrels ("wars" KJV) and conflicts ("fighting" KJV)

[1] Ephe 6:4

among you?" (Jas. 4:1). He then answers his own question to reveal to the readers exactly what is at the heart of their angry disputes (or what is *in their hearts* that produced their angry disputes). "Is not the source [of these quarrels and conflicts] the *pleasures* that wage war in your members?" "Yes!" is the intended reply.

We have angry conflicts with one another because our pleasures (i.e., desires which are not necessarily sinful in and of themselves) have become so intense that they are at war within our members. The term to "wage war" is a word that has as its root the idea of being "encamped". When our desires (as good as they may be) become so strong that they "camp out" in our hearts, those desires become sinful, idolatrous desires, not because they are sinful desires (*per se*) but because they are desired *inordinately*. Our hearts covet them so intensely that we are willing to sin (war and fight) either *in order* to obtain them or because *we are not able* to obtain them.

James, in Chapter 4, continues to focus on the Christian's motives by unpacking in more detail what he has just said. "You lust [a different word that also implies a desire for something that is not inherently sinful] and do not have, so you commit murder" [a biblical effigy for, and manifestation of, hatred—cf. Matt. 5:21-22; I Jn. 3:15]. "And you are envious [another synonym for desire with an implication of coveting, sometimes associated with anger—cf. Acts 7:9; 17:5] and cannot obtain: so you fight and quarrel." [verbal forms of the words fightings and quarrels in vs. 1, which mean to strive or dispute and to contend or quarrel respectively].

Having unpacked verse one, he continues to press home his point that the cause of their relationship problems is their selfish, idolatrous motives as evidenced by their self-centered prayer life. "You do not have because you do not ask. You ask and do not receive because you ask with wrong motives so that you may spend it on your pleasures [the same word for pleasure that was used in vs. 1 from which our English word *hedonism* is derived]. You adulteresses [their selfish motives have not only hurt their interpersonal relationships with each other, but have so affected their relationship with God that he views them as unfaithful spouses], do you not know that the friendship with the world [the love of the world to the point of idolatry] is hostility toward God [they have loved the world to such a degree that the love of God is not in them (cf. I Jn. 2:15), again demonstrating that their own desires are affecting their relationship not only with each other, but also with God]? Therefore whoever wishes to be a friend of the world makes himself an enemy of God."

On the other hand, God desires us to desire Him with the same kind of desire with which He desires us. James continues: "Or do you think that the Scripture speaks to no purpose: 'He jealously desires the Spirit which He has made to dwell in us?'" The Spirit of God earnestly desires that we not displace our love for Him with a love for anything that the world has to offer.

The best evidence that a Christian desires (loves) something more than he desires (loves) God is his willingness to sin against God either *in order to acquire that desire,* or *because he cannot acquire it.* "If you love Me keep My commandments," Jesus said (Jn. 14:15). One of the most common sins that demonstrates the presence of inordinate desire is anger.[5]

When you become sinfully angry at your wife it's almost certainly because there's something that you want, desire, long for or crave that she's either not giving you or keeping you from having. It may be a good thing, like Frank wanting his wife to roll the toothpaste up from the bottom instead of squashing it in the middle. Or like Sam, who wanted regular and continuous sexual relations with Linda. That which you want may in fact be something that the Bible says you should be able to enjoy, like sexual relations with your wife; receiving honor from her; time alone with the Lord, or respect from your children.

Now, we are discussing in this chapter a husband's responsibility to not become bitter and angry at his wife. Let's see if we can identify exactly what it is that provokes you to anger. Place a check next to the items listed below that push your "hot button." As you look at these items, ask yourself what it is that you want most from your wife, and what it is that provokes an angry response in you when you don't get it.

- ❐ To be more respectful to me
- ❐ To be my suitable helper
- ❐ To spend less time on the phone
- ❐ To spend less money
- ❐ To be more trusting of me
- ❐ To not be a people-pleaser
- ❐ To lose weight
- ❐ To be more affectionate
- ❐ To initiate sexual relations more frequently
- ❐ To enjoy sexual relations more intensely
- ❐ To be more feminine
- ❐ To take better care of her appearance
- ❐ To be more attentive to me
- ❐ To not have unrealistic expectations about me
- ❐ To be more godly
- ❐ To be less critical
- ❐ To be more forgiving
- ❐ To ask for my opinion more
- ❐ To not put the children's needs ahead of mine
- ❐ To follow my instructions more carefully
- ❐ To not have to have the last word
- ❐ To support my decisions more

- ❐ To be more submissive
- ❐ To not challenge or appeal my decisions
- ❐ To cook with variety
- ❐ To not be so bossy with me
- ❐ To not be so worldly
- ❐ To not disagree with me in the presence of others
- ❐ To not expect me to read her mind
- ❐ To not be so serious
- ❐ To better control her temper
- ❐ To better control her tongue
- ❐ To not be anxious
- ❐ To not forget important things that I tell her
- ❐ To be more of a giver / less of a taker
- ❐ To be more patient with me
- ❐ To be more self-disciplined
- ❐ To be more gracious
- ❐ To be a better disciplinarian with the children
- ❐ To not waste so much time
- ❐ To be more grateful
- ❐ To keep the house clean and attractive
- ❐ To verbally express more love for me
- ❐ To be less career-oriented
- ❐ To be more hospitable

- ❏ To be closer to me than anyone else.
- ❏ To take more interest in my friends or leisure activities.
- ❏ To pray and read her Bible more
- ❏ To be less perfectionistic
- ❏ To try harder to please me
- ❏ To be more discrete
- ❏ To admit when she's wrong
- ❏ To be more industrious
- ❏ To tell me what she is thinking (rather than my having to draw it out or her)
- ❏ To be more punctual
- ❏ To not be so moody or temperamental
- ❏ To more fully understand the pressures of my job
- ❏ To be more involved in church
- ❏ To cooperate with my leadership of the family
- ❏ To not be so friendly or flirtatious with other men
- ❏ To better prioritize her spiritual responsibilites

add further items...

"Now that I've identified my 'hot buttons' (my idolatrous desires), what do I do next?"

You must work on *dethroning your idols*. That is, you must prayerfully and actively replace those inordinate desires with desires that are in accordance with pleasing and glorifying God, rather than with pleasing and glorifying yourself. You must learn to change the way you think about your desires and the extent to which your wife must meet them. Rather than thinking, "My wife is a...(insert your favorite word) for not giving me what I want," you must learn to think, "Having a wife who doesn't...(insert your inordinate desire), is not the worst thing in the world. I must learn to love the Lord and to love her more than I love my...(insert your inordinate desire)."

How Does Anger Relate to Bitterness?

Do you think Frank exploded at his wife the first time she left the toothpaste tube undone? Probably not. What about Sam? Did he react so passionately the first time Linda turned down his sexual advances? Presumably, no. When Linda declined his sexual advances, it was as if a little computer screen flashed up in Sam's mind. On the screen he saw not just one offense that could be more easily overlooked, but rather a list of offenses categorized under the heading (in bold print), **"Specific Ways that Linda Has Turned Me Down Over the Years."** At the top of the list was Saturday morning's disappointment: "*Entry number 254.*" If Sam and Frank had responded biblically to all the previous hurts and disappointments, and brought their desires under the control of Christ, they wouldn't have become so embittered against their wives.

How about *you*? Have you forgiven your wife for the hurtful things she's said and done to you over the years? Do you use sinful anger as a warning device to help you identify and dethrone those idolatrous desires in your heart? If the answer is "yes" to those two questions, then you can rest assured that bitterness is a long way from rooting itself in the soil of your heart.

I'll conclude this chapter with another quotation from Richard Baxter. This should serve to remind you that when you covenanted with your wife in marriage, you did so knowing that she was a sinner and, as such, one who would be in need of your constant forgiveness.

> Remember still that you are both diseased persons, full of infirmities; and therefore expect the fruit of those infirmities in each other; and make not a strange matter of it, as if you had never known of it before. If you had married one that is lame, would you be angry at her for halting [limping]? Or if you had married one that had a putrid ulcer, would you fall out with her because it stinketh? Did you not know beforehand, that you married a person of such weakness, as would yield you some manner of daily trial and offense? If you could not bear this, you should not have married her; if you resolved that you could bear it then, you are obliged to bear it now. Resolve therefore to bear with one another; as remembering that you took one another as sinful, frail, imperfect persons, not as angels, or as blameless and perfect.[6]

Christian husband, love your wife, sinful as she may be at times, and do not allow her sins and idiosyncrasies to cause you to become embittered against her. Remember, she has to live with, love, and forgive a man who is also a sinner and very peculiar in his own ways.

Hot Button Identification

Review the "hot button" check-list discussed earlier in this chapter. The list represents common desires and expectations that husbands have for their wives. Most of these wants are basically good things which become sinful only when they are desired inordinately. Check those items which you desire so much that you've been willing to sin in order to get from your wife, or sin if your wife did not give you.

When you've identified each potentially inordinate desire, discuss each one with your wife, gently explaining to her why they are so important to you. Ask her to forgive you for all the times you became angry, or bitter, or manipulative as a result of your coveting them. Discuss with her how you should communicate each desire to her in the future, and how you should respond in the future, should she disappoint you by not fulfilling each desire.

Notes

[1] The hurt can be real or imagined, it makes no difference: the result is the same. If you do not deal with it biblically you'll become bitter. If I hurt you as a result of my sin, and you choose not to overlook it or cover it in love (Prov. 17:9; 1 Pet. 4:8) you must follow Lk. 17:3 and pursue me with the intent of granting me forgiveness, and I must repent. If you get your feelings hurt as a result of something that I did which was not a sin, you must repent of your unbiblical thinking which caused you to be offended at something that was not a sin.

[2] For a more detailed description of some of the more obvious evidences of bitterness on the part of a husband towards his wife, see *The Family in its Civil and Churchly Aspects*, by B.M. Palmer, (Harrisonburg, VA: Sprinkle Publications, 1991), pp.32-40.

[3] I have explained the defiling influence (Heb. 12:15) of marital disharmony on children in *The Heart of Anger* (pp. 21-22, 31).

[4] Jay E. Adams, *From Forgiven to Forgiving* (Amityville, N.Y.: Calvary Press, 1994), pp. 11-12.

[5] *The Heart of Anger*, pp. 105-107.

[6] Baxter, p. 433, [*clarification added*].

Chapter 7

How to Fight Back Without Getting Even

In the last chapter, perhaps you wondered, "How can I overcome my feelings of bitterness toward my wife?" In this chapter, we're going to look at the answer to this question in more detail.[1] Stay with me for a moment while I provide the necessary groundwork to do this.

Contrary to what you might have thought, when you "fell in love" with your wife, you were not struck with some kind of external stimulus such as "Cupid's arrow" or a "zap" from some other mystical marriage-broker. Rather, *you* created the romantic feelings that you had for her by means of both what you told yourself about her, and what you did *to*, *for* and *with* her. That is, your own heart produced those wonderful feelings as a by-product of your thoughts and actions. It's sort of like the root of bitterness principle (Chapter Six) in reverse. Any bitter, hurtful or resentful feelings you now may have toward her are also the by-products of your thoughts and actions. You most likely developed warm, loving feelings toward her during your courtship. If you're now bitter at her, it's because in one way or another, *you've stopped courting her*. Your lack of courtship has slowed down the "emotional love generator" in your heart. Additionally, the unkind and unforgiving thoughts you now think about her (in contrast to the kind and loving thoughts you experienced during courtship) throw a monkey wrench into the "generator" and prevent those loving feelings from developing. It's basically that simple.

If you want to revive the romance you once had for your wife, you'll have to change both the way you *think about her* as well as the *things you do for her.* You'll have to start courting her once again, and you'll have to start *right now*—even though you may have bitter feelings for her in your heart.

Who in the Bible Fell out of Love?

Can you think of someone in the Bible who fell out of love? The account I'm thinking of is found in the New Testament.

> *To the angel of the church in Ephesus write: "The One who holds the seven stars in His right hand, the One who walks among the seven golden lampstands, says this: 'I know your deeds and your toil and perseverance, and that you cannot endure evil men, and you put to the test those who call themselves apostles, and they are not, and you found them [to be] false; and you have perseverance and have endured for My name's sake, and have not grown weary. But I have [this] against you, that you have left your first love'"* (Rev. 2:1-4).

The church at Ephesus had lost their intense, fervent devotion to Christ. No doubt, the intensity of their emotional fervency for Him had declined. Notice though, the counsel the Lord did *not* give them. He did *not* give them some feelings-oriented solution to their problem, like: "You need to reach down into the depths of you're heart (or 'love cup') and stir up that warm fuzzy feeling that you had for Me when you first became Christians." Actually, Jesus did not command them to emote at all. Rather, He told them to change the way they *thought,* as well as the way they *behaved.*

> *Remember therefore from where you have fallen, and repent and do the deeds you did at first; or else I am coming*

to you, and will remove your lampstand out of its place—unless you repent (Rev. 2:5).

The same counsel that was given to the church at Ephesus can be rightly applied to husbands who no longer love their wives as they once did. Christ's counsel to the Ephesians is threefold. First, He tells them: "*remember...from where you have fallen.*" It's as if He's saying, "remember the way it used to be when you fervently loved Me." Memory can be a very effective spiritual weapon (Psa. 42:6, 119:55; 143:5; Lam. 3:21). Chances are, if your love for your wife has grown cold, you've forgotten the way things used to be. When you married your wife, you were in the habit of *doing* certain loving things for her that you're no longer doing and *thinking* certain lovely things about her that you're no longer thinking. The first step in recovering your lost love for your wife is to remember how far you've fallen out of love with her, and especially how far you've left off doing those loving things that you used to do.

The second thing that Christ commanded the Ephesian church was to "*repent.*" They were instructed to change their minds and their actions. So you too, must change any sinful thought patterns that you've developed concerning your wife, as well as those actions (sins of commission and omission) you're committing against her.

The third and final part of Christ's counsel to the Ephesians was to "*do the deeds you did at first.*" They were commanded to begin doing, once again, those things that they did at first— when their love for Christ was ardent and zealous. So also, *you* must do the deeds *you* did at first, to, with, and for your wife and replace any bitterness towards her with feelings of love. As you change the way you treat your wife and think about her, your feelings for her will change proportionately for the better.

Kim and I had been married for less than a year. It was Saturday morning, and she was hurt by something I'd done. No matter how I tried, I couldn't seem to resolve the conflict with words alone. After about 20 or 30 minutes, I decided to do something radical. I wrote her a note explaining that I was going to the store, making it clear to her that I would be back momentarily. I left the note on the kitchen table and went out to buy her some flowers. I distinctly remember the drive to the flower shop. I was hurt and very angry with Kim as I pled with the Lord: "Please help her to see how unreasonable she's being." I was rehearsing some of the conflict in my mind, partially cultivating that root of bitterness; yet I was in the process of showing her love. My mind was struggling with cursing her, but my body was in the process of blessing her. I was, as an act of my will and in direct contradiction to my emotions, trying to overcome what I perceived to be her evil with good: *"Do not be overcome by evil, but overcome evil with good"* (Rom. 12:21).

As I continued driving to the store, trying to fight bitterness, my emotions continued to torment me. I walked into the store resolutely determined to "fight back" biblically, but still struggling with bitter feelings. And then *it happened*. The moment I picked up those flowers, both my entire thought pattern and my emotional response immediately and radically changed.

"I can't wait to see the expression on her face when I give her these flowers (I thought); as soon as she sees them, she's going to melt. She won't be able to stay upset with me now. This is going to knock her socks off. She'll not be able to resist any longer!"

The drive home was quite different than the drive to the flower shop. Excitement and anticipation grew as I rehearsed what I was going to say to her (cf. Prov. 15:28). My heart began to swell with loving feelings that had eluded me all morning. I was actually *looking forward* to the ensuing conversation.

I walked through the door with an entirely different attitude than when I had left. As I presented the flowers to her, she was obviously moved. I knew that the flowers were not going to solve the problem, but would probably open the door for us to resolve the conflict biblically. When Kim realized that I was going to show her love in the face of her being less than loving to me, she softened. Within ten minutes, the conflict was brought to a total, biblical resolution.

"I still can't see myself doing this while I'm upset with her."

That's the time when it is probably most necessary. Let's look at the "overcome evil with good" passage more closely.

> *Never pay back evil for evil to anyone. Respect what is right in the sight of all men. If possible, so far as it depends on you, be at peace with all men. Never take your own revenge, beloved, but leave room for the wrath [of God,] for it is written, "Vengeance is Mine, I will repay," says the Lord. "But if your enemy is hungry, feed him, and if he is thirsty, give him a drink; for in so doing you will heap burning coals upon his head." Do not be overcome by evil, but overcome evil with good* (Rom. 12:17-21).

I'd like to focus your attention on the last verse: this is the summary statement of the preceding paragraph; the river into which the preceding verses converge: *"Do not be overcome by evil, but overcome evil with good."* This imperative contains two difficult commands which will need explanation. The first injunction is: *"Do not be overcome by evil."* Another way of saying this is, "you may not lose in your personal battles against evil." Think about that for a moment: You're actually commanded *not to lose* this particular battle you're fighting. Conversely, if you *do lose* in your fight against evil, you've sinned.

"Is that really what it means?"

Yes!

Before I explain further, however, I must point out that this entire paragraph (Rom. 12:17-21) is filled with the terminology of *war*. Although some believe that Christianity is pacifistic, the Bible is filled with battle terminology which instructs the believer to have the mindset of a soldier. This passage from Romans 12 is a prime example of such terminology.

In verse 17, you are warned against the improper use of

weapons and briefed on the importance of developing a *battle plan*. Verse 18 stresses the importance of *peace* (the antithesis and desired result of war). Verse 19 cautions you not to take personal *vengeance*, and provides you with guidance on the do's and don'ts of *retaliation*. Verse 20 provides you with instruction on how to *destroy your enemy* (with coals of fire). Verse 21 twice contains the war-time term for *conquer* (overcome).

Now, who is the enemy spoken of in this passage? The enemy is evil—that is, evil people and the evil that they do. So, here you're fighting evil (let's say some sin that your wife is committing against you), and God says that you may not lose. That is, you *may not allow her sin to overcome you.*

- You may not retreat.
- You may not surrender.
- You may not give up.
- You may not throw in the towel.
- You may not wimp out.
- You may not allow her evil to prevail against you.
- You may not allow her sin against you to provoke you to sin against her.

Symptoms of Battle Fatigue

How many battles have you lost? Do you have any symptoms of battle fatigue? Here are a few common indications that you may have been overcome by evil!

- Telling yourself things like, "She'll never change," or, "I just can't live with this woman any longer."
- Permitting yourself to become bitter at her.
- Relinquishing your spiritual leadership ("After all, she won't let me lead anyway").
- Unnecessarily limiting the scope of communication with her because of unsuccessful attempts to resolve conflicts in the past.

- Allowing anger to keep you from confronting her biblically.
- Allowing yourself to become sinfully angry, anxious or depressed about the hurtful things she does to you.
- Allowing your "hurt feelings" to keep you from fulfilling your biblical responsibilities as a husband and/or father.
- Resorting to sinful, retaliatory actions such as: *gossip, withdrawal, slander, name calling, pouting, temper tantrums, sulking, threatening, quarreling, abusive speech.*

If you have even one symptom of battle fatigue, you almost certainly have lost a battle by allowing your wife's sin to overcome you. You have responded to sin with sin, and are in violation of Romans 12:21a, which commands you to not be defeated by evil.

As difficult as that may be for you to believe, the second command in this verse may tempt you to greater incredulity, for it's even harder to obey.[2] The second injunction, Romans 12:21b is: *"Overcome (conquer) evil with good."* What Paul is essentially saying is, "You may not accept anything less than victory in your personal battles against evil; you must *win the war*." To put it another way, Paul is saying, "You may not cease from pursuing your opponent with good until you win the war; you're to pursue the enemy until he/she gives in." There's no place in this verse for stalemates; no place for standoffs; no impasses; no mutual (bilateral) disarmament, no deadlock; no cease-fire before the victory. You're not to be done in, but you're to do the other person in. The issue is not how long you can hold out in the face of her attacks, but rather, how you can use the resources that God has given you to fight with so that you can defeat the foe.

This second command not only requires you to win the battle, but also defines the means you're to use in order to secure the victory. You see, God is interested not only in whether you win or lose, but in how you play the game (or fight the battle, in this case). Means are very important to God. The only means whereby you may defeat the enemy (indeed, *can* defeat the enemy), is the

means of *doing good*. Your weapons must be only those arma-
ments that can be considered "good" in God's eyes. With this state-
of-the art weaponry provided by God, you can fight back harder
than your female opponent. Blow for blow, good is more powerful than evil.

"This retaliation doesn't sound very Christian to me. Besides,
Romans 12:17-19 seems to forbid all forms of retaliation."

Let's begin to unpack the entire passage.

Never pay back evil for evil to anyone (Rom. 12:17a).

This passage actually doesn't forbid all forms of retaliation. It
forbids retaliating *in kind*. You may not retaliate in kind—that is,
with evil. You may fight back, but you may only fight back with
good. The ammunition you load in your firearm must be bullets
that are biblically certified as "good." Your motive is not to hurt,
but to bless her with goodness until goodness overtakes her sin
and motivates her to repent (cf. Rom. 2:4).

Consider two more New Testament passages that contradict
the doormat approach.

*Not returning evil for evil, or insult for insult, but giving a
blessing instead; for you were called for the very purpose
that you might inherit a blessing* (1 Pet. 3:9).

Rather than returning evil for evil or insult for insult, you are
to (actively) give a blessing in return. This is hardly a passive
response.

*See that no one repays another with evil for evil, but al-
ways seek after that which is good for one another and for
all men* (1 Thess. 5:15).

The word "seek after" in this verse may also rightly be interpreted "persecute" as it is in Romans 12:14: *"Bless those who persecute you; bless and curse not."* The passage might well be under-

stood this way: "See that no one repays another with evil for evil, but always *persecute one another* with good." This is hardly the response of a doormat.

"But, what about Matthew 5:39, which commands us to turn the other cheek? What you're saying seems to contradict the words of Christ, doesn't it?"

Not at all. Matthew 5:39 is more of an aggressive command than you might think. It's actually an *offensive weapon* designed to win the war against evil. Jay Adams writes in his *How to Overcome Evil*:

> The false interpretation of turning the other cheek that equates that action with defeatism, doormatism ("all I can do is lie here and invite you to wipe your muddy boots on me"), pacifism or non-aggression, must be exposed for what it is—a non Christian misrepresentation of the truth. Everywhere the Bible teaches that the Christian must aggressively fight against evil and overcome it.
>
> The Christian can no more take a passive attitude toward evil than his Lord did. He came into this world to take captivity captive. He came to destroy the works of the evil one and render him powerless (Heb. 2:14). He "disarmed rulers and authorities, and made a public display of them"(Col. 2:15). There was nothing passive about the cross. The cross was *active*. He was sacrificing Himself for the sins of His people to free them from the chains of sin and the devil. Why then should they willingly submit to these shackles once more?
>
> The Bible teaches the *violent*, not passive, overthrow of the enemy. He must be smashed to smithereens, demolished, utterly devastated. No quarter may be given. His power and place are to be destroyed. The Christian position is the most violent and aggressive one of all.[3]

Remember that the enemy is not your wife, but the evil that she may occasionally inflict on you. It's not that you are to "do your wife in," but you are to "do in the evil that she does." To use more vivid metaphor, allow me to put it this way:

When your wife shoots her pop-gun at you, you may fire back with your pepper spray.

If she pulls out a water pistol, you can hit her with a douse of your flame thrower.

If she aims her pea-shooter at your forehead, you engage your missile-launcher.

If she brandishes a sling shot, you pick up your bazooka.

Should she resort to a SCUD Missile, you launch your Patriot Missile at her.

The next imperative in the passage (Rom. 12:17b) requires you to draw up a battle plan: *"Plan ahead to do what is right in the sight of all men."*

Few translations bring out the literal meaning of the verb that begins this command. It's actually a participle that literally means "to think of beforehand." God is saying that you must plan your next response to evil before the next battle. That's right, you must anticipate beforehand (cf. Prov. 15:28) how you're going to respond to the conflict, so that when you find yourself in the heat of the battle, you will not respond to evil in kind, but rather respond to it with good. This is how soldiers are prepared for battle in basic training. They are drilled on how to fight *before* the battle so that they'll respond automatically in the heat of combat.

Do you know exactly how you're going to respond to your wife the next time she sins against you? Have you prepared your arsenal? Have you cleaned and loaded your weapons? Have you practiced fighting with them? If not, you'll likely pick up the first familiar (but sinful) weapon at hand when the bullets start to fly, and thus be overcome by her evil rather than overcoming her evil with good.

The next command has two clauses—one is conditional, the other is unconditional.

> *If possible, so far as it depends on you, be at peace with all men* (Rom. 12:18).

The first stipulation is the conditional one, "*If possible...*live at peace with all men" (believers and unbelievers). It's not always possible for Christians to be at peace with unbelievers—even in marriage (cf. 1 Cor. 7:15). But there's no reason why two believers can't learn how to be at peace with one another. Indeed, they are commanded to "*make every effort to keep the unity of the Spirit through the bond of peace*" (Eph. 4:3 NIV).

The second clause is unconditional, "*so far as it depends on you,* be at peace with all men." You must "pursue peace with all men" (Heb. 12:14), regardless of their response to you. Your obedience to God does not depend on the response of your wife. Your love for her should not be conditional; it's not predicated on her love for you. Regardless of her willingness to be at peace with you, *you* should be willing to be at peace with her— especially if she's a fellow believer.

Now, if your wife is not at peace with you, don't assume first of all that it's because she's not at peace with God. It's possible that the reason she's not at peace with you is because of some things that "depend on you." Let me suggest, in the form of three questions, some reasons why she may not be at peace with you.

1. Have I *provoked* her to evil? Your wife's evil against you may, in part, be a sinful response to an evil that you have first committed against her. While she's not thereby exonerated, you must seek her forgiveness for anything you may have done to provoke her to evil in the first place.

2. Have I *protracted* her evil by a sinful response in return? Is it possible that, rather than responding with good to her sin, you responded in kind (perhaps with even more evil than she inflicted against you), and that such a sinful response on your part has contributed greatly to the lack of peace between you?

3. Have I *prolonged* the problem by not dealing with it quickly? According to Matthew 5:23-24, conflicts between believ-

ers are to be resolved expeditiously: *"If therefore you are present-*
ing your offering at the altar, and there remember that your brother
has something against you, leave your offering there before the altar,
and go your way; first be reconciled to your brother, and then come
and present your offering" (Matt. 5:23-24). The longer you wait to
resolve conflicts, the more bitterness and suspicion can take root
and fester.

The next command in our text is found in verse 19:

> *Never take your own revenge, beloved, but leave room for*
> *the wrath [of God] for it is written, "Vengeance is Mine, I*
> *will repay," says the Lord.*

Have you ever wondered why the Bible forbids you from taking your own revenge? Why does God insist on doing it for you?
There are at least two reasons. *First,* God has not given you (or
any one person) the *authority* to take personal vengeance on anyone. What Paul is addressing in this passage you'll remember, is
personal conflicts against evil people, or the evil that people do.
In the next chapter (13) of Romans, Paul deals with the corpo-
rate or governmental right of God-ordained authorities to execute vengeance: *"for he is a minister of God, an avenger who brings*
wrath on the children of disobedience" (Rom. 13:4). Haven't you
just seen such wording ("avenger" and "wrath"): *"Never take your*
own revenge, beloved, but leave room for the wrath [of God], for it is
written, 'Vengeance is Mine, I will repay,' says the Lord"?

You see, vengeance is not for you to take personally (individually). It's a *judicial* issue, not a *personal* one. Ultimately, God
is the One who will right all wrongs. Vengeance is lawlessness
because it doesn't recognize the lawful and righteous execution
of God's judgment which He will bring about in His time. In
other words, vengeance amounts to being impatient with God.
You must remember that wrongs cannot always be righted immediately (cf. 1 Tim 5:24).

Vengeance does not belong to you. It belongs to God.

"'Vengeance is Mine, I will repay,' says the Lord." If God were to say to you, "This is my crown," would you walk up to Him and take it off of His head?

"Of course not, that would be stealing (not to mention foolishness)!"

Well, what do you think that you're doing every time you take your own revenge? You're *stealing from God*. Don't do it. He didn't give you such authority.

The *second* reason you're forbidden to execute your own vengeance is because you really don't have the *ability* to do so. That is, you don't have all the facts necessary to make the proper judgment.

Take a look at 1 Corinthians 4:5:

> *Therefore do not go on passing judgment before the time, [but wait] until the Lord comes who will both bring to light the things hidden in the darkness and disclose the motives of [men's] hearts; and then each man's praise will come to him from God.*

There are things that are hidden from you which only the Lord knows. Suppose your enemy was suffering from a physical disorder that made it easier for him to become angry. While this would not exonerate him from culpability, it would require a bit more mercy than you would be disposed to give him, not having all the facts. Or, suppose he's done the same thing to twelve other people this month and deserves a more serious judgment than you'd think to give him. Additionally, you don't know his motives. They likewise might be better or worse than you realize. Only God knows what they are: *"Man looks at the outward appearance, but the Lord looks at the heart"* (1 Sam. 16:7). The amount of vengeance required by God's justice is predicated on His knowledge of men's motives, knowledge to which you've not been given access. Keep this in mind the next time you're tempted to be vindictive toward your wife.

We're now ready to unveil the ultimate weapon for dealing with those who fight against us with evil (verse 20).

> *But if your enemy is hungry, feed him, and if he is thirsty, give him a drink; for in so doing you will heap burning coals upon his head.*

"Haven't we seen this verse somewhere before?"

Yes and no. In Chapter Five, we saw and explained the Old Testament verse spoken by Solomon (and recorded by the men of Hezekiah) which Paul cites and amplifies in our passage. "Jesus tells us to love our enemies" and "Solomon tells us how to do it," I said. The point, you'll remember, had to do with loving people by *meeting their needs* (vs. fulfilling their desires). The ultimate weapon to use against those who do evil is to *love them*: to meet their needs. The best way to overcome the evil that your wife perpetrates against you is to *love her*—to meet her needs. Look again at that list you made of her needs and your resources (at the end of Chapter Five). Look again at the list of ways you can demonstrate love to your wife (Appendix C). Plan ahead to overcome her evil with good by meeting her needs in love. The worksheet at the end of this chapter will help you to begin building an arsenal in advance of the next conflict.

"OK, I understand the marching orders, but tell me, what about those 'coals of fire'? What are they?"

Since virtually everything I've written in this chapter I've "learned and received and heard" from my friend and mentor (and fishing buddy), Dr. Jay E. Adams, I'm going to let him answer that question in his own words: "The coals are your good deeds heaped on him." Dr. Adams continues:

> Remember, Paul has warfare in mind. In his day, they didn't have flame throwers, but they knew that fire was an effective weapon. If you could get coals (of smokeless undetectable charcoal, as the word here indicates) on your enemies' head, you would effectively put him out of busi-

ness as an enemy. You would subdue and overcome him. Picture your troops holding your heights above the pass. Secretly you have heated large beds of charcoal to white heat. As the unsuspecting enemy passes directly beneath, you shovel them on his head. You have him! You've defeated him! He is rendered powerless, helpless! You've stopped him in his tracts. That is the picture.[4]

Now that you have a basic understanding of your marching orders, let me set up a battlefield scenario so that you can see for yourself how to apply this passage in the context of your marriage. The examples employed in the following illustration may not be the best weapons for you to use with your wife. They are intended only to give you a basic idea of how to fight back without getting even. Part of your responsibility to live with your wife in an understanding way is to know which good deeds will most effectively overcome her particular sinful response.

Your wife informs you that she needs a new widget for the kitchen. You disagree that it's something that's really necessary, but after listening to her appeal, you concede to the purchase. The only stipulation that you place on her is that she not spend more than $25 on the widget.

First conflict: She comes home from the store with the most expensive version of the widget on the market. It costs $63.50. She just hit you in the neck with a stinging pelt from her peashooter.

Now what are you going to do? Are you going to unleash your pet rattlesnake on her with a string of unbiblical utterances? No. This time you're going to do what you've been planning on doing since the last time she blatantly ignored your instructions: You're going to pull out your slingshot and carefully load it with *good*. After forcing yourself to say something nice about the widget, which you still believe is superfluous, you're going to calmly sit her down and gently ask her if she remembered your instructions to be sure you have the details right, before you reprove her. If reproof is necessary, be sure she understands that she was not disobeying you, but the Bible which states that a woman must be submissive to her husband in all things that are not obviously sinful. (Eph. 5:22-24; 1 Pet. 3:1-6). After all, the Bible says in 2 Timothy 2:24-25: *"...the Lord's bond-servant must not be quarrelsome, but be kind to all, able to teach, patient when wronged, with gentleness correcting those who are in opposition,"* and such a biblical response is a good one.

Second conflict: Before you can finish the first sentence of your argument, she becomes highly defensive. As you try again, she raises her voice, accuses you of being "cheap," and stands up crying, "You don't love me! You never buy me anything I ask for without making me feel miserable about it! I need it and I'm not going to take it back!" Then she stomps out of the room and storms off to the bedroom, slamming the door so hard that three pictures and a plate fly off the wall. She has bruised your head with a .45 caliber slug. *Now* what are you going to do?

What you're going to do is prayerfully go back to your biblical arsenal and pull out your .357 magnum. You've thought this through already. So it's no big deal. You've practiced it countless times in your mind. You decide that while she's in the bedroom fuming at you, you're going to do the dishes for her. After that you'll vacuum the floor. Then you'll make her a cup of tea, bring it up to her on a tray along with a fresh flower that you just cut from the yard and placed in her favorite vase. "Yes," you say to yourself, "this will do her in. She'll never be able to resist." The anticipation grows. As you begin to do those loving things for her, your feelings begin to change. You notice a spring in your step and a song starting to come from your mouth. "This will do her in! Victory, sweet victory is near!"

Third conflict: As you walk into the bedroom with the tea and flowers she glares at you. Before you can utter a word, she blurts out, "You're so selfish. I'm sorry I ever married you. Please go away and leave me alone." She refuses to talk to you and gives you the cold shoulder. As you walk out the door you're stunned and confused that she could refuse such kindness. She has just thrown a javelin through your heart and you're bleeding pretty badly. You pray, "Lord, what do I do now? I wasn't prepared for this."

Your mind races for another weapon to pull out of your arsenal, but nothing you can think of seems appropriate for this battle, so you grab your Bible and begin searching for appropriate passages to help you plan your next move. You begin reading Galatians 6:1: *"Brethren, even if a man is caught in any trespass, you who are spiritual, restore such a one in a spirit of gentleness; [each one] looking to yourself, lest you too be tempted."* You prayerfully trace a string of 23 cross-references through the Bible. Little by little, the new battle plan emerges.

You decide that you're going to write her a letter. "She really loves it when I write her letters," you recall. "I'll assure her of my love for her, acknowledging any faults that I'm aware of, and let her know that I'm willing to do whatever is biblically necessary to resolve this conflict. I'm also going to remind her that as a Christian, she also has a responsibility to resolve this conflict biblically. I'll support my case with Scripture." When you finish the letter, you gently walk into the bedroom where she is lying on the bed crying. You put your arms around her, assure her of your love, give her the letter, and tell her that you'll be waiting in the living room for her to finish resolving the conflict according to biblical principles, assuring her that you have every intention to do so yourself. Then you walk out, leaving her to "stew in her own juices," reading the letter, looking at the flower, remembering the chores you've done for her, the tea you've brought to her; and most of all, the gentle spirit with which you've been imploring her to repent.

Then, *it happens.* As you're sitting on the sofa in the living room praying for a resolution, you hear the door in the bedroom beginning to open. In walks your wife with tears in her eyes. She walks over to you, throws her arms around you, thanking you for responding so lovingly to her, and asking you to forgive her for her sinful reactions. As you continue to talk, the conflict is brought to a biblical conclusion, and you both walk away closer to each other and closer to the Lord.

Now, the thought of viewing your wife as an enemy, as I have suggested in this chapter, may or may not be appealing to you. But remember, you're not only commanded to love you wife (Eph. 5:25; Col. 3:19)—you're also commanded to love your neighbor (Lev. 19:18),[5] as well as your enemy (Matt. 5:44). As I sometimes tell my counselees, "If you find it hard to love your wife, try loving her as your neighbor. If even that seems too hard for you, then love her as your enemy." The point is, that whether you do so as an enemy, or a neighbor, or a wife, you have no choice as a Christian but to love her and overcome her evil with good.

Overcoming Evil with Good "Arsenal"

List the various ways that you can "overcome evil with good" by responding to your wife in love when she sins against you in the future. Review Appendix C: "Specific Ways to Demonstrate Love to Your Wife" to help get you started acquiring some weapons for the next battle.

Notes

[1] We are once again indebted to Jay Adams and his little book, *How to Overcome Evil* (Phillipsburg, N.J.: Presbyterian and Reformed Publishing, 1977), for the bulk of material in this chapter. The material is also available on audio cassette from Sound Word Associates, P .O. Box 2035, Michigan City, Indiana, 46361. When properly applied to the marriage relationship, the principles found in Romans 12:14-21 are revolutionary.

[2] It is only possible through the enabling of the Holy Spirit, who indwells exclusively those who have put their trust in the Lord Jesus Christ for the eternal salvation of their souls. Only a true Christian can continue to love in the face of unrequited love. Only a Christian is able to show 1 Corinthians 13 love which "bears all things, believes all things, hopes all things and endures all things" in the face of evil.

[3] *How to Overcome Evil*, pp.22-23.

[4] Ibid, p. 104

[5] It is interesting to note, in light of this chapter and the last, how Leviticus 19:18 is held over against this "Golden Rule" of the Bible: *"You shall not take vengeance, nor bear any grudge against the sons of your people, but you shall love your neighbor as yourself; I am the Lord."*

Chapter 8

Pleasing Possibilities

When was the last time you thought about how you could please your wife? As I've already mentioned, the Bible assumes that a married man will be concerned about such things.

> *But one who is married is concerned about the things of the world, how he may please his wife* (1 Cor. 7:33).

No doubt, when you were courting her, you spent plenty of time figuring out how to please your wife. But now that you're married, how much time do you actively devote to thinking about the specific things you can do and say that would bring pleasure to her?

"Well, I do think a lot about how I can please her sexually."

That's great. But when was the last time you devoted any of your spare time planning to bring her pleasure in ways that don't necessarily provide you with the same kind of pleasure? You know, the way you probably did when you were courting! For that matter, do you even remember the non-sexual ways with which she likes you to please her? Have you learned any *new ways* since you've been married?

Before we continue looking at the specific applications of 1 Corinthians 7:33, let's take a closer look at the passage as it is found in its context:

*Now concerning virgins I have no command of the Lord,
but I give an opinion as one who by the mercy of the Lord is
trustworthy. I think then that this is good in view of the
present distress, that it is good for a man to remain as he is.
Are you bound to a wife? Do not seek to be released. Are
you released from a wife? Do not seek a wife. But if you
should marry, you have not sinned; and if a virgin should
marry, she has not sinned. Yet such will have trouble in this
life, and I am trying to spare you. But this I say, brethren,
the time has been shortened, so that from now on those who
have wives should be as though they had none; and those
who weep, as though they did not weep; and those who rejoice, as though they did not rejoice; and those who buy, as
though they did not possess; and those who use the world,
as though they did not make full use of it; for the form of
this world is passing away. But I want you to be free from
concern. One who is unmarried is concerned about the
things of the Lord, how he may please the Lord; but one
who is married is concerned about the things of the world,
how he may please his wife, and [his interests] are divided.
And the woman who is unmarried, and the virgin, is concerned about the things of the Lord, that she may be holy
both in body and spirit; but one who is married is concerned about the things of the world, how she may please
her husband* (1 Cor. 7:25-34).

This passage and the chapter which surrounds it, is one of
the most important texts in the Bible about marriage. However,
it has often been misunderstood (especially by individuals
unaware of New Testament history and the greater witness of
Scripture).

First, let's compare Scripture with Scripture. Paul says that
it's *good* for a man to remain single (v. 26). The apparent difficulty with what Paul is saying is that it seems to contradict what
God says in Genesis 2:18: *"Then the Lord God said, 'It is not good
for the man to be alone; I will make him a helper suitable for him.'"*
Paul says it's *good* to remain single, God says it's *not good*! Is there

a contradiction in Scripture? Is Paul, in fact, disagreeing with God himself? The solution to this seeming dilemma is found in the phrase *"in view of the present distress."* Paul qualifies his statement that it is good for a man not to marry with this very important caveat: Paul, speaking as a prophet, is giving an exception to the rule, that generally speaking, "it is not good for man to be alone."[1] His exception had to do with the tremendous persecution that had already begun at the time he was writing to the Corinthians and increasingly grew worse.

Let's review for a moment, our history. Christians under Nero were about to be tortured and put to death in some of the most horrific ways imaginable. Some of them were going to be crucified. Others were going to be dipped in pitch, and hung on poles. The poles were going to be placed in specially prepared holes in Nero's garden. Then, these Christians were going to be ignited as torches to illuminate the wild orgies that would go on underneath their burning bodies. Some believers were about to be wrapped in wild animal skins and torn apart by dogs. Still others were going to be fed to starving lions in front of crowded amphitheaters. They were going to be gladiators' toys who were ripped limb from limb before the cheering crowds in the Roman Coliseum.

This was the "present distress" to which Paul was prophetically referring when he said, that in view of these extraordinary circumstances, "it is good not to marry." He said to the Corinthians, "I am trying to spare you from such trouble in this life." Yet, even under those conditions Paul says, *"But if you should marry, you have not sinned"* (v. 28).

It's against this particular historical backdrop that we must interpret what Paul is saying to the Corinthians about the responsibilities of marriage.

Before returning to the theme of this chapter (which is *how to please your wife*), I must mention, even if briefly, another verse in this section of Scripture because it does deal with your responsibility as a husband.

> *"But this I say, brethren, the time has been shortened, so that from now on those who have wives should be as though they had none"* (1 Cor. 7:29).

Paul says that "the time has been shortened." The Greek word translated "time" is a "special season or opportunity." Of course, all of life is already short in the sense that it is *"[just] a vapor that appears for a little while and then vanishes away"* (Jas. 4:14). The length of life for some during times of persecution is shortened even more. Paul is saying in effect, "the period of time allotted to [some of] you to serve the Lord has been shortened. From now on, in light of this brevity of life, those who have wives should be as though they had none."

Paul is not, with this statement, wiping out all of the other biblical commands given to husbands which are articulated in the New Testament and expounded in this book. Rather, he is warning those who are married not to let the responsibilities of marriage interfere with their other biblical responsibilities to serve the Lord (cf. Lk. 14:20). He is saying, "You guys who are married ought to serve the Lord with the same fervor and zeal as your unmarried brothers in the church, even though you'll be more distracted with these additional family responsibilities."

"I see, but how exactly *can* I please my wife?"

The Greek verb used in verse 33 which is translated "please" is a word that has several nuances of meaning. Its root means "to fit in with." It may also mean "to conform," "to adapt," "to satisfy," "to soften one's heart to," "to meet with one's approval," or "to accommodate." The word implies a pre-existing relationship between the one doing the pleasing and the one being pleased.

While an unmarried Christian ought to have his mind focused almost exclusively on how he may please the Lord, a Christian who is married must focus his attention not only on pleasing the Lord, but also on pleasing his spouse. The Bible assumes that all married persons will have their interests divided between pleasing Christ, which is always top priority, and pleasing their spouses. Although the fact that you'll please your wife is a biblical assumption, too few husbands ever stop to consider the specific ways they can bring pleasure to their wives (except, as I've already implied, in the sexual arena). Here are a few questions that may help you come up with some concrete ways in which you may fulfill this implicit responsibility of every Christian husband.

- In what ways do I please my wife before I please myself?
- How do I alter my plans to "fit in with" those of my wife's?
- How do I conform myself to her likes and dislikes?
- In what (non-sexual) ways do I satisfy my wife?
- How can I "soften my heart" towards her in regard to her desires?
- To what extent do the things I do meet with my wife's approval?
- What adaptations am I willing to make in my life in order to please her?
- How do I accommodate myself to her wishes and desires?

One of the obvious investments that a man must make in his wife is *time*. How much time did you spend every day talking to your wife before you married her? Do you now invest *more* or *less* of your time talking to her on a daily basis than you did back then (before you became "one flesh" with her)?

"Well, the main reason I spent so much time talking to her while we were courting is because I was trying to convince her to marry me. That was my priority back then. Now that she's married to me, I have other priorities to attend to—like providing an income to take care of her needs."

Such reasoning is common, but it's also selfish. Now that you've got her, is it right for you to forget and neglect those unselfish things you used to do when you were courting her? Of course not! Now that you've procured her, one of the top priorities on your daily agenda should be to please her. This usually involves meeting her non-material needs and fulfilling some of her non-financial desires. To do this effectively, you'll need to invest some time regularly (I usually recommend at least 20 minutes each day for my married counselees) for uninterrupted communication. By "uninterrupted" I mean, no phone, no kids, no television, and no other distractions. If your schedule allows this to be done in the morning, I recommend you do it then. This is probably the best time of the day for most people. If the morning is not possible, the evening, when the children are in bed (or otherwise occupied), might be better. Let me suggest that you discuss this with your wife and plan to meet at the same time every day (if possible, set up a daily appointment at a specific time).

Another investment you can make if you want to please your wife is *effort*. Think about your courting days again. You spent lots of your physical and mental energy learning about her likes and dislikes, her interests, dreams and desires. You expended such effort not only in studying her, but also in doing those things you learned would please her. You probably expended energy on her that you would otherwise have spent on other things, like your favorite hobby, your friends, or your other responsibilities. You may have even deprived yourself of your normal and necessary sleep—all because you wanted to please her.

These days, when she asks you do something to please her, those very things you were once willing to sacrifice can become excuses for not being able to do so. You may not be as willing to expend the energy to please her that you were when you were first courting. Brother, these things ought not to be so!

A final investment that I'd like to mention with regard to pleasing your wife is the investment of your *thoughts*. How much of your spare thoughts are devoted to thinking about delighting her? Once again, remember when you were courting. Didn't you spend hours upon hours thinking about specific ways you could please her? Perhaps you even sought counsel from some of your friends or hers in your attempts to figure out how to do it. Didn't you come up with creative little things that you just knew were going to delight her beyond measure and send her into orbit? Remember how excited you were just *thinking* about the expression on her face or the excitement in her voice as you anticipated surprising her with that "something" that you knew would please her? What happened since then that has kept you from thinking such wonderful thoughts?

There are many possible answers to this question, but I'd like to suggest one that I believe is the most common: Could it be that in relation to your marriage, you have left your first love? Do you remember (from Chapter Seven) what Christ said to the Ephesian church who had fallen out of love with Him?

> But I have [this] against you, that you have left your first love (Rev. 2:4).

Do you remember his counsel to them?

> Remember therefore from where you have fallen, and repent and do the deeds you did at first (Rev. 2:5).

As we mentioned before, Christ's counsel to those who had lost their love was three-fold. *First*, He says, "Remember...from where you have fallen" (remember the way things were when you really loved Me). *Secondly*, He tells them to "repent" (change your thinking and the direction of your life). *Lastly*, He commands them to "do the deeds you did at first" (do those things you used to do when you first became a Christian—when you truly loved Me).

In order to better understand the specifics of what it means to "please" your wife, let's take a look at how the word is used similarly in two other New Testament passages. First, consider Romans 15:1-3:

> Now we who are strong ought to bear the weaknesses of those without strength and not [just] please ourselves. Let each of us please his neighbor for his good, to his edification. For even Christ did not please Himself; but as it is

*written, "The reproaches of those who reproached You
fell upon Me"*

The context of this passage is Paul's warning the Romans to
avoid two sinful extremes concerning the thoughts, opinions and
motives of others. These two extremes are sinful *judging* and sinful *contempt* (with the accompanying thoughts and feelings of
disdain). The weaker brother, whose conscience has not yet been
fully programmed according to the Bible, is commanded *not to
judge as sinning* the stronger brother, whose conscience has been
developed to biblical maturity (e.g., "What a sinner this guy is for
eating that pagan food!"). The stronger brother, who knows that
certain things aren't necessarily sinful to partake of if done with
thanksgiving to God, is charged not to despise or hold in contempt his weaker brother (e.g., "I can't believe this guy has a scruple
about what I like to eat—why doesn't he grow up and get a life?!").

After warning both sides against such uncharitable behavior,
he comes back and addresses the stronger brother again. "You
who are strong (and know the truth)," he says, "ought to help
your weaker brothers by limiting your Christian liberty if you
know that it will cause them to stumble. If they *do* partake before
their consciences have been reprogrammed biblically, they will
sin, because they partook of something they thought *might* have
been a sin. When they do, they have in fact sinned, because they
did not partake in faith—and you who encouraged them to do so
put a stumbling block before them, causing them to sin, and
thereby are guilty of sin yourselves. When you please *yourself*
rather than pleasing your neighbor for his good by bearing the
burden of your weaker brother, you are being *selfish*!"

The application here to you as a Christian husband is as follows: When you *don't* please your wife, it's probably because you're
being *selfish*! I know that it's my selfish preoccupation with my
own interests and agenda which most displaces my thoughts of
pleasing Kim. More often than I'd like to admit, I waste time thinking about—and doing—things that don't matter as much to the

Lord as pleasing her.

How about *you*? What do you spend most of your spare time thinking about? Do you spend half as much time thinking about how to please your wife now as you did before she was your wife? Do you do half the things now to please her that you used to do before you were married?

Another principle we can see in this passage is that *pleasing others involves bearing their burdens*. Remember, you're to treat your wife as if she were a "weaker vessel" (1 Pet. 3:7). By implication, that makes you the stronger of the two. You (as the stronger) ought to bear the burdens of your wife (as the weaker), being more concerned with how you may please her than with how you may please yourself. How often do you bear your wife's burdens by choosing to please her rather than pleasing yourself?

A third nuance of pleasing others that can be seen in this passage has to do with *your motive*.

Why should you want to please your wife?

"Because if she's happy I'll be happy! Right?"

Wrong! Although you probably *will* be happier to the degree that you please her (*"he who loves his wife loves himself"*—Eph. 5:28), you're not to try to please her out of such selfish motives. Rather, as "each of us" is to "please his neighbor for his good, to his edification" even so, your motive in pleasing your wife should be *for her good, in order to edify her*.

"How is my pleasing her, for her good, and how does it build her up?"

- It models genuine Christ-like sacrificial love to her which she can emulate (cf. 1 Jn. 4:19).
- It creates an environment around her that will make it easier for her to obey God.
- It helps prevent her from becoming resentful of your selfishness.

Of course, as with everything in life, your highest motive for doing anything is to please and glorify God (cf. 1 Cor 10:31).

The second passage where pleasing others is used in a good sense, is 1 Corinthians 10:32-33.

> *Give no offense either to Jews or to Greeks or to the church of God; just as I also please all men in all things, not seeking my own profit, but the [profit] of the many, that they may be saved.*

Here again, the context deals with the eating of foods (which in this case have been sacrificed to idols). Here also, Paul is urging the hearers and readers of his letter to be careful not to allow their Christian liberty to needlessly offend others (causing them to sin). But this time, he expands the scope of possible "offendees" to include not only believers ("the church of God") but non-believers ("Jews or to Greeks") as well. Paul was willing to lay aside his rights and freedoms in order to please "all men" (another reference to believers and unbelievers) in all things. How willing are *you* to lay aside your rights and freedoms in order to please your wife? Paul was once again unselfishly putting the benefit of others before his own. How often do you sacrifice your own pleasures in order to please your wife?

Let me say one more word about motive. It's your motive in this regard more than anything else, that determines whether or not you're rightly or wrongly pleasing man (cf. Gal. 1:10; Eph. 6:6; 1 Cor. 10:33). Do you want to please others because you're a men-pleaser and love "the praise of men more than the praise of God" (Jn. 12:43), or because you want to win them to Christ or benefit them biblically in some other way?

One more element of pleasing your wife I'd like to address, has to do with your knowing those things which are important to her. There are probably many things which are more important to her than they are to you—things which she values even more than you do. My wife, for example, places more value than I do on having our home organized so that things may be done "decently and in order." Perhaps this is related to her biblical responsibility to be a "keeper at home" (Titus 2:5). She places a higher value on such things than I do. A little bit of clutter is not as distracting to me as it is to her. Having a well-kept, well-groomed, and uncluttered home environment is more important to her than it is to me. If I want to please her, I will, as much as possible, accommodate her desires.

In light of this, I'd like to let you in on a tip that will help you learn a good number of those things that are important to her. Every time you and your wife have a conflict, ask yourself, "What is it that she's wanting from me that she thinks I'm not giving her?" Of course, you may have to ask her, if she doesn't make that clear during the course of the conflict. The answer to this question will usually yield the essence of what she values and the substance of what is most important to her.

Usually, when your wife initiates a course of conversation which leads to a conflict, it's because she *desires* something that you're not giving her, or somehow are preventing her from having. Now those desires may be righteous or unrighteous, they may be reasonable or unreasonable, they may be fundamentally good desires or they may be inordinate (good desires which she wants too intently—perhaps to the point of idolatry), but they are the desires of her heart and you must try to understand them. Those longings which are idolatrous, you, as her spiritual leader, must help her dethrone (in Chapter Nine, you'll find some additional help in cooperating with God in your wife's sanctification process). Those which are lawful you must endeavor to fulfill as a part of your responsibility to please her. As you learn those things which are important to her (those things which she values and upon which her desires are likely based), and as you begin to accommodate those values and desires which are not sinful, you'll be pleasing your wife in a most demonstrable way. So, the next time you have a conflict with her, don't consider the conflict resolved until you've ascertained at least one thing that she wanted, desired, or valued.

This chapter ends with a worksheet entitled, "Things That Are Important to My Wife." On that worksheet, you'll want to record those things that she values more than you do. You may immediately recall some things that you've already learned about her which need to be included on the list. After those initial entries, begin recording new insights you learn during any conflicts you will have with her in the future.

There is a second worksheet entitled, "Things I Can Do to Please My Wife." This is for you to record the various other "wife-pleasing things" you may have thought of as you read this chapter, as well as any other things you may think of in the future.

Things That are Important to My Wife

1.

2.

3.

4.

5.

6.

7.

Continue...

Things I Can Do that Please My Wife

1.

2.

3.

4.

5.

6.

7.

Continue...

Note

---

[1]Jesus in Matthew 19:10-12 gives three other exceptions to the rule when he speaks of the three kinds of eunuchs which He very deliberately sandwiched between the statements, *"All [men] cannot receive this saying, save [they] to whom it is given"* and *"He that is able to receive [it], let him receive [it]."* These two qualifying statements clearly imply that Jesus was giving an exception to the rule cited in Gen. 2:18.

Chapter 9

"Honey, You Need a Bath"

"My wife and I have been married for five years and she still hasn't learned how to treat me with the respect and honor that the Bible requires a wife to show to her husband."

When I hear statements such as this one, where a husband is complaining about some longstanding character deficiency in his wife, my usual response is to ask the husband to *consider his leadership.* "How is it that you've been married to this woman for so long and she still hasn't changed? What exactly have you done to help her with her problems?"

R.C. Sproul approaches this problem in much the same way:

> After marriage, the biggest single influence on the development of the wife's personality and character is the husband. When a man comes to me and complains that his wife has changed since they got married, I immediately respond, "Who do you supposed changed her?" In a sense, the wife a man has is the wife he has produced. If he has a monster, maybe he ought to examine his own nature.
>
> In the Ephesians passage, it is clear that the husband is called to be the priest of his home. The man is responsible for the spiritual well-being of his wife. Her sanctification is his responsibility. There is probably no male task that has been more neglected than this one...

> In seeking the sanctification of the church, there is a sense
> in which Christ seeks to change his wife. So the husband
> is called to change his wife. The change is to be toward a
> higher conformity to the image of Christ. We should seek
> to present our wives to Christ as holy and blameless, with-
> out spot or wrinkle![1]

Let's take a closer look at Ephesians 5:25-27. This portion of
Scripture has some interesting things to say about your role in
your wife's spiritual growth and development.

> *Husbands, love your wives, just as Christ also loved the*
> *church and gave Himself up for her; that He might sanctify*
> *her, having cleansed her by the washing of water with the*
> *word, that He might present to Himself the church in all*
> *her glory, having no spot or wrinkle or any such thing; but*
> *that she should be holy and blameless.*

Whereas verse 26 (*"that He might sanctify her, having cleansed*
her by the washing of water with the word") refers to the sanctifying work of Christ for His bride in *this world* (on earth), verse 27
(*"that He might present to Himself the church in all her glory, hav-*
ing no spot or wrinkle or any such thing; but that she should be holy
and blameless") refers to the sanctifying work of Christ for his
bride in the *next world* (in heaven). The first sentence of verse 28
(*"So husbands ought also to love their own wives as their own bod-*
ies.") is given so that husbands might apply what Christ has done
for the church to themselves, in relation to their wives. The ad-
verb "so" points out the relationship between what Christ has
done for the church and what husbands ought to likewise do for
their wives.

"How can these supernatural evidences of Christ's love for
the church be applied by me? I'm only human! Does God really
expect me as a mortal man to do any of these things for my wife?"

That question was asked and answered over 375 years ago by
William Gouge in his treatise, *Of Domestical Duties*. Gouge points
out that while it may not be possible for a husband to "so" love

his wife in *measure* (to the same extent or degree), he certainly can in *likeness*:

> In this large declaration of Christ's love, there are two general points to be noted.
>
> 1. That the church in herself was [in] no way worthy of love.
>
> 2. That Christ carried himself towards her that he made her worthy of such love.
>
> This ought to be the mind [set] of husbands to their wives.
>
> 1. Though they be [in] no way worthy of their love, yet they must love them.
>
> 2. They must endeavor with all the wit and wisdom they have, to make them worthy of love. I say *endeavor* because it is not simply in the husbands power to do the deed. Yet his faithful endeavor shall on his part be accepted for the deed."[2]

First, Gouge is saying that you must love your wife, not as King Ahasuerus loved Esther (after making a long and laborious search, then finding her to be "beautiful" [cf. Est. 2:2], and then having her further beautified for twelve months [cf. Est. 2:12] *before* he loved her). Rather, you must love your wife as Christ loved the church, knowing that she was full of spots and blemishes and other such things. Secondly, Gouge explains that even though you can't sanctify her the way God can (supernaturally), you must use all the means you've been given by God to make her worthy of your love.

As I pointed out earlier, Christ loved the church *first*; while she was yet sinful, He bestowed upon her his love.

> He did not choose to love her because there was something attractive in her that caught his eye: quite the contrary—His love arose exclusively and entirely from within

Himself. There was nothing within her which she possessed beforehand that moved Him to love her—not beauty, not goodness, not wealth—nothing! Neither was there anything in her that that He wanted or needed. He had no hope of her giving back to him anything except that which He first gave to her. Indeed, He delights in that righteousness with which, as a glorious robe, she is clothed; and in those heavenly graces, as with precious jewels, she is decked: but that righteousness and those graces are His own—they are His free gift which He presents to himself in all her glory.

In the same way, husbands should love their wives. Although there is nothing in a wife that would move him to love her, except that she is his wife: although he expects no future benefit from her, he should give his love to her. True love focuses on the object which is loved, and the good it may do to her, rather than the subject (one who is under surveillance) which loves, and the good that it may receive: for love does not seek its own. This kind of love should move husbands to do what is in their power to beautify their wives and so make them worthy of such love.[3]

While the commentators disagree about the exact meaning of the phrase, *"by the washing of water with the word"*(v.26), the few who even attempt to apply it, seem to agree that the practical application of the passage is some form of the husband's assistance in the progressive sanctification process of his wife.[4] As her spiritual leader, you must "set her apart" (or make her holy), purifying her through the Scriptures. You must help her, through the Word, to remove her spiritual *spots* and *wrinkles* and *any* [other] *such thing* (v.28) that does not conform to the image of Christ. The way that you do this is by obeying and using the Word in all of your dealings with her.

It's remarkable how many Christians believe that they can grow spiritually without a regular (and I mean *daily*) intake of Scripture. Many seem to think that they can grow in Christ, develop character and solve problems, with little if any time invested in reading, studying, memorizing and meditating on God's Word. They seem to have forgotten verses such as the following:

> The law of the Lord is perfect, restoring the soul; The testimony of the Lord is sure, making wise the simple (Psa. 19:7).

> It is written, "Man shall not live on bread alone, but on every word that proceeds out of the mouth of God" (Matt. 4:4).

> Like newborn babes, long for the pure milk of the word, that by it you may grow in respect to salvation (1Pet. 2:2).

> But we all, with unveiled face beholding as in a mirror the glory of the Lord, are being transformed into the same image from glory to glory, just as from the Lord, the Spirit (2 Cor. 3:18).

In this last passage, we read that the Holy Spirit transforms us into the image of Christ as we behold His image in the mirror of the Word of God. We are thereby "transformed into the same image from glory to glory" (from one level of spiritual maturity to another).

Now, the Holy Spirit may work in any way He wishes, but we ought to expect Him to work in our lives as He has said He would in the Bible: that is, *through the Bible*. It doesn't really matter how much you pray, how much you witness for Christ, how often you participate in the Lord's Table, if you're not in God's Word (or to say it more accurately, if God's Word is not dwelling inside of you; cf. Col. 3:16), you're cutting yourself off from one of the most powerful resources necessary for your spiritual growth. To put it another way, if the Word of Christ is not abiding in you, then you're not giving the Holy Spirit his most effective weapon: *"the sword of the Spirit, which is the word of God"* (Eph. 6:17).[5]

Zap Theology: The "Kiss and Make Up With God" Syndrome

Have you ever struggled to overcome a bad habit in your life? Sure you have! We all have. Many Christians, however, when they "struggle" with sin, don't really struggle at all. Rather, they simply confess their sin to God, pray that He will help them change, and promptly get off their knees expecting that God has somehow infused or "zapped" them with a special measure of grace that will enable them to never commit the same sin again, without any further effort on their part. This is what is sometimes referred to as "the kiss and make up with God" syndrome. [6]

Our sanctification is, of course, an act of God. However, it's also a *process* which requires our cooperation. It's not enough merely to *pray* that God will change us; we must also *do* what the Bible says is necessary to "put off" sin and "put on" Christ. Change is a two-fold process for the Christian: We actually *put off* our sin and *put on* its biblical antithesis. To put it another way, Christians don't "break" habits, pagans do. Christians replace *bad* habits with *good* ones.

It's not enough for the Christian who habitually lies to simply stop lying. He must make it his goal to become truthful: "*Therefore, laying aside falsehood, speak truth, each one [of you,] with his neighbor, for we are members of one another*" (Eph. 4:25). It's not enough for a thief to simply stop stealing. He must not only *put off stealing*, but he must also *put on diligence and generosity*: "*Let him who steals steal no longer; but rather let him labor, performing with his own hands what is good, in order that he may have [something] to share with him who has need*" (Eph. 4:28).

This "put-off/put-on" dynamic can only happen as the mind is renewed through the Scriptures:

> *That, in reference to your former manner of life, you lay aside the old self, which is being corrupted in accordance with the lusts of deceit, and that you be renewed in the spirit of your mind, and put on the new self, which in [the*

likeness of] God has been created in righteousness and holiness of the truth (Eph. 4:22-24).

The Word of God is necessary to produce lasting change in your life. The Holy Spirit takes the Scriptures that you've internalized (through Bible reading, study, memorization and meditation etc.) and changes (transforms) you from the inside: *"And do not be conformed to this world, but be transformed by the renewing of your mind, that you may prove what the will of God is, that which is good and acceptable and perfect"* (Rom. 12:2). You cannot properly be sanctified apart from God's Word.

Neither can your believing wife. This is why you must learn to use the Scriptures effectively, in the milieu of daily living. You must use them to teach, to convict, to correct, and to train her in righteousness: *"All Scripture is inspired by God and profitable for teaching, for reproof, for correction, for training in righteousness"* (2 Tim 3:16).

Before I explain further, I must first warn you about a peculiar doctrine that has been gaining influence in Christian circles for at least the last two decades. Varieties of this teaching have found their way into Christian books, magazines, seminars, and local churches. It goes something like this: Christian spouses should never try to counsel each other because counseling presupposes a problem, and therefore places one partner above the other (or damages the self esteem of one's mate).

Popular or not, this concept is simply unbiblical. The Bible abounds with verses that speak of believers' counseling one another (Rom. 15:14; Col. 3:16; 1 Thes. 5:11-14; Heb. 10:24). As I sometimes tell my counselees, "I'm just one beggar, showing another beggar where the bread is at. Tomorrow you may be on this side of the (counseling) desk and I on the other."

Furthermore, Ephesians 5:26 (*"that He might sanctify her, having cleansed her by the washing of water with the word"*) implies such counseling on the part of the husband toward the wife. On the other hand, Genesis 2:18, (*"Then the Lord God said, 'It is not good for the man to be alone; I will make him a helper suitable for him"*) leaves plenty of room for a woman to counsel her husband. If there's anything that God desires a wife to *help* her husband with, it's to be a better Christian. The use of the Scriptures in loving confrontation is a door that swings both ways in the context of a biblical marriage.

"How do I do that?"

Listed below are some specific sanctification ideas for you to consider. At the end of this chapter you'll find a worksheet to help you and your wife decide how you may best "wash her with the water of the Word." She may desire to modify some of the options I've mentioned. She may also have some additional ideas of her own.

Specific Ways a Husband May Sanctify His Wife by Scripture

- Be sure that your wife has enough time in her daily schedule for personal Bible study and prayer. This may involve getting up earlier or rearranging your schedule so that you can watch the children during this time.
- Spend time with her regularly (at least once a week) in Bible study.
- Encourage her to ask you for help in answering any questions she may have about Bible doctrine or application.
- Ask her to memorize a portion of Scripture together with you and to hold one another accountable.
- Make and explain your decisions on the basis of Scripture.
- Commend her for any and all biblical character traits which she possesses (reverence, self-control, discretion, love, joy, peace, etc.).
- Make every effort to provide her with valid scriptural reasons when you can't give her what she wants (explain those reasons to her).
- Be alert to even the smallest indications of spiritual growth and maturity in her and praise her for them.

- Be certain that you never criticize (reprove) her other than on scriptural grounds, encouraging her to do the same with you.
- Learn how to restore her, in accordance with such passages as Matt. 18:15; Lk. 17:3 and Gal. 6:1, when she does sin.
- Encourage her to be faithful in her attendance at church, where she can sit under the faithful preaching and teaching of the Word. Set a good example of faithfully attending yourself.
- Encourage other opportunities she may have to study the Scriptures (individually or with others).
- Provide scripturally-based music for her to enjoy when at home or in the car.
- Provide her with Bible study tools (and teach her to use them if she does not know how).
- Learn how to relate the Scriptures to life and life to the Scriptures. Talk of them in the milieu of every day life (cf. Deut. 6:7).
- If your wife enjoys reading, invest in biblically-sound books (and Christian biographies).
- Make the dinner hour an enjoyable time of discussing Biblical truth and personal applications of Scripture.
- Determine which areas in her life she desires to change most and why she desires to change them. Use these areas as springboards to search the Scriptures together for God's answers (be sure you also tell your wife the changes you'd like to see in your own life and seek her assistance and prayers).

"But my wife knows more about the Bible than I do! How can I teach her?"

Good question. Keep in mind that God has made you the spiritual leader of your home and has charged you with the responsibility of washing her with the Word. This alone should answer your question. You can teach her because God requires you to do so as the spiritual head of your home. (cf. 1 Cor. 14:35). As a Christian, you can learn to do anything which God requires of you. It's as if God has dressed you in a uniform. That uniform may be a few sizes too big. It may even fit your wife better than it does you. But remember, He gave it to *you*, not her. If your wife is a Christian she's required to salute the uniform even if it's too big. As you grow into the uniform, you both may feel more comfortable with the arrangement, but for now you must learn to function accordingly.

Moreover, being a spiritual leader to your wife does not require that you necessarily know more about the Bible than she does—at least not to get started. I know some men whose wives are so far ahead of them in Bible knowledge that they may never surpass them in knowledge. The real issue of being a spiritual leader is not so much Bible knowledge (as helpful as that truly is), but rather the direction in which you're going.[7]

The following illustration demonstrates this principle:

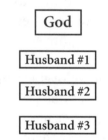

Which husband is closer to God?

"That's easy. Husband # 1 is obviously closer to God!"

Is he? The diagram you're looking at is a *snapshot*, not a motion picture. Suppose I were to tell you that Husband #1 has actually been drifting away from the Lord over the past four months; and Husband #2 has been in the same place for three years; but Husband #3 has been growing spiritually like a weed for the past two years. Which one is really "closer to God?"

Don't be intimidated by our own ignorance of the Scriptures. You can learn all you need to about the Bible to lead her effectively. It's probably not your lack of Bible *knowledge* that has kept you from using the Scriptures to sanctify your wife as much as your lack of *initiative*. Why not purpose today to use the

Scriptures as they were meant to be used in your dealings with your wife—to sanctify, cleanse and beautify her —that you may present her to Christ (not to mention to yourself) in all of her glory.

How to Cleanse My Wife with the Scriptures

Many husbands wonder what they can do to encourage their wives to grow spiritually. The best practical way to do so is to saturate (wash) her with the Word of God. Using the list of "Specific ways a husband may sanctify his wife with Scripture" as a starting point, record in your own words what you can do to fortify your wife and marriage with Scripture. Be sure to discuss each one with her before you put them on your list. Ask her to help you modify each item and ask her for any additional suggestions.

Notes

[1] R.C. Sproul, *The Intimate Marriage* (Wheaton: Tyndale House, 1986), pp.45-46.

[2] Gouge, p. 76

[3] I'm indebted to William Gouge, whose material I've adapted and expanded in the preceding two paragraphs (p. 415).

[4] Most believe the phrase refers to baptism (i.e., baptism, which has its ground or basis in the preached Word), others believe it is a reference to some form of ceremonial washing such as that mentioned in Ezekiel 16:9. The passage also has other exegetical difficulties which are beyond the scope of this book to explore.

[5] Incidentally, the word for "Word" in this passage is *rhema* the spoken Word (vs. *logos* the written Word). *Rhema* is the word for "Word" in Ephesians 5:26: *"that He might sanctify her, having cleansed her by the washing of water with the word."* As you speak the Word to your wife throughout the course of each day, the Word has its sanctifying effect on her and you thereby love her and sanctify her as Christ does the Church.

[6] This term was used by Jay Adams, in various lectures and personal conversations I've had the pleasure of having with him.

[7] I am indebted to Bill Gothard for this diagram which I learned years ago at one of his Advanced Seminars.

Chapter 10

Sexual Relations in Marriage

Would it surprise you to learn that having sexual relations with your wife is no less of an honorable act in God's eyes than reading your Bible or praying? The Bible is not prudish in its many proclamations about sex. Indeed, the very first command given to Adam and Eve in the Garden had to do with sex: *"And God blessed them; and God said to them, 'Be fruitful and multiply, fill the earth, and subdue it'"* (Gen. 1:28). Moreover, there is an entire book of the Bible, Song of Solomon, that addresses rather graphically, the subject of sexual relations in marriage.

Yet sadly, many Christians believe sexual relations in marriage to be dirty or taboo. They seem to have forgotten that God not only created sex, but that He did so in such a way as to make it one of the most pleasurable experiences in life.

Of course, the sinfulness of man has perverted God's design and often turned a tremendous blessing into a curse. What God designed to be a delight, man, because of his corruption, has often found to be a profound disappointment.

Sexual difficulties in marriage find their way to the marriage counselor's agenda quite regularly. Hardly one couple in ten who comes in for marriage counseling does not experience some kind of sexual problem in their relationship. What most of these couples fail to realize is that sexual difficulties are typically *symptomatic*. That is, they're not usually the real problem, but are the by-product of other problems in the relationship.

The alarm clock goes off at 5:45 am. Tom and Shirley struggle to get out of bed. They're especially tired this morning because last night they were up well past midnight arguing about a decision that had to be made. They had gone to sleep angry and did not successfully resolve the conflict. Rather than being pleasant with each other this morning, they are short and critical. Their speech is filled with sarcasm, false accusations, name calling, and other pejorative comments. Their verbal and non-verbal communication reveal the anger and bitterness that has recently crept into their hearts.

What Tom and Shirley don't realize is that with each hurtful remark they make, and with every unkind non-verbal expression they display, they're sabotaging their sexual relationship. It's as if they're littering their marriage bed with all manner of clutter and debris. The pajamas they slept in, wet towels from the morning's bathroom activities, coffee grounds from the percolator, the dirty breakfast dishes, and various sections of the morning newspaper, all end up getting tossed on the bed before 7:30 am. As Tom walks out the door, rather than his usual good-bye kiss he mutters, "I don't know how I ended up with such a contentious shrew of a wife." He just, in essence, opened up the bedroom door and dumped another pound of rubbish onto the pile. All day long, as Tom and Shirley review the events of the past few hours in their minds, they continue to trash their marriage bed. When Tom arrives home from the office, the pile of "junk" on the bed is three-feet high.

As the evening progresses, the pile grows even larger as a result of each of them giving the other the cold shoulder. By the time evening comes, if either one of them had any desire for sexual relations, they'd have to make love amidst all that garbage. Their sexual "problems" are not really *sexual* at all, they are *relational*. Marriage counselors know that, more often than not, sexual problems in marriage are indications of other problems in the relationship. When these other problems in the relationship are resolved biblically, the sexual problems tend to clear up almost by themselves.

There is one attitude in particular that adversely affects the sexual relationship between a man and his wife, which I've observed over and over again in many of the men I've known. I've struggled with it myself from time to time. For years, I've wondered why so many husbands *take their wives for granted*. R. C. Sproul, in his book, *The Intimate Marriage*, addresses this common occurrence quite succinctly:

> It is all too easy. for married men to view their wives with steadily diminishing importance once the wedding is over. Before that, the man expends an enormous amount of energy seeking to woo and win his wife. He enters the courting relationship with the zeal and the dedication of an Olympic bound athlete. He gives his girl his undivided attention, making her the center of his devotion. When the marriage is achieved, our athlete turns his attention to other goals. He figures he has the romantic aspect of his life under control, and now goes on to scale new heights. He devotes less and less time to his wife, treating her as less and less important. In the meantime the woman, being accustomed to the courting process, enters the marriage relationship expecting that to continue. As the marriage progresses, she finds herself devoting more and more attention to her husband than she did before the marriage, while he is devoting less attention to her. Now she is washing his clothes, cooking his meals, making his bed, cleaning his house—maybe even packing his suitcase. At the same time, he is becoming less affectionate (though perhaps more erotic), taking her out less, and generally paying less attention to her.
>
> This syndrome, when allowed to continue unchecked, frequently results in an affair. The affair, popularized by novels and romanticized by Hollywood and television, has become a national epidemic. At one time in my ministry I was counseling sixteen couples who were having

marital problems with a third party involved. In every case I asked the unfaithful partner the same question, "What is it that attracted you to this person?" In every single case the answer was essentially the same, "He made me feel like a woman," or "She made me feel like a man again." It's easy to make a woman feel like a woman during courtship. It's not so easy to do it in marriage. It simply cannot be done if the wife is considered secondary in importance. When Paul speaks of the necessity of the husband giving himself to the wife as Christ gave himself to the church, he is touching the very heart of marriage.[1]

One of the keys to keeping the romance in your marriage and not taking your wife for granted is to *never stop courting her*. This is perhaps the single best piece of sexual advice I can offer. Perhaps you've heard it said that "foreplay begins when you get out of bed in the morning, not when you get into the bed at night." Remember what you read in Chapter Nine?

> Contrary to what you might have thought, when you "fell in love" with your wife, you were not struck with some kind of external stimulus such as "Cupid's arrow" or a "Zap" from some other mystical marriage broker. Rather, *you* created (internally) the romantic feelings that you had for her by means of both what you told yourself about her, and what you did *to* and *for* and *with* her. That is to say, your own heart produced those wonderful feelings as a by-product of your thoughts and actions. You most likely developed warm loving feelings toward her during your courtship. If you're now bitter at her, it's because in one way or another, you have stopped courting her. Your lack of courtship has slowed down the "emotional love generator" (so to speak) in your heart. Additionally, the unkind and unforgiving thoughts you now think about her (in contrast to the kind and loving thoughts you experienced during courtship), throw a monkey wrench into the "generator" and prevent those loving feelings from developing. It's basically that simple.

> If you want to revive the romance you once had for your wife, you'll have to change both the way you think about her as well as the things you do for her. You'll have to start courting her once again, and you'll have to start right now—even though you may have bitter feelings in your heart for her.

Here's the bottom line: If you want to revive any of the passion you once had in your sexual relations but may have lost, you'll have to *daily and regularly court your wife.*

The loving attitudes that you display toward your wife (cf. 1 Cor. 13:4-7; Col. 3:12-14), from the moment you give her your wake-up greeting to the way you compliment her for the supper she's prepared, will likely determine the pleasure you both have the next time you have sexual relations.

Biblical Principles of Sex[2]

The following seven principles are largely based on a proper understanding of 1 Corinthians 7:1-6. Let's take a look at this passage before unpacking its meaning (other Scripture passages will be cited later where they are applicable).

> *Now concerning the things about which you wrote, it is good for a man not to touch a woman. But because of immoralities, let each man have his own wife, and let each woman have her own husband. Let the husband fulfill his duty to his wife, and likewise also the wife to her husband. The wife does not have authority over her own body, but the husband [does]; and likewise also the husband does not have authority over his own body, but the wife [does]. Stop depriving one another, except by agreement for a time that you may devote yourselves to prayer, and come together again lest Satan tempt you because of your lack of self-control. But this I say by way of concession, not of command (1Cor 7:1-6).*

Principle #1: Sexual relations within marriage are holy and good. God encourages relations and warns against their cessation.

> [Let] marriage [be held] in honor among all, and let the [marriage] bed [be] undefiled; for fornicators and adulterers God will judge (Heb. 13:4).

The NASB rightly brings out the imperative grammatical construction of this verse. Christians must view marriage as an honorable institution which was designed by God. They must not do anything that would rob the marriage bed of its honor and goodness (whether by thought, word or deed). When you cease to fulfill your marital obligations in this area the Bible says that you "defraud" your wife and expose her to unnecessary temptation (1 Cor. 7:5). Remember, according to this passage there are two biblical solutions to the problem of sexual immorality—two ways for you to "avoid fornication". One is self control (vv. 5 and 9), the other is regular marital sexual relations (v. 2) with your wife.

Principle #2: Pleasure in sexual relations is not sinful but assumed (the bodies of both parties belong to each other).

> Let your fountain be blessed, And rejoice in the wife of your youth. [As] a loving hind and a graceful doe, Let her breasts satisfy you at all times; Be exhilarated always with her love (Prov. 5:18-19).

God's intent is that you be sexually *satiated* by your wife. Let's suppose that today is Thanksgiving. You've been looking forward to this day for weeks because your mother has promised to make your favorite dessert. As the Thanksgiving day feast begins, you can hardly wait for the meal to end so that you can savor every luscious morsel of that final course. As you munch down each delectable morsel with ever-increasing passion, you soon lose sight of the fact that you've got to save some room in your stomach for that favorite dessert of yours. You continue to relish course after course until finally you're *totally satiated*. When the dessert is finally brought out from the kitchen, you're so full that you have to explain to your mother that you "couldn't eat another bite."

That is the kind of satiation that is implied when the Bible tells you to "Let her breasts satisfy you at all times" and "Be exhilarated always with her love." You are to be so "satisfied" with your wife that you couldn't easily be tempted by anyone else. Both the words "satisfy" and "exhilarated" in this verse also carry with them the idea of being *intoxicated*. This is the only verse in the Bible that I know of that encourages you to be drunk—not with alcohol, but with the pleasure that comes from having God-ordained sexual relations with your wife.

Principle #3: Sexual pleasure is to be regulated by the principle that one's sexuality is not to be self-oriented ("rights" over one's own body are given in marriage to the other party). Homosexuality and masturbation are out of accord with this fundamental principle. The idea here, as elsewhere, is that "it is more blessed to give than to receive."

Probably the greatest way that Christian husbands fail in the sexual part of their marriage is by being selfish. We live in an auto-erotic society. That is, a society that views sex primarily as something from which pleasure is to be received, rather than as an opportunity for which pleasure can be given. Masturbation is viewed not only as acceptable, but in some cases as therapeutic. Many men, even Christian men, view sexual relations with their wives as little more than an opportunity to masturbate. They are concerned only with pleasing themselves. They do not realize that God gave them their sexual organs, not primarily for their own pleasure, but rather for the pleasure of their wives (1 Cor. 7:4). They have never learned that in sexual relations, as in all other areas of life, it is more blessed to give than to receive (Acts 20:35).

Masturbation, although not identified by name in the Bible, must be viewed as sinful for at least three reasons. *First*, masturbation is a perversion of the intent of sex. It's selfish rather than loving—it's *taking* rather than *giving*. God did not give you your sexual organs so that you could please yourself with them, but rather so that you could bring pleasure to your wife, and so that she can express her love to you by giving you sexual pleasure. *Second*, masturbation almost always involves sinful lust. Jesus made it absolutely clear *"that everyone who looks on a woman to lust for her has committed adultery with her already in his heart"* (Matt. 5:28). *Third*, masturbation is an activity that causes Christians who practice it to experience guilt. The Bible is also very clear about the sinfulness of Christians who willingly participate in any activity for which their consciences condemn them.

> *Happy is he who does not condemn himself in what he approves. But he who doubts is condemned if he eats, because [his eating is] not from faith; and whatever is not from faith is sin* (Rom. 14:22-23).

In all my years of counseling Christian men, I've never known even one whose conscience did not bother him whenever he succumbed to this activity. Many Christian men have so habitually succumbed to this temptation that they have become caught in this transgression, and have consequently been hindered in their walk with God. Rather than confessing this struggle to, and getting help from, a godly counselor and/or their wives (who are often in a wonderful position as "suitable helpers" to assist them through various means), such men live with guilt for *years*, bound by lust and missing out on the joy and fruitfulness promised by God to those who have a clear conscience (cf. Acts 24:16; 1 Tim. 1:5-7,18-20).

Principle #4: Sexual relations are to be regular and continuous. No exact number of times per week is advised, but the

principle is that both parties are to provide such adequate sexual satisfaction that both "burning" (sexual desire) and the temptation to find sexual satisfaction elsewhere are avoided.

"Your homework assignment for this week is to have a physical relationship with your spouse at least X times this week—and when you do, I want you to be more concerned about pleasing her (or him) than you are about pleasing yourself."[3] I've said such words to counselees on more occasions than I can remember. Recently, I "warned" two couples that if the frequency of their sexual relations didn't improve over the next few weeks, I was going to assign sexual relations for homework at our next session. The grammatical construction of the injunction in 1 Corinthians 7 assumes that some of the readers were in the process of defrauding each other sexually, and is a command to "stop depriving one another."

Contrary to popular belief, all husbands do not have a greater desire for sexual relations than do their wives. A larger percentage of women than you might expect actually desire more frequent sexual encounters per week than their husbands do. Each person is different and each couple has their own unique set of internal and external factors that effect such desire. The biblical principle requires each partner to know and respond to the desires of his or her spouse. Part of your responsibility to live with your wife in an understanding way, you'll remember, is to know such information about "your woman," and respond accordingly. Part of her responsibility to be your "helper suitable" (or "completor") is to do likewise for you. Generally speaking, the partner with the lesser desire ought to be willing to yield to the wishes of the partner with the stronger desire in order to help the partner with the stronger desire not to "burn." ("*But if they [the unmarried and widows] do not have self-control, let them marry; for it is better to marry than to burn*" 1 Cor. 7:9.) Of course, as the next principle implies, the partner with the stronger or more frequent desire must also be willing to show love to his or her spouse by sometimes limiting the frequency of their sexual encounters in deference to her or him. The key principle for both partners is found in Philippians 2:3-4:

> *Do nothing from selfishness or empty conceit, but with humility of mind let each of you regard one another as more important than himself; do not [merely] look out for your own personal interests, but also for the interests of others.*

If your wife desires more frequency in sexual relations than you do, there will be times when you must be willing to minister to her sexually—even though you may be disinterested, tired, absorbed in some other interest or responsibility, discouraged or upset. If you're the partner with the greatest sexual desire, and your wife is willing to minister to you sexually during times when she is not as amorous as you are, or when she is "not really in the mood," you must take care not to be too disappointed or "get your feelings hurt" should the encounter not be as passionate, exciting or exhilarating as you'd like. Rather than experiencing such disappointment, you should be grateful for a wife who is willing to minister to you so unselfishly.[4] Rather than telling yourself, "If she really loved me, she would be making wild and passionate love to me," remind yourself that it's truly a *greater* demonstration of her love for you when she unselfishly makes love, even though she's not in a wildly passionate mood.

Of course you should always try to prepare her sexually (with sufficient affection and foreplay) so that she may have a more enjoyable time, but if she's simply interested in pleasing you, don't take it personally! Just enjoy it and be thankful for such an unselfish, caring wife. Show your appreciation with words of affirmation and gratitude, and with other physical expressions of your affection. Remember that many women seem to experience much more "sexual satisfaction" even if they don't achieve an orgasm than can most men. This may be difficult for you to comprehend, because as men, we often find it hard to conceive of having a pleasurable sexual encounter that does not end with an orgasm. "Sex without orgasm is like a banquet without food," is the way many men reason. This notion, however, is not scripturally based. This is probably not the way your wife thinks, neither should it be the way that you think about sex.

Principle #5: The principle of satisfaction means that each party is to provide sexual enjoyment (which is "due" him or her in marriage) as frequently as the other person requires. But, of course, other biblical principles (moderation, seeking to please another rather than oneself, etc.) also come into play. Consideration for one's mate is to regulate one's request for sexual relations. But this must not be used as an excuse for failing to meet genuine needs. On the other hand, requests for sexual satisfaction may not be governed by an idolatrous lust.

Moderation (self control) is to be exercised in all things (1 Cor. 9:25), including marital sex.

> *All things are lawful for me, but not all things are profitable. All things are lawful for me, but I will not be mastered by anything* (1 Cor. 6:12).

Just as you must control your desires for food, money, and other good and pleasurable activities by keeping them from becoming excessive, so also you must learn to moderate your desire for sex so that it does not consume a larger place in your life than is lawful. Remember that almost any good desire (like the desire for food, shelter, sleep, respect and even sex), can become idolatrous if we desire it inordinately.

Is not life (and body) more than sex? Not for some men I've known. Their minds are so inordinately consumed with sex that there's little thought given to the other biblical responsibilities of life, such as your ministering to your wife, children and neighbor. If this sounds like you, I recommend that you pray daily that the Lord would help you replace these thoughts and desires with those that are more in line with biblical reality. Consider also seeking the help of your wife and one of your church leaders.

Just as your wife must "consider" the intensity of your sexual desire (should yours be stronger than hers), so you should be considerate of those things that may interfere with her desire or ability to minister to you. There may be times when your wife offers to have sexual relations, but you will have to consider whether or not it is really in her best interest for you to have them.

"Is she too weary?" "Will it be more enjoyable for her if I wait until tomorrow when she is more rested." "Will postponing our encounter afford her with a greater sense of privacy?" "Has her day been filled with so much stress that it would really be selfish for me to expect her to do this?" A loving husband asks himself questions such as these before he accepts his wife's offer for sexual relations.

Principle #6: In accordance with the principle of "rights," there is to be no sexual bargaining between married persons ("I'll not have relations unless you..."). Neither party has the right to make such bargains.

When you got married, you gave up the right to use your body only as you see fit. You no longer possess sole authority over your own body—*your wife does.*[5] You are now *one flesh.* Your body belongs to her and vice versa. It is not for either of you to deny access to each other's body unless (or until) certain selfish desires are met.

Are you kinder, more gentle, more generous, more attentive, more tender, more affectionate with your wife when you are desirous of sexual relations than at other times? If so, you may be tempting her to use sex as a bargaining tool. If she attempts to use sex as a bargaining tool, you must consider whether or not you are truly loving her as Christ loves the church. The question to ask yourself is, "Would she be using sex to get what she wants if I were really meeting her needs and fulfilling as many of her legitimate desires as I could without sinning?"

Principle #7: Sexual relations are equal and reciprocal. Paul does not give the man superior rights to the woman. It is clear, then, that mutual stimulation and mutual initiation of relations are legitimate. Indeed, the doctrine of mutual rights involves also the obligation of mutual responsibility. This means, among other things, mutual active participation in the act of intercourse.

Many unscriptural taboos abound among Christians about sexual relations in marriage. Among these is the idea that the woman may not be the initiator or aggressor. Since the body of each partner belongs to his or her spouse, it follows that mutual stimulation and initiation of relations are legitimate, as is mutual, active participation in the act of intercourse.

On the other hand, God did design the husband to be more of an initiator and the wife to be more of a responder. How well do you initiate lovemaking with your wife? Here are some self-examination questions that you may want to ask yourself concerning your attempts.

- Do you initiate sexual relations often enough?
- Do you resent the fact that your wife doesn't initiate relations as often as you wish?
- Are you uncomfortable when your wife initiates lovemaking?
- How do you initiate sexual relations? Do you usually do so by making a verbal request?
- Do you always use the same "canned" invitation?
- Do you ever skip the routine invitation and try to arouse her romantically without using interrogatives, or any words at all?

The questions at the end of this chapter are a continuation of those suggested at the end of Chapter Two. They should help you to better understand and minister to your wife sexually. All of the questions may not be fitting or necessary for your situation. Be careful not to be overly sensitive or hurt by her answers. In the long run, your sex life should be enhanced as a result of the time you spend discussing and biblically resolving these issues. It is advised that you do *not* keep any written record of her responses to these questions. I've also included in Appendix J, "Hints, Suggestions, and Attitude Helpers About Sex," some additional thoughts that may help you to be a more complete lover to your wife.

Questions I Would Like to Ask Her

1. If you could change three things about our sex life what would you change?

2. Do you believe that I have been selfish sexually? If so, how?

3. Do I have any offensive odors, mannerisms, or habits that hinder your enjoyment of our sexual relations.

4. Is there anything that we've done sexually that you are uncomfortable doing?

5. Is there anything that we've not done sexually that you believe you would enjoy doing?

6. Do I provide enough affection and foreplay prior to intercourse?

7. Do you feel pressured to perform a certain way by anything I do or say?

8. Am I pro-active (aggressive) enough sexually?

9. Is there anything about my appearance that you are so displeased with that it hinders your ability to enjoy sex?

10. Is there any part of your anatomy that you are so displeased with that it hinders your ability to enjoy sex?

11. Have you ever had an orgasm? (You probably know the answer to this question already, but if you have *any* doubts you should ask).

12. Are there any other marital or personal issues that are hindering your ability to enjoy sexual relations with me?

13. Do I make enough of an effort to provide you with a pleasant, comfortable, and secure environment in which to make love?

14. What time of day and in what situations do you most/least prefer to make love?

15. Are you comfortable with the frequency with which we make love?

16. Am I creative enough in my attempts to initiate making love to you?

17. Is there anything else that I can do by way of word, attitude or action that would make our sexual relationship more meaningful?

Add further questions here…..

Notes

[1] R.C. Sproul, *The Intimate Marriage*, pp.42-43.

[2] The seven biblical principles of sex contained in this chapter were originally printed in *The Christian Counselor's Manual*, by Jay Adams (Grand Rapids: Zondervan, 1973), p. 392. Used by permission.

[3] "X" usually is a number derived as a result of my questioning both parties about the frequency with which they prefer to have sexual relations.

[4] This expression is not really accurate biblically. Your feelings don't actually get hurt. Rather, your thoughts which, in part, produce your emotions are usually out of harmony with Scripture. As I've alluded to in a previous footnote, if your wife really sins against you and thereby ends up "hurting your feelings," she is the one who must repent of her sin. If however you get your "feelings hurt" over something which she does that is not sinful (such as occasionally being less passionate than you are about sex), *you* must repent of your unbiblical thoughts which produced such painful emotions.

[5] Actually, you did so to an even greater degree when you became a Christian. The Pro-choice advocates seem to have forgotten these two points— if, in fact, they ever really knew them.

Chapter 11

Protecting Your Wife from Danger

"Where exactly does it say in the Bible that it's *my* responsibility to protect my wife?"

Implicit in the command to love your wife *as* Christ loved the church is the responsibility to protect her from danger: *"But the Lord is faithful, and He will strengthen and protect you from the evil [one]"* (2 Thes. 3:3; cf. also Lk. 13:34, 21:18; Acts 12:4-7, 18:10, 26:17; 2 Pet. 2:9). In addition, the husband's protection of the wife is implied in Ruth's request of Boaz to "spread his covering" over her (Ruth 3:9). This metaphor is used to describe a hen covering her chicks with her wings to protect them from harm (cf. Ruth 2:12). Jesus used it to describe his passion for the city of Jerusalem.

> *O Jerusalem, Jerusalem, who kills the prophets and stones those who are sent to her! How often I wanted to gather your children together, the way a hen gathers her chicks under her wings, and you were unwilling* (Matt. 23:37).

The clearest and most definite implication of the husband's biblical responsibility to protect his wife, however, is found in Ephesians 5:23:

> *For the husband is the head of the wife, as Christ also is the head of the church, He Himself [being] the Savior of the body.*

The Greek verb from which the word "savior" is derived means "to save." It involves keeping someone safe and sound, rescuing him/her from danger or destruction, saving that person from judgment, evil or injury; peril, disease and death. These are the kinds of things from which God expects you, as your wife's savior, to protect her. You're to shelter and defend her from any danger that would hinder her usefulness or mar her beauty. You're to gallantly treat her as a weaker vessel (or a fragile vase) who is in need of your preservation.

The Power of Influence

Do you recall the verse in the Bible that warns us about keeping "bad company?"

"I sure do. It's First Corinthians 15:33: *"Bad company corrupts good morals."*

That's it, but I believe you've misquoted it.

"I have?"

Well, most people I've heard only quote the second part of the verse. They usually forget the first four words: *"Do not be deceived..."* That little preamble is a very important warning. Paul is cautioning us to be careful. He says, *"Don't be misled!* You'd better pay attention to those with whom you keep company because, if you're not careful and hang out with the wrong people, you'll be influenced by them—and you won't even realize that it's happening."

The Bible in many places speaks about the power of *influence*. Here are a few of the more prominent general references.

> *He who walks with wise men will be wise, But the companion of fools will suffer harm* (Prov. 13:20).

> *Do not associate with a man [given] to anger; Or go with a hot-tempered man, Lest you learn his ways, And find a snare for yourself* (Prov. 22:24-25).

Do you not know that a little leaven leavens the whole lump [of dough]? (1 Cor. 5:6b)

The power of influence is probably more potent than you realize. It was certainly more powerful than I realized. Consider, for example, the differences in the way people speak and the words they use in different parts of the country. When I grew up in the suburbs of New York City, we would greet each other with a friendly "Hi!" I attended college in the Mid-west where the common greeting was "Hello." When I first came down to the South where my family and I now reside, I thought it was rather awkward that almost everyone greeted each other with the word "Hey" (a term that in New York was commonly considered to be almost disrespectful—"'Hey' is for horses.").

Then of course, there is the Brooklyneese expression, "Yooze guys," which contrasts rather starkly with the genteel "you all" of Mid-America. But what do I now say when I'm counseling couples or exhorting my audience from the pulpit? I say "Y'all", as in "Y'all need to do what the Bible sayez."[1] In New York it was "so long," in the Mid-west it was "good-bye," but in the South it's "Baaah." On Long Island when you're thirsty you drink a "soda," in Kansas City, you're sipping on a "pop," but in Atlanta, whether it be root beer or Sprite, or Dr. Pepper™, you're having a "Coke.™" When I was a kid I would get "mad," in college I got "angry." Now when I get angry, my wife says that I'm "ill." In New York, I would "push" the button in the elevator, in the Mid-west I would "press" the button, now I "mash" it. In New York, the term was "lazy," in Kansas City it was "slothful," while in the South, this person is commonly referred to as "a good 'ole boy."[2]

Now the point of all this is that when I first moved to the South twelve years ago, I was determined that I was *not* going to talk like a Southerner. It wasn't that I thought people down here talked funny, I just couldn't stand the thought of being teased by some of my family and friends in New York and Kansas City, every time I opened my mouth. So, I fought it. For months I steadfastly refused to utter Southern colloquialisms. Then, much to my surprise, it kicked-in. I began thinking in a Southern dialect. Little by little, my speech was "betraying me." Southern words, which I purposed I would never speak, started slipping out of my mouth. It soon became increasingly more difficult for me to keep them from coming out of my mouth. Finally, after eighteen months, I capitulated to the influence of my Southern friends. I decided to "become all things to all men, that I may by all means save some" and started "speaking Southern."

According to Proverbs 13:20, the door of influence swings both ways. That is, we may be influenced by good as well as evil: *"He who walks with wise men will be wise, but the companion of fools will suffer harm."* As their protector, you must protect your family from dangerous influences. As their spiritual leader, you can help them find refuge by providing them with godly influences.

Potential Areas of Danger

Because of the power of influence, God told His people to destroy those nations which originally inhabited the promised land. He did not want His people to learn the detestable practices of those pagan nations:

> *Only in the cities of these peoples that the Lord your God is giving you as an inheritance, you shall not leave alive anything that breathes. But you shall utterly destroy them, the Hittite and the Amorite, the Canaanite and the Perizzite, the Hivite and the Jebusite, as the Lord your God has commanded you, in order that they may not teach you to do according to all their detestable things which they have done for their gods, so that you would sin against the Lord your God* (Deut. 20:16-18; cf. also Exod. 23:32-33; Deut. 7:1-5).

God is serious about protecting His bride from danger. Have you ever seriously considered how you can protect your bride from the many dangers she may be facing? Do you even *know* what they are? Let's look at some of the more prominent ones.

Dangerous friends and associates. Do you know who your wife's friends are? You should. The people we select as friends will have a profound influence on our lives. My counseling files are filled with examples of wives who've been hurt because they've been influenced by depraved individuals—from people they've met in church, or in their community, or in their neighborhood; to people they work with, to parents and other relatives, and to lovers.

A family came to see me for counseling many years ago. The main problem was a deficient relationship between the father and his daughter. Week after week, I planned to devote our counseling session to improving this deficient relationship. Week after week, I was thwarted in my attempts because the wife seemed to have a different agenda than I did. Each week she had a new anxiety about her family that she wanted me to address during our meeting. Finally I smelled a rat. I called the pastor of her church who had referred her to me and explained the scenario to him. I asked him if he knew anyone in the church who might be infecting this woman with all of these worries. Immediately, he realized where the problem was.

"There's a woman in our church who has some unbiblical feminist views. She talks almost daily to the wife whose family you're trying to help. Leave it to me. I'll take care of it from my end."

Now, I'm not sure exactly what he did to diminish the apparent influence of this woman on my counselee, but starting with the very next session, I was able to stick to my agenda and deal with the conflict between her husband and daughter. Her relationship with her husband also was noticeably better from that point on.

Our discussion on influence would not be complete without at least a brief mention of a wife's ability to sway her husband.

How much does your wife influence you? The Bible gives several examples of men who've allowed themselves to be wrongly influenced by their wives. First there was Adam, who "listened" to Eve persuade him into eating the forbidden fruit (Gen. 3:6,17). Potiphar's wife, through deception, unjustly influenced him to put Joseph in prison (Gen. 39: 7-20). Sarai impatiently suggested to Abram that he go into Hagar her handmaid so that they might have a son. "Abram listened to the voice of Sarai," and Ishmael was born. As a result, the conflict between Ishmael and Isaac continues to this day, as we still witness the ongoing strife between Arabs and Jews (Gen. 16:2). Solomon's wives turned his heart away after foreign gods (1 Kings 11:3-4). Through Jezebel's wicked influence, Ahab sold himself to do evil in the sight of the Lord (1 Kings 21:25). Samson's wife successfully manipulated him into telling her the answer to the riddle he told at his wedding (Judg. 14:15-18). Herodias, who "had it in for" John the Baptist, shrewdly used her daughter to influence her husband Herod to behead the prophet (Matt. 14:1-11).

Now don't get me wrong. You do need to listen to your wife, and even allow yourself to be influenced by her. What you may not do is allow her to influence you to do anything that is sinful.

Developing inordinate relationships. Even close relationships with good people can threaten marital intimacy if one spouse develops a "one flesh" kind of relationship with such people. It may shock you to learn that the most common of such inordinate relations is the parent-child relationship. In my book, *The Heart of Anger,*[3] I talk about how relationships in the family are supposed to work:

> When two people leave their respective homes to establish a new home for Christ, they become a family *before any children arrive.* When children are added, Mother and Father become the heads of a new *decision-making unit.* This unit is not a democracy. The husband is the head of

this unit, and the wife is his helper. The two are one flesh.

As children are born, they are welcomed into the family, but *not* as a part of the decision-making unit. In other words, they are part of the family, but they are *not* "one flesh" with the parents.

According to Scripture, the relationship between husband and wife is a permanent relationship which is not to be broken (Matt. 19:3-6). The authority/submission relationship between parents and their children is a temporary one which eventually *is* to be broken according to Genesis 2:24. One day the children will also leave home. Therefore, the relationship between a husband and wife is the *priority* relationship. The relationships between parents and children, and the relationships between siblings, are important but *secondary* [emphasis added].

The first "friendship" you must protect your wife from cultivating too intensely is her friendship with your children. She is *your* lifetime companion, not theirs. *You* are to be her best friend, not the children. Now, I'm certainly not discouraging the natural and biblical development of a parent-child friendship—especially as the child matures. What I *am* warning you about is allowing either parent to develop a closer friendship with any of the children than with their spouse.

Another common area of potentially dangerous friendships is the *in-law* relationship. Again, let me state clearly that there is absolutely nothing inherently wrong with having an in-law as one of your close friends. In many cases, it's preferable. The danger comes when a married man or woman experiences more intimacy with, and/or dependence on, a parent than a spouse.

The last area of potentially dangerous "close friendships" I'd like to comment on is the "girlfriend" relationship. Your wife may need protection from developing inordinate relationships with other women—even professing Christian women. I have counseled countless women who, out of various motives, have developed "co-dependent"[4] relationships with other woman (and occasionally men) to their own detriment, and the detriment of their marriage. The impact of such "friendships" on the marital relationship can be *devastating*, and I'm in no way exaggerating. I've seen such relationships cause more Christian women to neglect their husbands, children, and church, than I care to remember. There are numerous separated and divorced Christians whose marriages would, in my judgment, still be intact were it not for such friendships.

Your wife is to depend on you to provide her with comforting emotional and spiritual support more than anyone else (except the Lord). If your wife ministers to other women, you must help her minister in such a way that she does not encourage those she serves to look to her more than God to meet their needs. If other women are ministering to your wife, be careful to monitor those ministries carefully, lest she begin looking to them to afford her with those things for which God has given you the responsibility to provide.

Bad theology. Several years ago I walked into a "family" Christian bookstore in Atlanta, to purchase a copy of Berkhof's *Systematic Theology* which I needed to prepare for a Nouthetic counseling exam.[5] As I walked into the store, I passed several large displays of Christian greeting cards, two large sections of bookshelves filled with books on Christian living, and three more sections of bookshelves devoted to self-help books before I got to the Bible reference display. On the other side of the store was a wall-display filled with Christian music. In the back of the store was all manner of books and games for children. I hunted for my systematic theology, but to no avail. Finally, I walked up to the sales desk and asked the clerk if the store carried the book.

"You know," she said, "I studied that book when I went to Bible college, but we don't carry it here."

Then I asked the next question. "Do you sell *any* systematic theology books in this store?"

Somehow, I was not surprised when she answered, "No."

Most people no longer get their theology from the pulpit. Rather, they get it from Christian books and magazines, Christian radio and television, Christian counselors (among whom are some of the worst theologians I've ever come across), and Christian "seminars" and "workshops" on various topics. It's not that learning theology from places other than church is wrong. Rather, it's that many preachers today don't teach theology from the pulpit, and many publishers, teachers and counselors have little or no interest in disseminating material that is theologically accurate. This is especially true in the area of self-help books and seminars, where pop-psychology carries more weight than Scripture. So, the problem is not simply that many people are not getting their theology from the pulpit, but also that the theology contained in these other sources is weak, if not heretical. As Paul predicted, in 2 Timothy 4:3-4, the time has come when Christians do not tolerate sound doctrine; but wanting to have their ears tickled, they accumulate for themselves teachers (and authors) in accordance with their own desires; they turn away their ears from *the truth*, and instead, turn aside to *myths*.

Look at Paul's departing words to the elders of the Ephesian church.

> *Be on guard for yourselves and for all the flock, among which the Holy Spirit has made you overseers, to shepherd the church of God which He purchased with His own blood. I know that after my departure savage wolves will come in among you, not sparing the flock; and from among your own selves men will arise, speaking perverse things, to draw away the disciples after them. Therefore be on the alert, remembering that night and day for a period of three years I did not cease to admonish each one with tears* (Acts 20:28-31).

The apostle admonished these pastors, charging them as shepherds, not only to feed the flock, but also to protect it from "savage wolves" who would be attacking, not only from without, but also from within the church. These wolves, who sometimes came "in sheep's clothing" (Matt. 7:15), would teach false doctrine (bad theology) for the purpose of influencing the sheep to follow them.[6] Paul instructed his companions to be alert to these dangers. Then he reminded them of his own example of a shepherd who continuously ("night and day...I did not cease") and compassionately ("with tears") protected the sheep by warning and admonishing them. Paul was a true spiritual leader. He was alert to the spiritual danger those under his care were exposed to and did his best to protect them from it. You too must be a spiritual leader to your wife and protect her from the false teachers of our day. Such teachers come from outside the realm of Christianity and some from within. They come to lead your wife astray. Sometimes, they purposely deceive. Other times, they are themselves deceived (cf. 2 Tim. 3:13). They come not only disguised as shepherds, but also as authors, counselors and lecturers. They are sometimes found in the pulpit, but more often in the church library, Christian bookstore, on the radio and television, in the classroom and seminar workshop—and in the counseling office.

Assuming too many responsibilities. There are 168 hours in each week. A person can only accomplish so much in that amount of time. If you or your wife consistently do not get all of your weekly responsibilities completed in that time, then there are only two possible explanations for your inefficiency. Either you're wasting time or you've assumed more responsibility than the Lord intended you to have. Of course, both explanations may simultaneously account for your lack of productivity.

Now if you're wasting time, you must stop doing so in order to bring your productivity up to biblical standards. If however, your inability to fulfill your biblical obligations is due to the assumption of responsibilities never intended by God, you must re-evaluate all of them in light of your biblical priorities, and reduce or remove those which are superfluous. That is, you may have to reduce the amount of time you devote to a particular task, or you may have to eliminate that responsibility from your life altogether.

I have seen Christian parents allow their entire schedule to be skewed because they feel obligated to attend every little league game in which their children participate. Whether it's baseball, football, soccer, or basketball, Mom and Dad will be at every game and almost every practice while personal Bible study and prayer, quality communication with their mates, church attendance and Christian service get neglected. Of course, I'm not suggesting that these parents *not* go to every game possible, only that they go to every game possible *without neglecting the other biblical responsibilities which God has given them.*

Then there are the countless Christian couples I've known who, rather than reducing their standard of living to bring their lives into harmony with the Scriptures and "seek first the kingdom of God and his righteousness," neglect their spiritual responsibilities, their children, and even their own physical health, all in the name of being "good providers."

"But how do we know which responsibilities to reduce or remove?"

The outline of the Book of Ephesians may provide us with some helpful guidance. Beginning in 5:18, we are commanded to be filled with (or controlled by) the Spirit. Our first priority each day is our walk with Christ. A parallel passage in Colossians 3:16, equates being filled with the Spirit to letting "the Word of Christ richly dwell within you."

Pastor and teacher John F. MacArthur has this to say:

> Paul's command to the Colossians, "Let the word of Christ richly dwell within you," was followed by a series of subsequent and dependent commands (Col. 3:16-25) that exactly paralleled those Paul gave in Ephesians 5:19-33 as being results of the filling of the Spirit. In both cases we see that singing, giving thanks, and submissiveness follow being filled with the Spirit and letting the word of Christ dwell in us. It is therefore easy to conclude that the

filling of the Spirit is not an esoteric, mystical experience bestowed on the spiritual elite through some secret formula or other such means. It is simply taking the word of Christ (Scripture) and letting it indwell and infuse every part of our being. To be filled with God's Spirit is to be filled with His Word. And as we are filled with God's Word, it controls our thinking and action, and we thereby come more and more under the Spirit's control. As Charles Spurgeon said, the Christian's blood should be "bibline," bleeding Scripture wherever he may be pricked or cut.[7]

Our personal time in the Word should be our top priority every day. Do you schedule your day around the Scripture, or do you try to squeeze the Bible into your busy schedule? The answer to this question may well determine the extent to which you are a Spirit-filled Christian.

After addressing the more general results of being Spirit-filled in Ephesians 5:19-20, Paul specifically targets the relationships in life that require submission to authority: "...and be subject to one another in the fear of Christ."

The first relationship he addresses is that of the husband and wife (vv. 22-33). This is followed by the parent/child relationship (6:1-4) and then the master/slave relationship (6:5-9), which we may rightly apply to our employer/employee relationships today. As John MacArthur pointed out, the same general outline occurs in Colossians 3:16-25. The *order* in which these relationships are addressed in both passages provides us with some general insight into the *priority* we should give each of these responsibilities in our daily schedules. The general outline looks like this:

1. Your personal relationship and walk with Christ. This is your ultimate priority every day. "'*You shall love the Lord your God with all your heart, and with all your soul, and with all your mind.' This is the great and foremost commandment*" (Matt. 22:37-38).

2. Your ministry to your spouse. You are one flesh with your spouse, not with your children or your job. Pleasing her is a responsibility you assumed when you said "I do." *"One who is married is concerned about the things of the world, how he may please his wife"* (1 Cor. 7:33).

3. Your ministry to your children. *"Fathers, do not provoke your children to anger; but bring them up in the discipline and instruction of the Lord"* (Eph. 6:4). It's your responsibility to diligently teach your children the Scripture in the milieu of daily living (Deut. 6:6-9).

4. Your ministry to your employers and/or employees. As men, our vocational responsibilities invariably consume more of our time than the first three priorities (Bible study, wife and children) combined. Notwithstanding the time constraints, we must not allow our vocation to keep us from fulfilling these responsibilities in their proper biblical order.

This same order of biblical responsibilities (especially the first three) are applicable to our believing wives. Their relationship with God should be their top priority each and every day. Your job, as a husband, is to help protect your wife from the distractions and superfluous responsibilities that would hinder her daily time in the Word. You should also protect her from the assumption of any additional responsibilities that would prevent her from faithfully discharging her responsibility to be a helper to you, or a mother to your children. Of course, your motive for doing this should not be based on your own selfish desires, but rather, God's desire for your wife's obedience (and benefit) as revealed in His Word.

Embarrassment. Boaz gave his men specific orders concerning Ruth (whom he later married): *"Even if she gathers among the sheaves, don't embarrass her"* (Ruth 2:15 *NIV*). King Ahasuerus, conversely, after his "heart was merry with wine," ordered his wife, Queen Vashti, to show off her beauty in front of his drunken friends. He gave no thought to protecting his wife from the embarrassment that such a pompous display would have caused her. Wives should be shielded by their husbands from all unnecessary embarrassment. Whether it be disrespectful expressions by the children, or insulting comments from friends and associates, or your own careless public criticisms or jokes about her idiosyncrasies, you must protect her from all such pejorative remarks. Be mindful also of the clothing you ask her to wear, that it doesn't dishonor her, and of the responsibilities you request of her, that they are befitting her as the weaker vessel.

Other Potential Areas of Danger

There are many additional dangers that your wife may be facing. Here are just a few of them. May I suggest that you go over each one with your wife asking for her input? Look up the related Scripture references together and discuss in specific terms how you may safeguard her from each danger. The exercise at the end of this chapter is provided to help you record the specific areas for which your wife desires and needs protection.

Bad attitudes from the children. One of the most important areas in which husbands can protect their wives is defending them against verbal assault by the children. These attacks come in the form of criticism, manipulation, vindictive acts of disobedience and various other disrespectful forms of communication. Your job in such cases is two-fold. First you must reprimand the child for his sin against God. Second, you must instruct the child to ask forgiveness of his mother. You may have to intervene in the middle of a conflict between them if it appears that your wife is struggling to gain control of the dispute (Deut. 21:18-21; Exod. 20:12).

Not getting enough sleep. Sleep loss can have a profound impact on our lives. In addition to somatic difficulties, it can affect our ability to think clearly. Hallucinations are common to many who regularly are deprived of sleep. When we are physically weak (as was Elijah after the humiliation of the prophets of Baal) we are more easily disposed to sin, and obeying God can become difficult for us. Of course, we are still culpable for our sin, even when we are physically exhausted or ill. (I Kings 19:1-8; 1 Cor. 3:16-17)

Eating too much. When Christians develop bad habits, they sometimes need others in the body of Christ to hold them accountable and to assist them in the rehabituation (put-off/put-on) process. Husbands and wives are often the best equipped to provide for each other such accountability and assistance. From prayer to Bible study, from memorization to counting calories (or fat grams), to reviewing food journals, a husband can do much to protect his wife from overeating (Gal. 6:1 ff; Prov. 23: 21; Rom. 13:13-14; Heb. 12:16-17; 1 Cor. 6:12-13).

Dangerous places. In addition to exposure to physical injury, dangerous places include a locality where your wife might be especially vulnerable to spiritual harm. The danger is most likely to occur at places where other people have opportunity to tempt or influence her to sinful words, actions, attitudes, thoughts, and motives (Gen. 39:11-12; 2 Peter 2:6-9).

Dangerous activities. The world offers many activities which are filled with potential danger. Television programs, motion pictures, the internet, talk radio, video cassettes, CD ROMs and DVDs, books, magazines, sporting events, personal hobbies and other recreational pastimes can range widely from benefit to danger (Eph. 5:16; Col. 4:5).

Dangerous music. The music in your home can also have a powerful influence on each member of your family. The lyrics of today's and yesterday's pop music are decidedly anti-Christian.

Even some of today's so-called Christian music is filled with weak (if not heretical) theology. Do not underestimate the power of music to influence your thinking (Phil. 4:8; 1 Thes. 5:21).

Gossip. Tid bits of gossip may taste as sweet as luscious pieces of candy. But like rat poison, when "they go down into the inner-most parts of the body," they contaminate everyone who ingests them (Prov. 18:8; Prov. 26:22).

In-laws and relatives with bad attitudes. Extended family members can have unbiblical attitudes from which your wife may need protection. Anger, criticism, gossip, contentiousness, inordinate curiosity, and meddling are some of the more common "in-law" related problems (Gen. 2:24; Gen. 26:34-35).

Feelings. One of the greatest enemies to an undisciplined person is his feelings. Rather than being obedience-oriented (following what the Bible says), many Christians are feelings-oriented (following their own feelings). They do what they feel like doing and not what they don't feel like doing. Such individuals typically have a difficult time budgeting their money, time, words and/or food intake. They often need extra accountability (and external control) until they can, by God's grace, develop self (internal) control (Matt. 26:39; Luke 17:3-10; John 5:30).

Sinful habits. In addition to the sinful habits already listed, you should help protect your wife from other proclivities, such as nicotine and alcohol addiction, masturbation, using profanity, temper tantrums, chronic anxiety, and gossip (Prov. 5:22; 2 Peter 2:29).

Sinful thoughts and desires. Worry, resentment, sensuality, jealousy, fear, and vengeance are all examples of sinful thoughts and desires (Rom. 13:14; Heb. 4:12).

Inordinate (or idolatrous) desires. The Bible has much to say about inordinate desires. An inordinate desire is a desire for something good or necessary which has gone from lawful to lustful. Love of money, love of approval, love of pleasure, love of control, love of food, and love of sleep are all examples of idolatrous desires which are specifically identified in the Scriptures as sinful (John 12:43; 1 Tim. 6:10; 2 Tim. 3:4; 3 John 9-11; Prov. 20:13).

Materialism. The belief that one's happiness is necessarily and directly related to the abundance of things which one possesses (Luke 12:15-20).

Perfectionism. An all-or-nothing mentality whose subjective standard is higher or more exacting than the Bible (Matt. 25:26).

Legalism. Elevating man-made laws to the same level of culpability as God-given commands (Matt. 15:1-10).

Mysticism. The belief that we can receive from God direct commands other than those prescribed by Scripture, regarding our direction in life. Additionally, any belief in unbiblical "secret knowledge" obtained through means other than the revealed Word of God (Col. 2:8).

Humanism. The godless philosophy of this age which deifies man, dethrones God, and dismisses such concepts as the existence and worship of God, the inspiration of Scripture, supernatural creation, sin and its consequences, eternal life and the reality of heaven and hell (Rom. 1:21, 22).

Feminism. The humanistic tenant that submission on the part of the wife to her husband is demeaning to women because it violates the "equality of the sexes." Feminism rejects outright the

God-ordained role distinctions between men and women (1 Cor. 1:19-23; 1 Cor. 15:26-28; 1 Peter 3:1-6, 22; Eph. 5:22-24)

As David "rescued" his two wives Abinoam and Abigail from the Amalekites (1 Sam. 30:18), so you may have to rescue your wife from those who've taken her captive. As the Levite pursued his unfaithful concubine who had returned to her father's house "in order to bring her back" (Judg. 19:1-3), you may have to retrieve your wife from returning to her former ways of living. As King Ahasurerus protected queen Esther against the wicked Haman (Esth. 7:7-8), so you must protect your wife from those ungodly men and women who would do her harm. As Joseph sought to protect Mary's reputation, your job is to guard your wife's reputation, and protect her from disgrace, as much as it's in your power to do so.

Guidelines for Protecting Your Wife

1. Be sure that you properly love and understand her. As a rule, the more you love and understand your wife, the more willing she will be to allow you to protect her; the more selfish and inconsiderate you are, the more she will resist your attempts to protect her. If you're consistently violating Ephesians 5:25-33 or 1 Peter 3:7, she will likely oppose your attempts to protect her. She may wonder whether you are "protecting" her out of genuine love or for your own selfish purposes. She may even translate your attempts to protect her as attempts to control or dominate her. If, on the other hand, you are consistently demonstrating Christ's sacrificial love day in and day out, she will probably see your desire to protect her as another evidence of your love for her. She will likely find it easier to cooperate with your attempts to protect her, the more she believes that Christ is protecting her through you. Perhaps the most effective way for you to convince your bride that Christ is indeed using you to protect her, is to become increasingly more like Christ in the way you love her.

2. Be certain that you explain the biblical basis for the danger you are trying to protect her from. What's wrong with this statement?: "I don't want you to hang out with that weird woman with the purple hair."

First, what you want is not as important as what God wants. *Secondly*, "weird" is not a name with which the Bible classifies anyone. *Thirdly*, having purple hair doesn't in and of itself constitute a real biblical danger. Since it is not necessarily a sin for someone to have purple hair, it isn't, therefore, a sufficient biblical reason to prohibit your wife from developing a friendship with such a woman.

Dangers from which you protect your wife must be the kinds of dangers from which Christ would protect His church; they must be *biblically valid* dangers. You should be prepared to cite chapter and verse to substantiate the biblical validity of the danger you believe your wife is facing. If you're not sure whether or not the concern is truly based on Scripture, you may need to search the Scriptures (and even get some wise counsel) to help you determine the exact nature of the danger, if any. You may also have to ask your wife to give you some time to research the issue more thoroughly, in order to give her a more complete answer.

3. If possible, help her find a biblical alternative to the hazard you're attempting to remove from her life. It's usually not enough for us to remove the dangerous influences from our lives. In addition to making *"no provision for the flesh in regard to [its] lust"* we must *"put on the Lord Jesus Christ"* (Rom. 13:14). We must not only eliminate any feeding factors that (by feeding our lusts) might tempt us to sin, we must also add to, or continue, those things, events, activities and associations that will promote godliness (conformity to the character of the Lord Jesus Christ).

Practically then, this means not just removing from our lives dangerous influences but also replacing them with *godly* influences. In terms of your responsibility to protect your wife, this means that you should encourage her to replace potentially harmful associations with more beneficial ones. The same is true in relation to any potentially dangerous events, reading materials, television programs, music, social activities, thought patterns and every other weight or sin that can easily beset her. It's your job to help her find biblically beneficial alternatives to the deceptively dangerous hazards that threaten her physical and spiritual well being.

4. Guard your heart against selfishly "protecting" her out of inordinate desire or sinful fear. Love is not selfish. Neither is it jealous (1 Cor. 13:4-5). There is however, a godly jealousy spoken of in the Scriptures. The Holy Spirit is intensely jealous for us.

> *Or do you think that the Scripture says in vain, "The Spirit who dwells in us yearns jealously?"* (Jas. 4:5)

His jealousy, however, is not a selfish jealousy. He knows that when we desire and develop a "friendship with the world" more than a relationship with Christ, it will be to our detriment. He is jealous in the sense that He does not want us to displace God in our hearts with anything else. When we do misplace our affections for God with other temporal desires, those desires will lead us further away from Him and further into spiritual danger.

The Apostle Paul also had a similar kind of jealousy for the Corinthians:

> *For I am jealous for you with a godly jealousy; for I betrothed you to one husband, that to Christ I might present you [as] a pure virgin. But I am afraid, lest as the serpent deceived Eve by his craftiness, your minds should be led astray from the simplicity and purity [of devotion] to Christ* (2 Cor. 11:2-3).

Paul's jealousy was not based on what he might lose but rather on what might befall the Corinthians should they be deceived and led astray from Christ. His jealousy motivated him to protect them because he wanted what was best for them—not because he was selfishly afraid that he was going to lose something.

This is the kind of selfless jealousy that you should have for your wife. You should desire to protect her, not primarily because *you* are afraid of what *you* might lose should she be exposed to some danger, but rather because *you are deeply concerned for her well-being.*

Areas in Which She Needs My Protection

In which areas does your wife need and want your protection? Review the list of potential dangers with your wife. Ask her to tell you exactly *what* the dangers are from her point of view and *how* she would like you to shield her from them.

Potential Danger   **How I Can Protect Her**

1.   1.

2.   2.

3.   3.

4.   4.

5.   5.

6.   6.

7.   7.

Add to this list any other areas...

Notes

[1]Incidentally, the secret to speaking Southern is simply elongating monosyllabic words at the end of your sentences, transliterating them with two or three syllables.

[2]The term in not necessarily synonymous with lazy. Not all "Good ole boys" are lazy!

[3] Priolo, *The Heart of Anger*, pp. 25-26

[4]The more biblical term is usually "idolatrous" relationships, in that they are often characterized by one of the women depending on the other to do for them what only God can do (cf. Isa. 31:1-3; Jer. 17:5; Col. 3:5).

[5]I am a certified member of the National Association of Nouthetic Counselors, an organization of biblical counselors who formulate their counseling model, not from the hundreds of current secular psychological theories, but rather from a sound exegesis of Scripture. We believe that the Bible is the only complete and authoritative textbook which was written specifically to provide both the answers to man's behavioral problems and the means for man's behavioral changes.

[6]These wolves in sheep's clothing were probably other pastors or spiritual leaders. It was the *shepherd,* not the sheep, who wore wool garments (sheep's clothing) for the purpose of keeping warm. False teachers disguise themselves as true shepherds.

[7]John F. MacArthur, *The MacArthur New Testament Commentary: Ephesians* (Chicago: Moody Press, 1986), p.252.

Chapter 12

How Much is She Worth to You?

Note: The Feminists Have it Dead Wrong!

I was somewhat incredulous several months ago at the media coverage of the largest men's prayer vigil ever held in Washington D.C. My incredulity was due to the amount of time given to various "Christophobic" feminists who were promoting their view that the biblical doctrine of submission on the part of the wife to her husband was somehow a dangerous threat to women. The truth is, that throughout history, Christianity has consistently elevated the place of women in the society into which it was introduced. It's only the recent American onslaught from secular humanism that has caused many to become suspect of biblical Christianity as it relates to gender roles.

> It was an important advance made in society when the Christian religion gave such a direction as this [giving honor unto the wife], for everywhere among the heathen, and under all false systems of religion, woman has been regarded as worthy of little honor or respect. She has been considered as a slave, or as a mere instrument to gratify the passions of man. It is one of the elementary doctrines of Christianity, however, that woman is to be treated with respect; and one of the first and marked effects of religion on society is to elevate the wife to a condition in which she will be worthy of esteem.

Christianity has done much to elevate the female sex. It has taught that the woman is an heir to the grace of life as well as the man; that, while she is inferior in bodily vigor, she is his equal in the most important respect; that she is a fellow-traveler with him to a higher world; and that in every way she is entitled to all the blessings which redemption confers, as much as he is. This single truth has done more than all other things combined to elevate the female sex, and is all that is needful to raise her from her degradation all over the world. They, therefore, who desire the elevation of the female sex, who see woman ignorant and degraded in the dark parts of the earth, should be the friends of all well-directed efforts to send the gospel to heathen lands.[1]

If you've been instructed in the elementary principles about domestic responsibilities delineated in the Bible, you probably know already that one of the two principal responsibilities that are outlined in the New Testament for your wife is that she is to honor or reverence you (her other predominant duty is to be submissive to you). What you may not realize is that *you* are also commanded to honor her.[2]

> You husbands likewise, live with [your wives] in an understanding way, as with a weaker vessel, since she is a woman; and grant her honor as a fellow heir of the grace of life, so that your prayers may not be hindered (1 Pet 3:7).

Before explaining further, let me point out that it's precisely this lack of honor that so often disposes a husband to be domineering, dictatorial and harsh in his attempts to be the manager of his home. Rather than being the "loving leader," a husband who does not honor his wife as the Bible commands tends to become a bully. If your wife accuses you of abusing your spiritual leadership, you should read this short chapter with special interest. It may be that your lack of respect for her, and for the position and place that God has given her in your life, has impaired your ability to lead her effectively.

To better explain what is involved in your responsibility to honor your wife, let's go back to our example of the fragile vase. Would you take an expensive Waterford crystal vase and plunk it down in a sink full of greasy dish water? No, you would treat that valued vessel with more honor than you would the more common and durable, less attractive vessels. You would carefully wash and dry it by hand, and return it to a prominent place in your home. You would honor it in this way because it's valuable and *more precious.*

The word translated "honor" in 1 Peter 3:7, is translated "precious" in 1 Peter 2:7:

> *This precious value, then, is for you who believe. But for those who disbelieve, "The stone which the builders rejected, this became the very cornerstone."*

Because of who Christ is and what He has done for us, we honor and esteem Him highly. He is precious to us who are believers. How *precious* is your wife to you? To what extent do you honor her and esteem her highly for who she is and for what she has done for you?

Peter says that you must honor your vessel by treating her as if she were precious—and indeed she is—not only to you, but also to God. Keep in mind that your believing wife has been bought with the precious blood of Christ and must be honored as one of God's heirs. As one commentator explains:

> The honor or preciousness that the husband must bestow on his wife is not only the recognition of her place in God's ordinance of marriage; it is the honor that is theirs as one of God's precious and holy people.[3]

As a rule, the weaker or more fragile your wife is, the more tenderness you must use in your treatment of her. If your wife's fragility is the result of her spiritual immaturity, you must, of course, help her to "grow out of" her superfluous frailty (review Chapter Six, "Honey You Need a Bath" for suggestions on how to help her grow spiritually). You must, however, continue to treat her with the gentleness that is commensurate with her weakness. If, on the other hand, her fragility is more *constitutional* (and not the result of any unbiblical thoughts or motives) you must endure with her through all of life, asking God to give you the ability to tenderly honor her weaknesses.

Your wife is not referred to as a "*weak*" vessel but as a "*weaker*" vessel. You're not the "*strong*" one, but the "*stronger*" one. You may be stronger than her, but being a sinner, you are weak in your own ways. Keeping this in mind will help you walk in humility before your wife.

Another element of honoring your wife as a weaker vessel has to do with the fact that she is God's special vessel or *instrument of blessing* in your life. One of the definitions of the word "vessel," is "an implement or instrument that has been specially adapted or designed for a particular use or purpose." God has given your wife to you as a *helper* and, as such, uses her in your life in a variety of ways. She is the vessel which He created and instructed to be your companion, to take care of your home, to meet your many physical needs and desires, and to share your joys and sorrows. She is God's vessel through which you may have children and give them guidance, as well as physical and spiritual nourishment and protection. She is the vessel through which He intended to bring you the greatest earthly pleasures. As Solomon explains, *"Enjoy life with the woman whom you love all the days of your fleeting life which He has given to you under the sun; for this is your reward in life, and in your toil in which you have labored under the sun"* (Eccl. 9:9). You should honor her because she's God's ordained instrument for your good. She's designed to be your *greatest reward* this side of glory and your fellow heir of the grace of life.

As a Christian, you are commanded to show this same kind of honor to the fellow believers in your church:

Be devoted to one another in brotherly love; give preference to one another in honor (Rom. 12:10).

When you "give preference to" or "prefer" others with honor, you bestow upon them the eminence they deserve. In every area where it's legitimate to do so, you are to prefer giving honor to others rather than yourself. In those areas where they're more gifted, more capable, more able and more proficient, you step back and allow them to receive the glory that's theirs to receive. Even if you truly believe that you're *as* deserving or *more* deserving of honor, you must not resent or envy them. Rather, rejoice that God has been pleased at this time to grant them such honor instead of you.

If others are deserving of honor and are not given the honor they've earned, you should seek to bring their honorable deeds to light. Instead of waiting for others to honor you, you should beat them to the punch by attempting to honor them *first*. You should attempt to put *them* in the spotlight rather than yourself. This is how Paul tells us that we are to "honor" the other Christians in our lives.

Peter, using the same word, commands you as a husband to show this kind of honor to the "other" Christian to whom you are married. Actually, you're to honor your wife in this way, as a weaker vessel, even if she is *not* a Christian. You're to set her in a place of honor, just as that expensive Waterford crystal vase is set in a place of honor in your home. Picture it, if you will, behind a glass-enclosed cabinet, or on a pedestal with a ceiling-mounted spot light illuminating its intricate beauty.

How valuable is your wife to you? How much *value* do you place on her? In what ways do you *esteem her* as deserving more honor than yourself? In what ways do you *prefer her* to be *honored* more than yourself? How thankful are you to the Lord for giving her to you? How much better off are you now than you were before you married her? How many of your needs and desires that you've taken for granted has she fulfilled? How much more blessed (and how much less miserable) are you now than when you were single? The answers to these questions are largely cognitive, but they're extremely important. The things you tell yourself about how much your wife is worth to you (how much you value her) will largely determine the degree of honor and glory that you bestow upon her in tangible ways every day of your life.

So then, the first thing you must do if you've not been honoring your wife practically, is to change the way you *think* about her. You should begin to value her more than you have. You probably should remind yourself more often than you currently do, how much she does for you, and how much you've selfishly taken her for granted, and how blessed you are that God has given her to you. Only then will you be able to *genuinely* demonstrate to her and to others the honor that the Bible says she deserves.

Here are a few more questions you might ask yourself once you've repented of any ungrateful attitude(s) you've developed toward God and your wife. How do I honor my wife? How *exactly* do I demonstrate the value that I place on her to others? In what ways do I see to it that she gets such honor? If you don't have many answers to these questions, I recommend that you take a look at the following list of suggested ways you may practice giving your wife the honor she deserves. You may even consider reviewing this list with her, asking her to comment on each option and add to the list any additional ways she would like you to honor her.

Specific ways that husbands may honor (show respect for) their wives.

- Learning and using proper etiquette.
- Refusing to use harsh or condescending forms of communication when talking to her.
- Praising her before others (especially your children).

- Being attentive to her when she's talking to you (*stop* what you are doing, if possible, *look* her in the eyes—and *listen* intently to what she's saying).
- Being considerate of her time and schedule in light of her other biblical priorities in addition to being your wife.
- Asking for and considering her opinion, especially when making plans and decisions that involve her.
- Providing her with enough financial resources to facilitate her biblical responsibilities.
- Protecting her from sin and temptation.
- Being considerate of (and helping her prioritize) her schedule.
- Not embarrassing her in front of (or revealing her weaknesses to) others.
- Dwelling on her positive qualities as much as possible, and overlooking her negative idiosyncrasies.
- Praising her and commending her to others (Prov. 31:29).
- Helping to establish and maintain her "good name" according to Proverbs 22:1.
- Not allowing the children to talk disrespectfully to her (cf. Eph. 6:2).
- Using kindness and gentleness in your dealings with her (Col. 3:12-13 and 1 Cor. 13).
- Attributing the best possible motive to her actions (1 Cor. 13:7: "love believes all things") especially when she does not follow your clear directives.

May God enable you to increasingly honor your wife, in these kinds of ways, and in accordance with the clear directives of His Word.

How Is My Wife to Be Honored?

- In what ways should I prefer to honor my wife?
- What are the areas in her life that deserve special honor?
- In what ways is my wife to be considered a weaker vessel?
- How exactly is she to be treated as a fragile and valuable vase?
- In what other ways may I show my respect for her? How else can I honor her?:

1.

2.

3.

4.

5.

6.

7.

8.

9.

10.

Add further ways to this list…..

Notes

[1]Barnes, Albert, *Notes on the New Testament*, Vol 10, (London: Blackie & Son, 1884), pp. 162-164.

[2]The Greek word for "honor" used by Paul to exhort the wife to "reverence her husband" in Ephesians 5:33 is a word which carries with it the connotation of reverential fear. The Greek word used by Peter in chapter three and verse seven of his first epistle is a word which has more to do with the value placed on (or preciousness of) an item such as a "fragile vase." The practical outworkings of these two kinds of honor often appear to be similar if not identical in daily living.

[3]Edmund P. Clowney, *The Message of 1 Peter* (Leicester, England: Inter-Varsity Press, 1988), pp.134-135.

Chapter 13

"Me, a Spiritual Leader?"

What does it mean to be a spiritual leader?

Rather than giving one short answer to this commonly asked question, I'm going to ask you to think of spiritual leadership from several perspectives. Like a pizza that is sliced into several pieces, each piece comprising a part of the whole pie, spiritual leadership can be defined one slice at a time.

Actually, you've already chomped down at least six "slices" in the process of getting to this chapter, without realizing it. When you stop to analyze it, most of the chapters in this book have dealt with the various responsibilities of spiritual leadership. Let me explain by briefly summarizing what we've already considered in previous chapters about your responsibility to be a spiritual leader.

- Chapters One and Two: A Spiritual Leader is a man who lives with his wife in an understanding way.
- Chapters Three and Four: A Spiritual Leader is a man who knows how to communicate biblically.
- Chapters Five, Six and Seven: A Spiritual Leader is a man who loves his wife as Christ loves the church
- Chapter Nine: A Spiritual Leader is a man who can discern the spiritual condition of his wife and lovingly lead her to spiritual maturity.
- Chapter Eleven: A Spiritual Leader is a man who is aware of the

dangers his wife is facing and knows how to protect her from those dangers.
• Chapter Twelve: A Spiritual Leader is a man who honors his wife as a weaker vessel (i.e., treats her as a fragile vase).

To these working definitions of spiritual leadership, I will only add two more. The first definition focuses on an aspect of spiritual leadership that has to do with your being the *head* of your wife.

> The husband is the head of the wife, as Christ also is the head of the church, He Himself [being] the Savior of the body (Eph. 5:23).

What does it mean to be the *head* of your wife? Being your wife's head means that you're responsible. You're responsible to *preside* over her, and you're responsible to *provide* for her. You're ultimately responsible for what is happening in her life. You're responsible to be aware of what your wife is doing and how she's doing it. You're responsible, as I have already explained, to dwell with her according to knowledge, to sanctify her, and to protect her. But most of all, as her head, you're responsible to *love her*.

As usual, Jay Adams says it well:

> Look back to Ephesians 1:22, where Paul describes that headship of Christ over the church. If a husband wants to know what headship over his wife must be like, and how it parallels the headship of Christ over the church, he can find out in this verse. It says: "God put all things in subjection under his feet and gave him as head over all things *to* [or better, *for*] *the church*, which is his body." In other words, all things that have been given to Jesus Christ are given to him *for his church*, and he exercises headship over His church *for her blessing, for her benefit, and for her good.* The power, authority, glory, honor, and headship at the very right hand of the Father have been given to Him that He may exercise and mediate them *for His*

church. His headship is a headship *oriented toward the church.* The church is His body. The head *feeds* the body, *nourishes* the body, and *cares* for the body. The head doesn't run off on it's own, but the head is *always concerned about the body.* Always sending out the messages that *will bring restoration* and *provide for* the safety and welfare of the various parts of the body, the head *preserves* and *cares for* the body.

The headship of Jesus Christ involves a *deep concern* for the church. That is the kind of leadership that husbands are called to exercise over their wives. They're heads over wives *as Christ is head* over His church, which means that they do not exercise an independent headship, standing aloof on a pedestal while their wives kneel and scrape on the floor beneath. Rather, it is a headship that *ministers* to the wife, a headship that is *concerned* about her. It is a headship in *love* that is *oriented toward doing all that one can for his wife.* Christ *loved* the Church enough to die for her. Will he not freely give her all things then? Of course, says Paul. And so it should be for one's wife. No tyrannical or arbitrary headship is allowed. *Headship means love; that is, the giving of oneself*[1] [*emphasis added*].

By giving you the position of "head," God has given you a uniform. It's a uniform that's probably still too big for you, one you've yet to fully grow into. You've yet to love your wife as Christ loves the church. Yes, it's true that your wife must learn to distinguish between your *position* as her head, and your *personality*, which is still trying to catch up to that position. And, yes, she has to salute that uniform even if it's seven sizes too big for you. But you must continue to do *all you can* to fill out that uniform. You must learn to be the loving leader that God requires you to be. The more you *do*—the more you fill out that uniform by living up to that position of honor that God has graciously given you— the easier it will be for your wife to do the two most difficult things God requires of her: to be submissive to you (Eph. 5:22-24; 1 Pet. 3:1), and to show you respect (Eph. 5:33; 1 Pet. 3:4-5).

A *Spiritual Leader* is a man who assumes responsibility for the management of his own household.

Scripture records the characteristics of the kind of men that are qualified for church leadership. Both pastors and deacons are required to demonstrate proficiency as household managers.

> He must be one who manages his own household well, keep-ing his children under control with all dignity (but if a man does not know how to manage his own household, how will he take care of the church of God?)...Deacons must be good managers of [their] children and their own households (1 Tim. 3:4-5,12).

All men are to *manage* their household. Church officers are to do it *well*. A spiritual leader then, is a *manager*. He manages his family in accordance with biblical principles. It's not that he does everything himself, but he sees to it that each member of the household fulfills his or her biblical responsibilities. Neither is he a micro-manager who must have his hand in every project. Rather, he's *aware* of everything that's going on in his home. He knows what needs to be done, but he also knows how to *delegate* responsibilities to those who are capable and responsible to ful-fill them.

> "Headship" does not mean crushing a wife's talents and gifts. It does not mean making all of the decisions with-out reference to her or the children, or giving to her no power to make decisions or to do anything on her own. Precisely the opposite is true of the Biblical picture. A good manager knows how to put other people to work. A good manager knows how to keep his children and his wife busy too. Certainly that man sitting among the el-ders of the gate was a good manager. He had recognized in his wife all sorts of abilities, all sorts of gifts from God that he had encouraged her to develop and use. And she was using these for the benefit of her husband and the

whole household. That is what a good manager does. He will be careful not to neglect or destroy his wife's abilities. Rather, he will use them to the fullest. The good manager will recognize that God has provided his wife as a helper for him. He remembers the Scripture that reads, "Whoever finds a wife finds a good thing." He does not consider her someone to be dragged along. Rather he thinks of her as a useful, helpful, and wonderful blessing from God. She is a helper, as a helper he will *let* her help. He will encourage her to help.[2]

In his book, *A Homework Manual for Biblical Counseling*, Dr. Wayne Mack has a section entitled, "Sorting Out Responsibilities." I have given this material as a homework assignment countless times over the years to help couples do that very thing. Wayne has graciously granted permission for me to reproduce this handout as an appendix to this book. I encourage you to sit down with your wife and work through the material together. Doing this will be a tremendous step in being a good manager who wisely delegates responsibilities to his "helper suitable."

When there are problems within his household, a good manager sees to it that they're solved scripturally. When there are conflicts in his home, he sees to it that they're resolved biblically. He helps with the coordination of scheduling. He sees to it that everyone in his household is treated with justice and equity. Additionally, should someone be temporarily unable to pull his or her load, he is willing to roll up his sleeves and "pinch hit" for one of his incapacitated team members. Simply put, a good manager is willing to do such things that may not fall within his usual responsibilities, such as changing diapers, fixing meals, vacuuming floors, or going grocery shopping.

According to the Scriptures, he also must be able to "control" his household. When I was in Bible college, I had an interesting conversation with the wife of one of my professors. This dear lady had an aversion to the word "control" in reference to the husband and wife relationship. As a counselor, having counseled

many men who have abused their authority and became tyrannical, dictatorial, dominating bullies who hurt their wives terribly,
I can certainly sympathize with such a sentiment. As a student of
the Bible, however, I can't get away from the fact that the Scriptures do, in fact, teach that a man is to rule over his wife:

> To the woman He said, "I will greatly multiply Your pain
> in childbirth, In pain you shall bring forth children; Yet your
> desire shall be for your husband, And he shall rule over you"
> (Gen. 3:16).

To better understand the meaning of this verse, let's take a
closer look at the phrase, "your desire shall be for," as it appears
one chapter later in Genesis 4:7:

> "If you do well, will not [your countenance] be lifted up?
> And if you do not do well, sin is crouching at the door; and
> its desire is for you, but you must master it."

Scholars disagree about the exact meaning of this text. Some
hold that the issue to which God is speaking is *primogeniture* (the
rights given to the eldest son). This view holds, that by virtue of
his being the firstborn, Cain should not have been envious of
Able because he had privileges of primogeniture. His brother,
among other things, would have to be subject to his rule. This
seems to be the interpretation held by the translators of the KJV:
"And unto thee [shall be] his desire, and thou shalt rule over him."
The other view, which I favor, connects this sentence to the
previous phrase, *"sin is crouching at the door."* According to this
interpretation, sin would be desiring to rule (control) Cain, but
Cain would rather be responsible to master (control) it. Of course,
since *"no prophecy of Scripture is a matter of one's own interpretation"* (2 Pet. 1:20), there can only be one intended meaning of
Scripture. Only one (if either) of these views is the one meant by
the Holy Spirit. Both interpretations, however, essentially do the
same thing with the phrase "desire shall be"; they both interpret

it as "ruling over" someone or something.

Now, putting that nuance of meaning back into Genesis 3:16, we can state the basic meaning this way: *"Yet your desire shall be to* control *your husband, but he shall rule over you."* I believe that, as a result of the fall, a woman's proclivity is to control her husband. But God has said that it's not to be that way. The husband is to control (manage) his wife. Let me hasten to add, lest you become too smug in your headship, that as a result of the fall, your proclivity as manager of the home is to become overbearing, domineering, and dictatorial with your authority. This is something you must constantly be on your guard against, for it's an abuse of your power. It's also antithetical to the second working definition I promised to give you in this chapter.

When you think about being a manager, perhaps you envision someone who's the boss and who has the right to give orders. The problem with this concept of leadership is that it's more pagan than Christian. True, in a sense, as the head of your family, you're technically "the boss." You are not, however, the *owner* of the family; God is, and He has some pretty stiff guidelines about the kind of "boss" you're to be. Yes, you have the right to give directives, but you have the responsibility of doing so only in accordance with biblical principles (See Appendix F: "Guidelines for Giving Directives to Your Wife," for the limitations God places on your "right" to give your wife instructions). Yes, you may "overrule" her decisions, but you may only do so out of pure, unselfish motives and for biblical reasons.

**A *Spiritual Leader* is a man who
has learned to be a servant to his wife.**

If you're truly a servant to your wife, you'll not become that overbearing, domineering, dictatorial bully I warned you about. Being a servant and being a bully are mutually exclusive. Let's take a look at an important lesson the Lord taught His disciples about leadership and then make some application to your being the loving leader of your wife:

> Then the mother of the sons of Zebedee came to Him with her sons, bowing down and making a request of Him. And He said to her, "What do you wish?" She said to Him, "Command that in Your kingdom these two sons of mine may sit, one on Your right and one on Your left." But Jesus answered and said, "You do not know what you are asking for. Are you able to drink the cup that I am about to drink?" They said to Him, "We are able." He said to them, "My cup you shall drink; but to sit on My right hand and on [My] left, this is not Mine to give, but it is for those for whom it has been prepared by My Father." And hearing [this], the ten became indignant with the two brothers. But Jesus called them to Himself, and said, "You know that the rulers of the Gentiles lord it over them, and [their] great men exercise authority over them. It is not so among you, but whoever wishes to become great among you shall be your servant, and whoever wishes to be first among you shall be your slave, just as the Son of Man did not come to be served, but to serve, and to give His life a ransom for many" (Matt. 20:20-28).

In this passage, what exactly were John and his brother asking for? Answer: *The preeminent position of honor in the kingdom of heaven over all the saints of God who had ever lived before and after them!* Now that's ambition!

Jesus, after explaining to the brothers that such a position would require tremendous personal sacrifice, and that only God the Father could grant it, called all the disciples to Himself. Why did He do that? To teach them all a lesson. The indignation of the other ten disciples (v. 24) underscores the obvious desire for preeminence on the part of John and James. But this indignation on the part of the *other ten* also reveals their own struggle with the lust for preeminence. Notice that Matthew says that they were not "concerned with" or "puzzled by," but that they were "indignant with" the two brothers. In response, Jesus said to them, *"You know that the rulers of the Gentiles lord it over them and [their] great men exercise authority over them."*

During the time of Christ, practically every Gentile government had for its system of administration some form of dictatorship. The disciples, therefore, were very well acquainted not only with autocracy, but with the abuse of power that often went along with it. The term "lord it over" is one word in the Greek. It literally translates, "to rule down on." The word means to "bring under one's power," to "hold in subjection," and to "exercise lordship or dominion over someone."

Whereas the term "rulers of the Gentiles" refers to those who had positions of governmental authority, the term "great men" refers to those who had obtained positions of honor and distinction in society for other reasons than governmental authority. They have achieved the status of "great men" because of their wealth, lineage, intellect, education, or charismatic personality. But regardless of how they got there, they were held in high esteem by society, and used their "greatness" to influence and control others in a way that Jesus strongly censures.

The verb translated "exercise authority" conveys the idea of exercising one's authority *against* someone (i.e., antagonistically or oppressively). These great men used their influential positions to exercise an oppressive, domineering, dictatorial, and self-serving kind of authority. However, this was not the way the disciples were to exercise the authority given them by God.

Jesus continues: *"It is not so among you, but whoever wishes to become great among you shall be your servant, and whoever wishes to be first among you shall be your slave."* Jesus is explaining to the disciples that both they and the Gentiles have it all wrong. Their selfish motives had inverted and perverted the only real way of obtaining greatness.

When Jesus says, *"and whoever wishes to be first among you shall be your slave,"* He is speaking to their unmortified ambition. "It's one thing to have a will to be great or even first in the kingdom of heaven when, in fact, you also have a willingness to become the servant and the slave of all," Jesus says. "However, it's quite another thing to love the first place among all the citizens in the kingdom of heaven because you desire to lord it over them all."

Now Jesus proceeds to give them the two crucial points. Point one comes in these words:

> Whoever wishes to become great among you shall be your servant.

The greatness is, of course, from God's point of view. John MacArthur explains this:

> [Jesus]...was speaking of an entirely different kind of greatness than the sort James and John were seeking and that the world promotes. This kind of greatness is pleasing to God because it is humble and self-giving rather than proud and self-serving. The way to the world's greatness is through pleasing Him and serving others in His name. In God's eyes, the one who is great is the one who is a willing servant.[3]

Notice this same humble, non-dictatorial spirit in the apostle Paul. Paul reminds the Thessalonians that he and his co-workers in the gospel *"did not seek glory from men, either from you or from others, even though as apostles of Christ we might have asserted our authority"* (I Thess. 2:6). Again, when writing to Philemon and urging him to forgive his runaway slave Onesimus and receive him back as a brother, Paul entreats his friend and says, *"though I have enough confidence in Christ to order you [to do] that which is proper, yet for love's sake, I rather appeal [to you]."*

A "servant" is one who has laid aside *his rights* and who *executes the commands of another*. In our Lord's day, this term described a person who held the lowest position of hired labor at that time, much like house-cleaner.

The second point Jesus makes here in Matt. 20:20-28 is found in these words:

Whoever wishes to be first among you shall be your slave.

Listen to a few definitions of the word translated "slave" from the Greek lexicons: *One who gives himself up to another's will; One devoted to another, to the disregard of his own interests; One who is in a permanent relation of servitude to another, with his will being altogether consumed in the will of another.*

The voluntary humiliation of one's self, to the lowest position among the saints, lies at the very heart of what our Lord is teaching here. If you want to be considered "great" by God, if you want to please Him more than please man, you will, like our Lord, become a servant. Christian man, if you want to be a "great" spiritual leader to your wife, *you will become her servant.* It's just that simple.

> *Have this attitude in yourselves which was also in Christ Jesus, who, although He existed in the form of God, did not regard equality with God a thing to be grasped, but emptied Himself, taking the form of a bond-servant* (Phil. 2:5-7).

This emulation of the "attitude" or "mind" of Christ is the very point Jesus emphasizes as He concludes this lesson to His self-serving disciples: "Just as" Jesus says. "Just as" what? *"Just as the Son of Man did not come to be served, but to serve, and to give His life a ransom for many"* (Matt. 20:28). Jesus is saying: "Follow my example. I did not come seeking a position. I did not come so that others could meet my needs, but so that I could meet theirs." If anyone had the right to *demand* the service of others, He did. But rather than insisting on *His right to be served,* He *gave His life in service to others.* That's the kind of leadership God is looking for. This is the kind of leader you must be to your wife—*a servant leader.*

Wayne Mack has captured the heart of this passage quite well:

> According to this passage, *a leader is first and foremost a servant*. His concern is not for himself; his concern is not to give orders, to boss other people around, to have his own way. His concern is to meet the needs of others. Indeed, if the best interests of others are not on his heart, if he is not willing to sacrifice himself—his personal needs, wants, desires, aspirations, time, money—if the needs of others are not more important than his own, he is not qualified to lead[4] [*emphasis added*].

This same servant-leader concept can be seen elsewhere in the New Testament (cf. 1 Pet. 5:3; 1 Thes. 2:5-11). In the thirteenth chapter of John, Christ can be seen "taking on the form of a servant" as he washes the disciples' feet.

> *And so when He had washed their feet, and taken His garments, and reclined [at the table] again, He said to them, "Do you know what I have done to you? You call Me Teacher and Lord; and you are right, for [so] I am. If I then, the Lord and the Teacher, washed your feet, you also ought to wash one another's feet. For I gave you an example that you also should do as I did to you. Truly, truly, I say to you, a slave is not greater than his master; neither [is] one who is sent greater than the one who sent him. If you know these things, you are blessed if you do them"* (Jn. 13:12-17).

How to Become a Servant to Your Wife

Now that you understand the necessity of serving (ministering to) your wife, let's look at some of the specific ways you can become more of a servant-leader.

1. Make a list of the ways that you've abused your authority over your wife. Here are a few common ones to get you started:

• By asking her to do things that are sinful.
• By asking her to do things that violate her conscience.
• By prohibiting her from doing things out of selfishness rather

than out of love.

- By being unreasonable and then hiding behind your headship ("I don't have to explain myself because I'm the head of this household").
- By making decisions without getting her input.
- By not allowing her to appeal your decisions.
- By asking her to do things without showing consideration of her weaknesses.
- By not treating her as a weaker vessel (fragile vase).
- By giving her an inordinate number of directives and prohibitions.
- By barking out orders instead of using gentle entreaties.
- By using harsh or condescending forms of communication.
- By using critical and haranguing rebukes when she does something wrong rather than comforting her and encouraging her to change in loving ways.
- By being physically abusive to her.
- By not seeking the assistance of outside counsel about unresolved conflicts, and forbidding your wife to do so.

2. Ask her forgiveness for the specific ways you've lorded your authority over her and for not having a servant's heart. Remember to use the format discussed in Chapter Four:
First: Acknowledge that you have sinned against her.
Second: Identify your specific sin by its biblical name.
Third: Acknowledge the harm your offense caused her.
Fourth: Identify an alternative biblical behavior to demonstrate repentance.
Fifth: Ask her for forgiveness.

3. Regularly pray for her and for your attitude toward her, asking God to give you the wisdom and humility to be a servant.

- Pray for her salvation (if she's not a believer).
- Pray for her health and safety.

- Pray for her spiritual growth.
- Pray for her to be obedience-oriented rather than feelings-oriented.
- Pray for her to be discerning.
- Pray that she will be protected from bad influences and that she will be a godly influence on others.
- Pray that she will be a godly mother to your children.
- Pray that she would develop specific character traits that are consistent with the character of Christ.
- Pray that God will give her the grace to increasingly become a Proverbs 31 and a Titus 2 woman.
- Ask her regularly for additional items for prayer that she may have.

4. Make it your goal to help her achieve her God-honoring goals. Become excited about helping her be successful. Ask your wife for her goals and how you can help her achieve them. Ascertain and list those goals, and then seek to assist your wife in meeting them, by the grace of God.

5. Look for opportunities to minister to her in other ways. Invest your time, effort, thought and money in ministering to her; discover what her needs are and use your resources to meet them.

6. Assist her in fulfilling her chores and other responsibilities.

> Some husbands think that there is something unmasculine about doing the dishes, cleaning the house, taking care of the children, or going shopping...[They] will not lift a finger to do anything they consider to be women's work. He can be in a room where the baby begins to cry, and the wife can be at the other end of the house, but the husband will not find out why the baby is crying. Instead, he calls, "Jane, the baby is crying. Come here and do something about it." And she has to drop what she is doing and come all the way to where he is.[5]

This kind of husband does not understand true biblical leadership.

7. Learn to esteem her more highly than you esteem yourself.

- Look for those virtuous qualities in her that you are most in need of yourself, and seek her help in acquiring them.
- When making a decision, consider how that decision will affect you own interests *and* hers.
- Commend her for those qualities that are biblically worthy of praise. Remind yourself of them frequently.
- Guard your heart from developing a pattern of critical, condemnatory, accusatory, judgmental thoughts about her. Such thoughts make it very difficult for you (if not impossible) to esteem her better than yourself.

As this chapter comes to a close, I'd like to tie these two working definitions of spiritual leadership together, showing you how they relate to one another. Perhaps you wondered, as you were reading about your responsibility to be a manager (definition #1), "How am I ever going to get my wife to come under my authority? How can I bring and keep her under my 'control?'" The answer to that often-asked question is found in definition #2: You control her by *being a servant to her*; by *loving her the way Christ loves the church*. That is really the best way to motivate her to be submissive to you. As you model being a servant (as you fill out that uniform) she will, in all likelihood, increasingly find it easier to submit to your authority. She will, like the church does to Christ, love you because you first loved her.

Specific Ways I Can Serve My Wife

1. Assist her with some of her chores.

2. Assist her with some of her other responsibilities.

3.

4.

5.

6.

7.

8.

9.

10.

Add to this list further examples of how you can serve your wife...

Notes

[1]Jay E. Adams, *Christian Living in the Home,* (Phillipsburg, New Jersey: Presbyterian and Reformed Publishing Co., 1972), pp. 95-96.

[2]Ibid. p. 91.

[3]John F. MacArthur, *The McArthur New Testament Commentary, Matthew 16-23* (Chicago: Moody Press, 1988), p. 24.

[4]Mack, *Strengthening Your Marriage,* p. 27.

[5]Mack, p. 34.

Chapter 14

Hang in There

Have you ever felt that your marriage was like a box in which you were trapped, and that that box was getting smaller and smaller with every passing day? Did you ever wonder whether or not that box was going to get so tight that it would suffocate or crush you? I have met many who have felt that way. It is for them that this chapter is written. Of course, you'll profit by reading this chapter even if the box that God has you in right now doesn't relate to your marriage. You also will benefit from this chapter if you're ever tempted to throw in the towel on trying to make your marriage work, so please stay with me for the final few pages.

Putting two sinners together in the close proximity of a marital relationship can, at times, produce a lot of pressure. How have you handled that pressure?

Here you are in a box. You're cramped, you're uncomfortable, you're becoming increasingly more frustrated with each passing hour. You want the pressure you're feeling to be lifted so that you can have some relief. You want God to get you out of the box for good! The Bible has some very important things to say to you about that box.

> *No temptation has overtaken you but such as is common to man; and God is faithful, who will not allow you to be tempted beyond what you are able, but with the temptation will provide the way of escape also, that you may be able to endure it* (1 Cor. 10:13).

The first thing God wants you to know is that you're not the only one who has ever been encased in this kind of box. The trouble you're in isn't new, it's "common to man." That is, although it may have a few unique components, it is, nonetheless, a kind of trouble that has encased or imprisoned many others before you. Indeed, even as you read this, there are others (yes, even other Christians) who are basically in the same box as you, right now.

Another thing God tells you in this verse about your box is that He has limited the trouble you're in, and He's done that in two very important ways. This divine promise, however, only applies to Christians. That is, those who by faith, are depending only on the redemptive work of Christ on the cross for their salvation.[1] For them, God has limited the *scope* and *duration* of their trouble.

God's faithfulness to you means, first of all that, He *"will not allow you to be tempted beyond what you are able."* That is, He will not allow the temptation to become so difficult that you will not be *able* to deal with it biblically. In other words, He will not let your box become so small that it will crush or smother you!

Secondly, God's faithful promise to you is, that as a Christian, your trial will come to an end. He will "provide the way of escape ...that you may be able to endure it." God promises that some day, some way, your trial will end; that He's going to let you out of the box.[2] He doesn't tell you *how*, or *when*, only *that* He will do it.

The "box" you are in:

Limited in Duration

Limited in Scope

Sooner or later, God is going to let you out of the box. He may provide your way of escape by sending a bulldozer crashing through the wall. He may push a button which will silently trigger a trap door in the floor of the box. He may send a giant can-opener to tear off the top of the box and throw a ladder down for you to climb out. Perhaps He will send an army of angels to march around the perimeter of your box, and after a shout, the walls will come crashing down like the walls of Jericho. He may simply snap His fingers and the entire box will disappear.

The question I want to ask you as you contemplate your box is this: "What are you doing while you're in there?" While you're waiting for God to get you out, are you cooperating with His plan or, like so many, have you impatiently pulled out your pocket knife in an attempt to tunnel your way out of the box, before God, through righteous means, extricates you in His own way?

Because I have tried to address in this book every New Testament passage that contains a specific command to the husband, I am also going to include in this chapter an explanation of 1 Corinthians 7:11b: *"The husband should not send his wife away."*

You, Christian husband, should not send away (divorce) your wife, even if she is an unbeliever: *"If any brother has a wife who is an unbeliever, and she consents to live with him, let him not send her away"* (1 Cor. 7:12)[3]. The debate over divorce and remarriage still goes on to this day. Often it produces more heat than light. But one thing that almost all agree upon, is that marriage is a very difficult thing to dissolve.

Nothing short of marital infidelity or desertion by an unbelieving spouse constitutes a biblical (i.e., non-sinful) divorce.[4] Even if you're married to a woman who does not profess to be a Christian, as long as she is pleased to live with you, you must "hang in there" and try to make the marriage work.

In all of my 13 years as a professional marriage counselor, I've never seen an unbiblical divorce cause less pain and suffering than it would have taken to "fix" the marriage. To be sure, it's difficult to stick it out. It requires much endurance and lots of hard work. But as hard as it is to stay married, it's much harder to pursue a sinful divorce because *"The way of the unfaithful* ('transgressors' KJV) *is hard"* (Prov. 13:15 NKJV.).

When counseling a person who's even thinking about initiating an unbiblical divorce, I usually ask him or her two questions.[5]

The *first* question goes like this: *Do you want God's best?* Most people answer "Of course!," but have never stopped to consider that their self-centered, rebellious action of initiating a divorce is not only a serious sin against Almighty God, but it's one that will have a profoundly injurious impact on their future life and happiness. Sin causes both temporal and eternal misery. Grace is not, as many suppose, sin without consequence. You shouldn't expect God to bless your disobedience by removing all of the natural (and supernatural) consequences of your sin. It doesn't matter how miserable you think you are in your current circumstances, if you pursue an unbiblical divorce you will, in the long run, be even more miserable than you are now, though you *may* experience some momentary relief from your suffering. Remember though the warning of Galatians 6:7: "*Do not be deceived, God is not mocked; for whatever a man sows, this he will also reap.*"

The other question I like to ask those who want to unnecessarily give up on their marriage is, "*Are you willing to demonstrate to God and the whole world that you have a hard heart?*" Most Christians understand the clear implications of that question. Jesus, when being questioned by the Pharisees concerning regulations of divorce, demonstrated that the covenant of marriage was not such an easy contract to get out of as some of them had believed.

> And [some] Pharisees came to Him, testing Him, and saying, "Is it lawful [for a man] to divorce his wife for any cause at all?" And He answered and said, "Have you not read, that He who created [them] from the beginning made them male and female, and said, 'For this cause a man shall leave his father and mother, and shall cleave to his wife; and the two shall become one flesh'? Consequently they are no longer two, but one flesh. What therefore God has joined together, let no man separate." They said to Him, "Why then did Moses command to give her a certificate of divorce and send [her] away?" He said to them, "Because of your hardness of heart, Moses permitted you to divorce your wives; but from the beginning it has not been this way.

And I say to you, whoever divorces his wife, except for im-
morality, and marries another woman commits adultery"
(Matt. 19:3-9).

When a Christian initiates an unbiblical divorce, it's *always* because he's hardened his heart against God.

Some time ago, I was in my office trying to convince a woman that she didn't have biblical grounds to divorce her husband. No matter how hard I tried to get her to look at what the Scriptures teach, she would not be persuaded. As I began pressing home the Scriptures, trying to convict her with them (*"all Scripture is inspired by God and profitable for...conviction"*...2 Tim 3:16), she seemed to be impervious to them. Although I was throwing everything in the Book at her, she seemed impenetrable; I couldn't get the truth of God's Word around the road blocks she had apparently set up in her heart. Finally, she tried to justify her sinful plans by saying, "You don't know my heart, only God does, and He understands." To which I responded, "You're right about that! God does know your heart and He understands that it's *hard*!"

Now, at this point, you as a man might say: "I know that it would be a sin, but I believe that God will forgive me if I divorce my wife."

Not so fast! Let's think this through for a moment. Suppose you were the president of a bank and I walked into your office one day with a somber look on my face.

"Do you remember when your bank was robbed three weeks ago?," I ask.

"I certainly do," you reply with a suspicious tone in your voice and look in your eye.

"Well, I don't know how to say this exactly but...Well, uh, I'm here to confess to the crime and beg you to forgive me. I'm *really, really* sorry. Look, I know I don't deserve it, but do you think you could find it in your heart to forgive me? Please!"

"I see. Well, where's the money you stole?"

"Money?"

"Yeah, I want my money back."

"But I came to ask you to *forgive me*. I really don't want to return the money. Can't you forgive me and forget about the money?"

"Of course not, you've got to be willing to make restitution before I can even consider forgiving you."

Do you see now, how foolish it is for you to expect God to forgive your sinful divorce without your first being willing to repent and (if possible) reconcile with your wife?

"But if I stay married to that woman I'll go crazy!"

You're more likely to "go crazy" by stepping out of God's revealed will than you are by obeying His Word and suffering for righteousness. Removing yourself from the place where the Word of God say's you belong is a serious thing: *"Like a bird that wanders from her nest, So is a man who wanders from his home"* (Prov. 27:8). It's his self-centeredness and discontentment that causes a man to forsake his wife and family, separate himself from them, seek his own desire, and look for greener pastures elsewhere (cf. Prov. 18:1).

I have counseled many Christian men on the other side of such a sinful divorce who were unwilling to reconcile with the wife they dumped before they entered a subsequent marriage. Yet, I can not recall even one, who when all things are considered, is better off now than he would have been had he been willing to hang in there, endure the pain involved with straightening out his life, and reconciling his marriage.

Recently, a man who was estranged from his wife came to me for counseling from another church in the area. I asked him why he was coming to *me* rather than the counselor at his evangelical church. His answer made me angry.

"That counselor," he said, "told me that a good divorce is better than a bad marriage."

The problem is that many Christians are unwilling to suffer for righteousness. They seemed to have forgotten, if they ever knew it in the first place, that part of the package that comes when you are enrolled in biblical Christianity is that God calls you to *suffer* (Matt. 5:10-12; 16:24; 2 Tim. 3:12; 1 Peter 2:19-25). Sometimes that suffering comes in the form of having to endure a difficult marriage. Unless and until God provides a biblical window through which you may exit (i.e., your wife's sexual infidelity or desertion) you'd better plan on being there for the long haul.

Endurance is another one of those biblical concepts that has somehow eluded many Christians today. Suffering and endurance go hand and hand in the Bible. An important element of endurance is the ability to weather a trial without resorting to sinful means of deliverance (Cf. 1 Sam. 24:1ff). That is, when God puts you in a box, if you have endurance, you will not take out your sinful little pocket knife and try to extricate yourself in ways that dishonor God. Rather you'll "hang in there" until God provides you with a God-honoring way to get out of the box. In relation to a difficult marriage, this usually involves learning how to make the marriage work. To get started, you must first get the beam out of your own eye (Matt. 7:5) by working hard at becoming a biblically complete husband.

One other element of endurance I'd like to mention has to do with the way you *perceive* the trial; how you view being in the box. An enduring person has the ability to keep a biblical perspective about his troubles. He or she does this by refusing to magnify a tolerable trial so that it appears intolerable and unbearable.

> "For consider Him who has endured such hostility by sinners against Himself, so that you may not grow weary and lose heart. You have not yet resisted to the point of shedding blood in your striving against sin" (Heb. 12:3-4).

In all likelihood, the difficulties you're going through and that tempt you to throw in the towel on your marriage are not nearly as intolerable as you've imagined. Sure they're painful, but you must be careful not to feel a flesh wound as though it were a knife through the heart. You will also do well to consider that God may be using the trials of your marriage to chastise and sanctify you for your own good and for His glory. He wants to produce in you the fruit of righteousness that tastes like peace.

> *...you have forgotten the exhortation which is addressed to you as sons, "My son, do not regard lightly the discipline of the Lord, Nor faint when you are reproved by Him; For those whom the Lord loves He disciplines, And He scourges every son whom He receives." It is for discipline that you endure; God deals with you as with sons; for what son is there whom [his] father does not discipline? But if you are without discipline, of which all have become partakers, then you are illegitimate children and not sons. Furthermore, we had earthly fathers to discipline us, and we respected them; shall we not much rather be subject to the Father of spirits, and live? For they disciplined us for* a short time as seemed best to them, *but He [disciplines us] for [our] good, that we may share His holiness. All discipline for the moment seems not to be joyful, but sorrowful; yet to those who have been trained by it, afterwards it yields the peaceful fruit of righteousness* (Heb. 12:5-11).

Take heed that you don't think like Cain, who foolishly complained that his punishment was too great to bear (Gen. 4:13). The truth is, you're still not getting all that you deserve for your sins! Christ has taken that punishment upon Himself. If you are enduring chastisement, you are doing so for your own benefit and for God's glory. Consider also that if God is indeed using your marriage to discipline you, what good would it be to run away? God will only come after you and discipline you even more severely—probably with an even bigger (and more painful) paddle. If you divorce your wife unbiblically and marry another, you will not only be committing adultery, but you will be setting yourself up for God to continue the discipline process in the next marriage. Believe me and believe the Bible: It's just not worth it. Unless you truly have biblical grounds of divorce, it's much easier to endure whatever it takes to repair this marriage than to run away from it and to start all over again.

If a fresh start is what you want, why not *start* being the kind of husband that the Bible requires of you? If, indeed, you are a Christian, then you can learn to do *anything* that the Bible requires. You *can* learn how to live with your wife "in an understanding way." You *can* learn how to love your wife "as Christ loves the church", giving Himself up for her and bearing with her sin (cf. Lk. 9:41; Rom. 5:8). You *can* learn how to love her with the same intensity that you love yourself. You *can* learn how to replace any bitterness in you heart towards her with the kindness, tenderness, and forgiveness of Christ. You *can* learn how to show her honor as a "weaker vessel". You *can* learn how to "sanctify" and "cleanse" her by washing her "with the water of the Word." You *can* learn how to improve your sex life and stop defrauding her (and yourself) in this area. You *can* learn how to be the spiritual leader and manager of your home that God wants you to be. And if you do, sooner or later you'll have the kind of marriage that's not only very satisfying to you, but one that is also pleasing and glorifying to the Lord; that truly demonstrates to all the spectacular, loving relationship that exists between Christ and His church.

As this book comes to an end, I'd like you to take a moment to use a bit of sanctified imagination. Imagine what it will be like when, by God's grace, you can present both to your own self and to Christ Himself (in heaven), your wife *"in all her glory, having no spot or wrinkle or any such thing"* (Eph. 5:27b) because she is *"holy and blameless"* (Eph. 5:27c). May God bless you as you endeavor to become, by the power of the Holy Spirit and with the unfailing assistance of the Scriptures, a more *complete* husband.

Notes

[1]If you are uncertain about what this means or about whether or not you are truly a Christian, if you've, not yet done so (this is your final reminder), please take a moment to read appendix A "How Do I Get Saved."

[2]Even those Christians who are suffering with incurable or terminal illnesses have hope that someday God will let them out of the box of their fleshly tent (their physical body) and deliver them into the freedom (cf. Rom. 8:18-22) of their heavenly home ("a building from God, a house not made with hands, eternal in the heavens;" Cf. 1 Cor. 5:1-4).

[3]From a two part cassette series entitled, "How to Live with an Unbelieving Spouse".

[4]Although all divorce is the result of sin, not all divorces are sinful. For a more complete explanation of the traditional Protestant view of divorce see *Marriage Divorce and Remarriage in the Bible*, by Jay Adams (Grand Rapids: Zondervan, 1980).

[5]Ever since I can remember more professing Christian woman initiate unbiblical divorces than do professing Christian men. This is a sobering reality. Don't think, "It will never happen to me and my wife." Marriage is a precious thing and should be treated with care.

Appendix A:
How Can I be Saved?

Throughout this book, reference is made to the fact that a man cannot be the kind of husband God requires apart from the enabling power of the Holy Spirit. You may find yourself asking the question, "How does this happen? How does a person receive the power necessary to live a life that is pleasing to God?" This appendix is intended to answer that question

The Spirit of God indwells only those who, because of His grace, have put their faith in the substitutionary death of the Lord Jesus Christ. They are saved by grace through faith.

All of the verses listed in this appendix are found in the New Testament. Listen to them for a moment:

> *For by grace you have been saved through faith; and that not of yourselves, it is the gift of God; not as a result of works, that no one should boast (Eph. 2:8-9).*

> *Jesus answered and said to him, "Truly, truly, I say to you, unless one is born again, he cannot see the kingdom of God" (John 3:3).*

God says that our sin has separated us from Him. God is both holy and just. His holiness disposes Him to hate sin. His justice requires Him to punish sin. The wages or punishment of sin is *death* (Rom. 6:23). For God to overlook sin without requiring the appropriate punishment would violate His justice.

Therefore, just as through one man sin entered into the world, and death through sin, and so death spread to all men, because all sinned (Rom. 5:12).

For the wages of sin is death, but the free gift of God is eternal life in Christ Jesus our Lord (Rom. 6:23).

It is written, "YOU SHALL BE HOLY, FOR I AM HOLY" (1 Pet. 1:16).

Try looking at it this way: Would you consider a judge to be just if, out of partiality to a convicted murderer, he sentenced him to only 30 days in jail rather than the minimum sentence required by law? Should such an unjust judge be allowed to sit on the bench? How about God? Would God, "the Judge of all the earth," be just *not* to punish sinners who transgress His law? Of course not! For God to let sinful men and women off the hook without demanding that they pay at least the minimum penalty for their crimes would render Him unjust. The minimum sentence for sin according to the Bible is death. Simply put then: God *must* punish sin because His justice requires Him to do so.

"And inasmuch as it is appointed for men to die once and after this comes judgment" (Heb. 9:27).

The Lord knows how to rescue the godly from temptation, and to keep the unrighteous under punishment for the day of judgment (1 Pet. 2:9).

And I saw a great white throne and Him who sat upon it, from whose presence earth and heaven fled away, and no place was found for them. And I saw the dead, the great and the small, standing before the throne, and books were opened; and another book was opened, which is the book of life; and the dead were judged from the things which were written in the books, according to their deeds. And the sea gave up the dead which were in it, and death and Hades

gave up the dead which were in them; and they were judged,
every one of them according to their deeds. And death and
Hades were thrown into the lake of fire. This is the second
death, the lake of fire (Rom. 20:11-14).

On the other hand, God is loving and merciful. He *"is not*
willing that any should perish but that all should come to repen-
tance" (2 Peter 3:9 *NKJV*). So how can God forgive sinners in love
and mercy, when His justice requires Him to punish them for
their sins? The answer is to *find a substitute!*

> *Men of Israel, listen to these words: Jesus the Nazarene, a*
> *man attested to you by God with miracles and wonders and*
> *signs which God performed through Him in your midst,*
> *just as you yourselves know—this Man, delivered up by the*
> *predetermined plan and foreknowledge of God, you nailed*
> *to a cross by the hands of godless men and put Him to death.*
> *And God raised Him up again, putting an end to the agony*
> *of death, since it was impossible for Him to be held in*
> *its power (Acts 2:22-24).*

> *Christ died for our sins, according to the Scriptures*
> (1 Cor. 15:3).

If God could find someone who was willing to pay the price
for the penalty of sin and who did not have to die for his own sin,
then He could punish the substitute in place of the sinner. But
who is without sin? Only God. So God, in His love and mercy,
took upon Himself the form of a man in the person of Jesus Christ
(Phil. 2:7), lived a sinless life, and then died on the cross as a substitute for sinners who were incapable of redeeming themselves.
Then, after He was buried, He rose from the dead, and in so doing demonstrated His power over death.

> *For Christ also died for sins once for all, the just for the un-*
> *just, in order that He might bring us to God, having been put*
> *to death in the flesh, but made alive in the spirit (1 Pet. 3:18).*

This same resurrection power is available to those who truly believe this Gospel of God's grace. For those who believe, it is power not only over death, but also over sin--the very sin that enslaves us, and that Christ died to save us from. You see, it's only when a person becomes a Christian that the Holy Spirit indwells him, giving him the power to change and to obey God.

Have you become a Christian? What keeps you from doing so? Listen again to the good news which is proclaimed to you and to everyone who hears it:

> *If you confess with your mouth Jesus as Lord, and you believe in your heart that God raised Him from the dead, you shall be saved; for with the heart man believes, resulting in righteousness, and with the mouth he confesses, resulting in salvation. For "WHOEVER WILL CALL UPON THE NAME OF THE LORD WILL BE SAVED" (Rom. 10:9-10, 13).*

> *For God so loved the world, that He gave His only begotten Son, that whoever believes in Him shall not perish, but have eternal life...He who believes in the Son has eternal life; but he who does not obey the Son shall not see life, but the wrath of God abides on him" (John 3:16, 36).*

Appendix B:
Guidelines for Asking Questions of Your Wife

Someone has said that questions are to communication as food is to eating. If, as we have learned, revelation is a prerequisite to relationships, then it follows that questions are an indispensable tool for experiencing one flesh intimacy. In other words, the more skill you have in asking questions, the more you will be able to "draw out" (Prov. 20:5) of your wife the information you need to understand her, and the more you will be able to experience the joys of marital intimacy. The guidelines presented in this appendix, if followed, will help you fine tune your questioning skills, without coming across like an interrogator.

1. Avoid asking "why" questions. Avoid asking "why" questions when looking for data. Jesus never asked a "why" question when seeking information. He used "why" questions to convict people of their sin. "Why" questions tend to put people on the defensive and make it easy for them to respond with justifications and excuses, rather than *reasons*. Questions that begin with "what" and "how" are usually more effective for securing thoughts and motives ("*What* went through your mind when I ignored you at the party?" or "*What* were you expecting from me when I hurt your feelings?" or "*What* did you want from me that I didn't give you, when you became frustrated with me?" or "*How* did you feel when I forgot to call you like I promised?").

2. Learn to create new questions which flow out of your wife's answers to your standard "stock" questions. Do you know how to ask questions both *extensively* (covering broad general categories) and *intensively* (zeroing in on the specific information that you're seeking)? Every husband should have a set of basic "stock" questions (like those suggested at the end of Chapter Two) to draw out of his wife the information he needs to live with her in an understanding way. But sometimes these questions are not sufficient to get all the pertinent information. He must learn how to "fine tune" his questioning skills. He must develop additional, more specific interrogatives based on the information that she's revealing as a result of his asking the "stock" questions.

Suppose, for example, a husband asks his wife, "What is your opinion about my buying a new set of golf clubs?" Then, she responds with, "It doesn't really matter because, based on our past discussions about your golf, I don't think you're likely to consider my opinion before you make your decision." What does he say next? Many husbands would immediately become defensive and say something cutting in response. Few would respond in sincerity by asking another question to understand her perspective. Here are a couple of examples of follow-up questions to this dilemma: "Sweetheart, what have I done that leads you to believe that I make decisions about my golf without considering your opinion?" or "Honey, you make it sound as though I routinely make decisions about my golf without considering your opinion; I'm not aware of doing that, can you help me to see where you're coming from?"

3. Be careful not to interrupt her before she's finished answering. In Chapter Four, I warned you about the danger of interrupting your wife to give her your opinion before she was finished expressing herself thoroughly. Here, I'd only like to add that you must be sure when questioning her that she has enough time to adequately answer each question before you move on to the next one.

4. Be careful not to use "yes or no" type questions when the information you're seeking is more detailed than yes or no. Sometimes "yes or no" type questions are necessary. They help save valuable time by quickly ruling out superfluous information that is not germane to the issues at hand. Understanding your wife, however, (her thoughts, feelings, motives, desires, concerns, anxieties, plans, etc.) usually involves asking questions that allow the expression of a much greater amount of data than a simple yes or no. Keep in mind that one of your goals is to have her reveal to you that highly specific and sometimes very complex information (the thoughts and motives of her heart) which you as her husband need, in order to minister to her effectively. Such information can't be thoroughly expressed with the words yes and no. Of course a "yes or no" type question can be worded in such a way that it presumes a more thorough answer than simply "yes" or "no":

- Can you think of any additional ways in which you would like me to commend and praise and compliment you?
- Do I ever embarrass or offend you by the manner or frequency with which I commend and praise and compliment you?

5. Be a learner and a servant. You are to be a *loving leader*, not a *dictator*. The wording of your questions should not be harsh, but gentle and respectful, more like a physician trying to assist his patient, than a Gestapo interrogator trying to intimidate his subject. Remember that you're a student, trying to learn as much as you can about your wife. Here are a few examples of questions that communicate a learner/servant attitude.

- Have I done anything that has helped lead you to worry (or whatever else it is, with which she is struggling)?
- What can I do to make it easier for you not to worry in the future?
- If, in the future, I perceive that you're worrying, what's the best way for me to bring that to your attention?

- Of all the ways I demonstrate my love to you, which ones are the most meaningful?
- In what other way(s) would you like for me to demonstrate my love for you? Can you help me to understand why these things are so meaningful to you?
- Are you pleased with the way in which I express my affection to you privately and publicly? Can you think of any other ways in which you would like me to express my affection? Can you think of any ways that I embarrass or offend you by my expressions of affection?
- What can I do as your husband that would make your life more fulfilling?

Appendix C:
Common Ways in Which Husbands
Sin Against Their Wives[*]

The following checklist will help you identify some of the ways you have sinned against your wife and family. Although not exhaustive, this list represents some of the more common areas of sinful behavior and neglect among Christian husbands. The wording is already in the second person ("you" rather than the third person "her" or " my wife") to facilitate confessing your sins directly to her later on. As you prayerfully read over each item, put a check next to those offenses which you believe are applicable to you. Fill in any blank spaces with more precise information. Confess each transgression to God and then prepare your heart to confess them, when appropriate, to your wife.

Remember, the more specific you can be, the more your wife will realize the degree to which you're serious about changing and the extent to which you are cognizant of how your sins have hurt her. This should make it easier for her to truly forgive you. Also, the more specifically you can identify your bad habits, the easier it will be for you, by God's grace, to change. Don't forget to add to the list any additional offenses which are not mentioned specifically on the list. When you are finished, look back over the checked items for specific patterns of behavior (common denominators) which may indicate a particular life-dominating sin (such as selfishness, anger, irresponsibility, lack of self control, etc.).

- ❏ I've not been a good example of a Christian to my family.
- ❏ I don't have a consistent personal devotional life (Bible reading and prayer).
- ❏ I'm inconsistent with church attendance.
- ❏ I don't lead family devotions regularly.
- ❏ I'm not as involved in Christian ministry as I should be.
- ❏ I've been bitter and unforgiving toward you.
- ❏ I don't reveal my heart to you as much as I should, especially in the area of _____.
- ❏ I've not cultivated your friendship (companionship) enough.
- ❏ I have a closer relationship (I am more "one flesh") with _____ in some ways than I do (than I am) with you.
- ❏ I fail to realize why _____ is so important to you.
- ❏ I don't ask for your advice or opinion as often as I should.
- ❏ I don't show enough concern for your interest in _____.
- ❏ I don't give you enough assistance with _____.
- ❏ I've taken your love for granted by _____.
- ❏ I've neglected your desire/need for _____.
- ❏ I do not show you my love in the tangible ways that I know please you, such as _____ and _____.
- ❏ I've not nourished you or cherished you as the Bible commands me to.
- ❏ I've been hypocritical with you in regards to _____.
- ❏ I'm still too dependent on my parents for _____.
- ❏ I become irritable with you about _____.
- ❏ I've been lazy in doing yard work or odd jobs around the house.
- ❏ I've been lazy in _____.
- ❏ I've been selfish sexually by _____.
- ❏ I expect you too often to drop what you are doing and give me attention.
- ❏ I become irritated when you're not ready to leave on time, but expect you to be patient when I'm not ready on time.
- ❏ I've unreasonable expectations, such as _____.
- ❏ I don't give you enough candy, flowers, gifts and surprises.

- ❑ I don't keep my _____ neat and orderly.
- ❑ I don't express myself clearly and thoroughly.
- ❑ I interrupt you when you are talking.
- ❑ I'm inattentive to you.
- ❑ My attention often wanders when you're talking to me.
- ❑ I'm often too preoccupied with _____.
- ❑ I'm too harsh with you.
- ❑ I'm impatient with you, especially when _____.
- ❑ I raise my voice rather than responding to you softly and graciously.
- ❑ I use biting sarcasm when I talk to you.
- ❑ I respond to you before I understand what you're really saying.
- ❑ I rebuke you publicly rather than trying to lovingly correct you in private.
- ❑ I judge your thoughts and motives without knowing them.
- ❑ I don't cover in love (or overlook) many things that you do which irritate me.
- ❑ I don't put the best possible interpretation on the things that you do, but tend to be critical and even suspicious of you at times.
- ❑ I lecture and criticize you when you do something wrong rather than comforting and encouraging you to change lovingly.
- ❑ I use manipulation and intimidation to win arguments rather than trying to resolve conflicts biblically.
- ❑ I say and do things that are vindictive in nature such as _____.
- ❑ I don't treat you as though you were a weaker vessel (a fragile vase).
- ❑ I don't show you enough respect, especially by _____.
- ❑ I don't show you enough affection in our home.
- ❑ I don't show you enough affection in public.
- ❑ I'm usually affectionate to you only before I desire to have sexual relations with you.
- ❑ I don't make it a point to spend time every day having significant communication with you.

❑ I spend too much time away from home.
❑ I'm slow to offer you help with the housework and dishes.
❑ I haven't helped enough with _____.
❑ I initiate plans without your input.
❑ I make plans without consulting God through prayer and the Word.
❑ I tease you too much in front of others.
❑ I leave food, clothing and other apparel lying around the house.
❑ I selfishly play music too loudly.
❑ I haven't been exercising leadership in our family in that I _____.
❑ I murmur and complain about _____.
❑ I haven't taken you out to dinner or shopping or _____ often enough.
❑ I'm too critical of your family.
❑ I haven't made enough effort to get along with your family.
❑ I don't invest enough time in trying to advance my career.
❑ I invest too much time in trying to advance my career.
❑ I'm not as thankful as I should be for all of God's mercy and blessings.
❑ I'm selfish when it comes to offering you help but often expect you to help me whenever I need it.
❑ I give into depression rather than trying to overcome it.
❑ I haven't been very sensitive to your problems, moods and feelings.
❑ I haven't been as sympathetic as I should have been to your _____.
❑ I seldom express my appreciation for you or compliment you.
❑ I spend too much money on _____.
❑ I'm too stingy with my money in that I _____.
❑ I don't try hard enough to find things for us to do together.
❑ I don't kiss you when we meet or depart from one another.
❑ I've shown too much interest in other women by _____.
❑ I've said unkind things to you.

❑ I've said unkind things about you.

❑ I've not been totally truthful with you about _____.

❑ I use profanity.

❑ I call you names.

❑ I drink too much.

❑ I smoke too much.

❑ I watch too much television.

❑ I'm too legalistic, especially in the area of _____.

❑ I make excuses or simply refuse when you ask me to do certain things that you want me to do, such as _____.

❑ I have bad manners especially when it comes to _____.

❑ I criticize you for your faults and mistakes rather than investing the time and effort to lovingly help you correct them.

❑ I'm difficult to satisfy when it comes to _____.

❑ I get angry or withdraw or _____ when a problem or disagreement arises between us.

❑ I'm too ambitious about _____.

❑ I've blamed you for my mistakes such as _____.

❑ I don't seek help when I have a serious problem.

❑ I don't often admit when I am wrong.

❑ I'm too distrustful of you especially when it comes to _____.

❑ I become angry when you do not discipline the children as I think you should.

❑ I haven't invested enough time discussing with you our philosophy of raising children.

❑ I haven't cultivated the children's friendship enough.

❑ I'm inconsistent when it comes to disciplining the children.

❑ I don't teach God's Word or discuss it with you and the children as often as I should.

❑ I don't spend enough time playing with the children.

❑ I've not helped you enough with the children's _____.

❑ I make promises to you and the children and do not follow through with them.

❑ I don't give enough of my _____ to the Church.

❑ I've not invested enough time cultivating biblical friendships for us to enjoy.

❑ I become angry or resentful when you are too tired to have sexual relations.

❑ I lose my temper or _____ when you or the children do not treat me with respect.

❑ I'm not easily entreated by you or the children.

❑ I'm sometimes unreasonable with you or the children.

❑ I get my feelings hurt too easily (I'm too sensitive because of my pride).

❑ I haven't done enough reading that would help me to improve as a husband, father and Christian.

❑ I compare you and the children unfavorably with others.

❑ I take things too seriously and often make mountains out of molehills such as _____ and _____.

❑ I have not worked hard enough at correcting my annoying habits and mannerisms, especially _____ and _____.

❑ I do not take care of myself physically as I should.

❑ I often neglect your sexual needs and am mostly concerned about my own.

❑ I don't express my love to you when I do not feel love for you.

❑ I don't try to overcome your evil (sin) with good.

❑ I don't protect you enough, especially in the area of _____.

❑ I don't always remember birthdays, anniversaries and other special occasions.

❑ I sometimes resist or resent your helpful suggestions.

❑ I haven't handled our family finances biblically, especially in the _____ area.

❑ I don't run errands gladly.

❑ I'm too selfish with your time.

❑ I allow my anxiety over your safety and the safety of the children to selfishly prohibit you from doing certain things such as _____.

❑ I haven't made ministering to you and the children enough of a priority.

List Additional Areas of Failure.

Notes

* The material in this appendix has been adapted and expanded from *A Homework Manual for Biblical Living*, volume 2, by Wayne A. Mack (Phillipsburg, NJ: P&R Publishing), "Sample Log List: Husband and Father," pp 35-38. Used by permission.

Appendix D:
Specific Ways to Demonstrate Love to Your Wife*

Are you loving your wife the way she wants to be loved or are you only loving her the way you want to love her? (Are you loving her from *her* frame of reference or from *yours*?) Evaluate the various ways that you express love to her. Put an X in the box next to the expression you're already showing regularly. Place a check in the box next to the expressions that you believe your wife would most appreciate. You may even want to go over the list with your wife asking her to check those expressions that would be most meaningful to her.

❑ Telling her frequently that you love her.

❑ Giving her a regular amount of "mad" money to spend in any way that she chooses.

❑ Leading the family in Bible study and prayer regularly.

❑ Greeting her with a smile, a hug, a kiss and an expression of your love for her, such as, "I sure missed you today."

❑ Smiling and being cheerful when you come home from work.

❑ Giving her a lingering kiss.

❑ Helping her with some of her domestic duties without her having to ask.

❑ Taking care of the children for at least three hours each week so that she has free time to do some of the things that she enjoys.

❑ Taking her out on a dinner date or some other fun activity of her choosing once each week.

❑ Doing the "fix-it" jobs she wants done around the house (within two weeks of her request).

❑ Expressing your love for her with physical affection throughout the day: Holding her hand; Sitting close to her; Inviting
her to sit on your lap; Putting your arm around her; Patting
her on her _____; Touching her; Rubbing her; Playing with
her_____; Caressing her _____; Other:_____.

❑ Talking with her about her concerns willingly without belittling her for having those concerns.

❑ Looking at her with an adoring expression.

❑ Preparing yourself adequately for sexual relations with her
(bathing, brushing you teeth, clipping your fingernails, shav-
ing, putting on after-shave lotion or cologne, dimming the
lights, locking the door, etc.)

❑ Being gentle and tender and holding her before and after sexual
relations.

❑ Spending enough time in foreplay before sexual relations.

❑ Expressing your love for her in writing with notes and cards
and letters.

❑ Telling her frequently and specifically what it is that you love,
appreciate and cherish about her.

❑ Commending her in specific terms for the various way she
pleases you and helps you through life (commending her to
others as well).

❑ Learn to be attentive to and recognize her spoken and implied
desires. Fulfill as many of them as you can.

❑ Being a good example of a Christian for her and the children
to model.

❑ Talking favorably about her to the children when she can hear
you and when she can't.

❑ Maintaining your own walk with the Lord through confession
and repentance of sin, Bible study, prayer, church attendance
and fellowship with God's people.

❑ Handling your affairs decently and in order.

❑ Scheduling and using your time wisely and according to biblical priority.

❑ Making plans carefully and prayerfully (with input from her and the Bible).

❑ Asking her advice when you have problems to solve or decisions to make.

❑ Following her advice unless to do so would violate biblical principles.

❑ Developing a biblically positive and realistic outlook on life.

❑ Acknowledging that there are some specific areas or ways in which you need to improve.

❑ Admitting when you're wrong and asking for her forgiveness.

❑ Asking for her prayers and assistance in overcoming sinful habits.

❑ Disciplining yourself to change those areas in your life that are out of harmony with Scripture.

❑ Disciplining yourself to change some of those areas in your life that irritate your wife even though they are not out of harmony with Scripture.

❑ Talking to her about your insights, interesting experiences in life, reading materials, etc.

❑ Teaching her how to do things that you enjoy (fly fishing, hunting, golf, tennis, etc.).

❑ Cultivating an interest in something that she enjoys but you find uninteresting or boring (like art or history or gardening or classical music).

❑ Developing an interest in some new hobby or activity together.

❑ Fix her a bubble bath while you prepare a romantic dinner.

❑ Planning a mini-honeymoon or getaway where the two of you can do whatever you want to do.

❑ Noticing her appearance (dress, hair, make-up, etc.) and complimenting her for it before she asks you to.

❑ Going shopping with her (with a cheerful attitude about it).

❑ Relating your experiences at while you were at work or while you were apart.

❑ Reminiscing about the early days of your marriage.

❑ Expressing appreciation for her family and relatives.

❑ Taking her out for breakfast, coffee, or dessert.

❑ Agreeing with her about buying a new item of clothing or some other item she wants.

❑ Buying her a piece of clothing or some other personal item she has mentioned.

❑ Thanking her when she supports your decisions and cooperates enthusiastically.

❑ Initiating sexual relations and seeking to be especially solicitous of her desires.

❑ Thanking her for having sexual relations--especially when she's sought to please you.

❑ Buying or making gifts for her.

❑ Remembering anniversaries and other occasions that are important to her.

❑ Cheerfully watching the television program that she wants to watch.

❑ Cheerfully going to the restaurant or activity that she wants to go to.

❑ Being cooperative, appreciative and responsive when she shows you affection.

❑ Being cooperative and responsive when she wants to have sexual relations.

❑ Running errands gladly.

❑ Pampering her and making a fuss over her.

❑ Being willing to see things from her point of view.

❑ Speaking the truth to her in love (do not withhold relevant information).

❑ Giving her your undivided attention when she wants to talk.

❑ Making sure that you have time regularly (daily) to be alone with her for uninterrupted and undistracted communication.

❑ Responding graciously (rather than impatiently or angrily) when she makes suggestions or discusses problems.

❑ Forgiving her quickly and thoroughly when she sins against you.

❑ Cheerfully staying up past your bedtime to solve a problem or share her burdens.

- ❏ Getting up in the middle of the night to take care of the children so that she may continue to sleep.
- ❏ Holding her close while expressing your love to her tangibly and vocally especially when she's hurt, discouraged, weary or burdened.
- ❏ Planning vacations and trips with her.
- ❏ Helping her yourself occasionally, rather than instructing the children to "Help Mommy."
- ❏ Telling her a good joke or something interesting you've learned.
- ❏ Joining with her in a team ministry at church.
- ❏ Doing a Bible study or research project together.
- ❏ Reading a book together (don't start with this one unless you're real courageous).
- ❏ Handling your money wisely.
- ❏ Establishing a family budget (with her input).
- ❏ Helping her deal with some spiritual difficulty (fear, resentment, anger, distrust, etc.).
- ❏ Keeping yourself attractive, clean and physically fit.
- ❏ Being a cooperative and helpful co-host when entertaining guests at your home.
- ❏ Asking her to pray with you (and for you) about certain things.
- ❏ Spending time with the children in play, communication, and study.
- ❏ Avoiding public disagreements with her.
- ❏ Cooperating with her in establishing and fulfilling personal and family goals.
- ❏ Being available and eager to fulfill her desires wherever and whenever possible and proper.
- ❏ Beginning each day with cheerfulness and tangible expressions of affection.
- ❏ Remembering to tell her when you must work late.
- ❏ Refusing to work late on a regular basis.
- ❏ Being punctual for meals and appointments.
- ❏ Calling her whenever you're going to be more than just a few minutes late.

❑ Taking care of yard work properly and of your own initiative.

❑ Helping the children with their homework.

❑ Refusing to compare her unfavorably with other people.

❑ Keeping your priorities biblically in line (as a rule, your personal walk with God, your wife, and your children, should come before your ministry and vocational responsibilities).

❑ Looking for things that the two of you may do together.

❑ Being willing to stay home with her rather than going out with her (or vice-versa).

❑ Being polite, mannerly and courteous with her.

❑ Refusing to be overly dependent on your family or friends.

❑ Developing mutual friends.

❑ Giving her the freedom to and assistance in developing healthy personal friendships.

❑ Developing a set of accountability people (men and women) that may be called by either one of you if conflicts arise between you that cannot be readily solved by yourselves.

❑ Providing some form of adequate health, life and disability insurance.

❑ Letting her sleep in once in a while by getting the children breakfast and, if possible, off to school.

❑ Putting the children to bed at night.

❑ Giving in to her desires more frequently and allowing her to have her own way, unless to do so would be sinful.

❑ Showing patience and forbearance with her by not nit-picking , fault-finding, and giving the impression that she has to be perfect before you'll love her.

❑ Developing a more lighthearted or sober-minded attitude (depending on which she believes is more necessary).

❑ Allowing her to purchase some things for the house that you believe are really not necessary (but within reason).

❑ Waiting a while longer (for her to ask) before giving her advice (rather than giving it at the first indication of a problem).

Notes

* The material in this appendix has been adapted and expanded from *A Homework Manual for Biblical Living*, volume 2, by Wayne A. Mack (Phillipsburg, NJ: P&R Publishing), "Ways a Husband May Express Love to His Wife," pp 42-45. Used by permission.

Appendix E:
How to Instruct Your Wife in Gentleness*

> *And the Lord's bond-servant must not be quarrelsome, but be kind to all, able to teach, patient when wronged,* **with gentleness correcting those who are in opposition,** *if perhaps God may grant them repentance leading to the knowledge of the truth (emphasis added, 2 Tim. 2: 24-25).*

If pastors must use gentleness when they instruct their sheep, how much more must husbands use gentleness when dealing with their wives? If opposition in the church requires meekness, opposition in the home requires much meekness. Here are some guidelines to keep in mind when you, as a husband, find yourself having to instruct (or correct) your wife.

1. Be mindful of your wife's understanding and capacity for learning what you're trying to teach her. Where she has a limited or diminished capacity to comprehend the data, give her "precept upon precept; line upon line; here a little, [and] there a little" (Isa. 28:10 *KJV*). A little at once, given often (perhaps every day), may in time help her to grasp the totality of what you're trying to teach her. As you desire that she increase her knowledge of what you're teaching her, she probably desires for you to increase your love for her. Remember, the first attribute of love is *patience!* (1 Cor. 13:5).

2. Instruct (and correct) her privately (Mat. 18:15 *KJV*), so

that you don't broadcast her ignorance (and sins) to others. Such discretion should demonstrate your love toward her and foster "one flesh" intimacy.

3. Encourage her to be present (when appropriate) as you are instructing other family members.

4. Consider the time you choose to instruct her. There is, "A time to be silent, and a time to speak" (Eccl. 3:7). You may have to wait until she can give you her undivided attention, or is more rested, or less preoccupied with other responsibilities, or will be less likely to react sinfully to your instructions. The more you can reduce the likelihood that she'll respond wrongly to you, the less likely you are to be harsh. But remember, you can't allow a sinful response on her part to justify harshness on your part.

5. If you become exasperated or sinfully angry in your attempts to teach her, acknowledge that to her without accusing (or shifting the blame to) her. Ask her forgiveness if necessary.

To paraphrase William Gouge:

> How cruel is a husband who harshly and roughly instructs his wife, as if to violently thrust into her head deep mysteries which she, for various reasons, may not yet be able to understand; and then become so angry with her, for her lack of comprehension, that he proclaims her ignorance before the children, friends and strangers.

Notes

*The idea for this appendix came as I was reading a portion of William Gouge's book, *Of Domestic Duties*. Under the treatise "Duties of Husbands," he has a section sub-titled, "of an husband's manner of instructing his wife," (pp. 372-373) which I have again taken the liberty herein to amend and expand.

Appendix F:
Guidelines for Giving Directives to Your Wife[1]

Wives, [be subject] to your own husbands, as to the Lord. For the husband is the head of the wife, as Christ also is the head of the church, He Himself [being] the Savior of the body (Eph. 5:22-23).

The directives which you, as a husband, give to your wife, whether they are *affirmative* (requesting her to do something) or *negative* (forbidding her to do something) must all be governed by Christ-like sacrificial love and the Scriptures. You should, therefore, give careful consideration to the matter and manner with which you direct your wife. You may not arbitrarily order her around according to your own fancy, whims or selfish desires. You are to be a loving leader, not a tyrannical, domineering, dictatorial bully. Just as pastors are to lead their flock without "lording it over" them (1 Pet. 5:3), so you must not abuse your authority as the head (or manager) of your home. You've been appointed to your position by God. The authority that you have been given is to be administered in accordance with His means and objectives and for His glory.

In light of this, the directives you give to your wife ought to be regulated by the following biblical guidelines:

1. The directives and prohibitions you give to your wife must be lawful according to the Bible. God doesn't give anyone *absolute* authority: not the President, not the Supreme Court, not the

Governor, not the Pastor, not the Father and not the husband! God does not give anyone the authority to command or influence someone to sin. All such efforts are to be disobeyed by the Christian (cf. Acts 4:19, 5:29). Your wife is not required by God to obey any directives that clearly violate Scripture. You may not give her any directives that would cause her to sin (cf. 1 Tim 5:22; 3 Jn. vvs. 9-11).

On the other hand, you should discourage your wife from doing anything that the Bible clearly teaches is a sin. To overlook this would be for you to neglect being her spiritual leader. You may not be able to prevent her from sinning, but you certainly must use all biblically-based resources at your disposal to keep her from sinning.

2. The directives you give to your wife must be lawful in her eyes. You may not rightly ask your wife to do something that she believes is sin. To do so would be to cause her to violate her conscience and tempt her to sin (cf. Rom. 14:14-23; 1 Cor. 8:1-13). If your wife has a scruple about something, your loving response should be to patiently go with her to the Scriptures to determine whether or not her scruple is biblically valid. If so, you must change your instructions. If not, you should encourage her to continued Bible study until she has effectively reprogrammed her conscience biblically. For her to obey you, believing that such obedience to you *may* be disobedience toward God, would, in fact, be a sin for her (Rom. 14:23). The "holding principle," found in this passage teaches us never to act until we're sure that what we're about to do is not sin.[2]

3. The prohibitions you give to your wife should be those things that you can demonstrate biblically are unlawful to her. It is your job to explain the biblical basis of your prohibition.

"Honey, I would love for you to be able to buy that new widget, but we simply don't have the money in our budget this month.

I believe it would be poor stewardship for us to get it now—especially since we really don't need it. Perhaps in a month or two we'll be able to get it without going into debt. We agreed, based on Proverbs 22:7, that we would not purchase anything that we really didn't need if we had to go into debt to do so. Of course, if the Lord provides us with some extra money before then, I'd be happy for you to have it sooner."

If you can't give her a biblical reason why she should not do something, you'd do well to examine your motives and rethink your objection in light of Scripture.

4. The directives and prohibitions you give to your wife must be rightly based on biblical precepts or principles (they must be biblically reasonable). You may not pressure your wife to do things that are not based on biblical precept. Any instructions you give her may be rightly questioned by her for their biblical basis. For example, suppose you wasted several hours watching TV one evening. Then, later on, you and your wife are lying in bed and you remember that you've forgotten to take out the trash. If you were to then say to her, "Honey, tomorrow is garbage pick up, would you please take the trash down to the curb," she may rightly ask you for a Scriptural explanation for such a request. You may not then simply say to her, "It's not a sin for you to take out the garbage, therefore you must do what I ask since the Scriptures require a wife to submit to her husband."

On the other hand, it would be biblically reasonable (Jas. 3:17) for you to ask your wife to prepare a special meal for the company you'll be entertaining next week, because such a request is in keeping with her being a "worker at home" (Tt. 2:5) as well as with the biblical command to "be hospitable to one another without grudging" (1 Pet. 4:9). You really should not be giving your wife directives without giving thought to whether or not they have some basis in Scripture. You may not simply say, when she asks for an explanation for your request, "because I'm the head of this family and what I say goes!" Do not underestimate the importance of investing the time and effort necessary to explain the biblical (and logical) reasons for your request. If your wife is a Christian, it will be easier for her to obey you once she's convinced she's also obeying and pleasing God by fulfilling your biblically-based request.

Many men prohibit their wives from doing things out of their own selfish desires or fears. It's good to always examine your motives before you say "no" to your wife. For you to prohibit her from driving to the store because you selfishly want her to stay home to wait on you is wrong. However, asking her to wait until tomorrow because the roads are too hazardous due to inclement weather, is quite different. In the former case, you really have no biblical basis to prohibit her. In the latter, you're protecting her body (the temple of the Holy Spirit) from danger in accordance with 1 Corinthians 3:16-17.

5. The directives and prohibitions you give to your wife which are not clearly delineated in the Scripture should be appealable. You must entertain your wife's appeals for any requests you make of her which are not specifically directed (commanded) by Scripture. "But the wisdom from above is first pure, then peaceable, gentle, *reasonable* ["easy to be entreated" *KJV*], full of mercy and good fruits, unwavering, without hypocrisy" (Jas. 3:17). If you've not yet taken the time to explain the biblical basis for your request, you must do so when she makes an appeal. You might also encourage her to make the arguments for her appeals on the basis of Scripture.

There may be times when your wife can give you a better biblical argument for doing something than you can give her for not doing it. You may have overlooked some relevant data which she has access to and you don't, or some portion of Scripture that is more relevant than the one(s) on which you base your prohibition. Consider all her appeals to those prohibitions that aren't unmistakably spelled out in Scripture.

6. The directives and prohibitions you give to your wife should be in keeping with her abilities and in consideration of her weaknesses. You ought not ask your wife to do anything which is beyond her strength and ability (i.e., "Before I get home from work this evening I'd like you to move the baby grand piano from the living room to the master bedroom."). God does not require of us things which are not able to handle (cf. 1 Cor. 10:13). Neither should you request of her anything that she, because of her weaknesses, cannot do. (i.e., Pressuring her to fix your supper when she has a 103 degree temperature).

7. The directives you give to your wife should be honoring to her as a weaker vessel. The things you ask your wife to do should not be unbecoming of her (1 Cor. 13:5). You're to treat her as if she were a *weaker vessel* (fragile vase) rather than a stronger one (an old, beat-up, tin garbage can). You are to treat her as *special* rather than *common*—with honor rather than dishonor. You should not ask her to do things that are indecent or shameful—things that would disgrace her. King Ahashuerus dishonored Queen Vashti when he, under the influence of alcohol, requested that she show off her beauty before his guests. His request was unseemly and dishonoring to his wife. Consider whether or not your request befits the honor with which your wife is due before you entreat her.

8. Guard your heart against peremptory pride which interprets virtually all appeals or challenges as personal attacks against one's authority.
"How dare you challenge my authority."
"But Honey, I was only trying to give you my opinion."
"No you're not, you're being unsubmissive!"
I've seen this over and over in my counseling ministry. I've fought it in my own heart regularly. According to one dictionary definition, the word "peremptory" means: *Putting an end to all debate or action; Not allowing contradiction or refusal; Imperative;*

Having the nature of or expressing a command; Urgent; Offensively self-assured; Dictatorial.[3]

Before you give directives to your wife, examine your heart for such prideful motives. Remember, the position you've been given as the spiritual leader of you're home is *delegated* authority. Are you certain that what you're asking her to do is something God would want her to do? Also remember that if your wife is truly challenging your authority, she's really challenging God's authority. You should be more grieved about her sin against God than you are angry at her sin against you.

9. The directives and prohibitions which you give to your wife should be infrequent. William Gouge likens authority to a sword, which will be blunted when used too frequently, and therefore fail to do its job when really needed.[4] A husband's sword is by his side, sharpened and polished, but it remains in its sheath, and will be taken out only when it is necessary to use it. He does not take it out to cut things that he can tear with his hands. Neither does he pull it out of its sheath and flash it around so that others will see how sharp it is and be excessively fearful of the one who wields it. Like a pastor who is "among" the sheep and uses his authority "over" them (Acts 20:28; 1 Thes. 5:12) *only when necessary*, so a husband should be by his wife's side, as a joint heir with her of the grace of life (1 Pet. 3:7). His authority should be used only when absolutely necessary. To do otherwise is to provoke your wife to anger and tempt her to disregard your directions.

10. The wording of your directives and prohibitions should be in the form of entreaties rather than commands. Notice how Paul words this request to his "beloved friend and fellow laborer" Philemon:

Therefore, though I have enough confidence in Christ to order you [to do] that which is proper, yet for love's sake I rather appeal [to you]—since I am such a person as Paul, the aged, and now also a prisoner of Christ Jesus—I appeal to you for my child, whom I have begotten in my imprisonment, Onesimus, who formerly was useless to you, but now is useful both to you and to me (Philem vvs. 7-9).

Following these guidelines will help you to be a spiritual leader who not only pleases God, but makes it easier for his wife to be biblically submissive to his leadership.

Notes

[1] The idea for this appendix came as I was reading a portion of William Gouge's book, *Of Domestic Duties* published in 1622. Under the treatise "Duties of Husbands," he has a section sub-titled, "Of an husbands manner of commanding his wife in any thing," (pp. 373-375) which I have taken the liberty herein to amend and expand.

[2] See *A Theology of Christian Counseling*, by Jay E. Adams, (Grand Rapids: Zondervan, 1986), p.31.

[3] *The American Heritage Dictionary of the English Language*, Third Edition, (Houghton and Mifflin Co., 1992).

[4] Gouge, p.378

Appendix G:
Things to Say to Defuse an Argument with Your Wife*

A gentile answer turns away wrath, but a harsh word stirs up anger (Prov. 15:1).

Listed below are some transition sentences that may help you when you're attempting to resolve conflicts with your wife. The list may be personalized according to the need of the moment. "Let no unwholesome word proceed from your mouth, but only such [a word] as is good for edification according to the need [of the moment] that it may give grace to those who hear" (Eph. 4:29).

- "I really appreciate your concern about this."
- "Thank you for being interested in this problem."
- "I'm glad you are concerned about this."
- "Am I hearing you correctly?"
- "Am I hearing you right? Is this what you are saying?"
- "Would you repeat that please?"
- "Could you repeat that in a different way?"
- "I see this is important to you; therefore, it is to me."
- "Let me think about that for a minute."
- "Thank you for taking time to share this with me."
- "Do you have any suggestions as to what I could do to improve in this area?"
- "Did I hear you say it upsets you when I _____.Thank you for telling me."

- "Are you saying that you want me to discuss these kinds of is-sues with you before I make a decision? (Be thankful!)
- "How could I do (have done) that differently?"
- "What, exactly, is it you see that I'm doing or saying wrong?"
- "I wasn't clearly seeing that."
- "Thank you for bringing that to my attention"
- "I'm glad you pointed that out to me."
- "When did that happen? I wasn't aware of that. (Be careful about
- the use of this statement; be sure that it is true before you use it!)
- "I see that's important to you, so I'll make it a point to be more aware of it in the future."

Notes

* The material in this appendix has been adapted from *Things To Say To Defuse An Argument*, a counseling handout from *Faith Baptist Counseling Ministries* in Lafayette, Indiana. Used by permission.

Appendix H:
Righteous Anger Vs. Sinful Anger

I'm indebted to David Powlison, of the Christian Counseling and Educational Foundation, who provided the idea for the following diagram. It is one of the best tools I know to help people determine whether or not their anger is sinful.

Righteous Anger	Sinful Anger
When God doesn't get what He wants. God's will is violated. Motivated by a sincere love for God.	When I don't get what I want. My will is violated. Motivated by a love of some idolatrous desire.
Christ is Lord of my life *Be angry, and do not sin.* Eph. 4:26	I am the lord of my life *What is the source of quarrels and conflicts among you? Is not the source your pleasures that wage war in your members?* Jas. 4:1

If your anger is due to your recognition that a holy God has been offended by another's behavior, that anger is righteous. In other words, if we are angry because God's *revealed* will (not His *decreed* will; for everything that happens has been foreordained by Him) is violated, our anger is righteous.

On the other hand, if your anger is the result of not having your personal desires met, that anger is likely to be sinful. For example, if we're angry because someone prevented us from having what we really wanted, our anger is sinful. Of course, it's possible to have both righteous anger and sinful anger residing in our hearts at the same time. In such cases, you would be wise not to respond to an offender until you are certain that you have purified your motives and can speak from a more righteous motive than a selfish one.

Appendix I:
Hints, Suggestions, and
Attitude Helpers About Sex*

1. Don't be intimidated if your wife initiates sex, for her pleasure or yours.
2. While you enjoy viewing her body, she may not care as much to see yours: talk to her about it.
3. When anticipating sexual relations, be mindful of the effects of: personal hygiene; scent (pleasant or unpleasant); room lighting (dark, full light, dim light, candle light)
4. In the areas where you don't know what your wife's preferences are, ask her. This is a tangible way to demonstrate the "other oriented" nature of biblical sexual relations.
5. Ask for her feedback when you touch her: what feels good, where to touch, rub, massage, fondle, and how gently or firmly to do so. On the other hand, communicate to her your feelings and preferences in these same areas.
6. Ask your wife how she wants you to dress, cut and wear your hair, preferences regarding facial hair, etc. While you may not be able or willing to accommodate her in all these areas, your willingness to listen and acquiesce where possible are tangible expressions of love.
7. Be creative in letting her know that out of all the women in the world you are delighted to have *her* for your wife, are thankful to be her husband, and that you desire to satisfy her romantic desires and sexual needs: a) leave a note under her pillow, on her desk, table, or wherever she will be sure to see it with expressions of love and gratitude for specific things she has done or for aspects of her character. b) call her during the

day to remind her that you love her and are thinking of her. c) remind her frequently of: your loyalty to her, that she's the only woman in your life, that you remember your wedding vows. d) give her plenty of non-sexual touching, such as hugging, pats, light kisses, back rubs and hand holding.

8. Communicate repeatedly and in very specific ways your susceptibility to visual sensual stimulation. When you're together, take opportunities to point out what stimulates you.

9. Have soft cotton cloths nearby during sexual relations to absorb any secretions and lubricants.

10. Understand and believe your wife when she tells you that she enjoys satisfying your sexual desires even when she is not interested in sex for herself. Don't push her to *desire* sex as frequently as you do: remember that her sexual appetite is probably, though not necessarily, not as strong as yours.

11. Don't be afraid to admit ignorance of the finer aspects of your wife's or your own anatomy. Be willing to investigate, whether by means of your wife's body, a book, or a doctor.

12. Focus on your walk with Christ, and you will find fulfillment in your role as husband and companion.

Notes

*I'm indebted to my dear friend Milton Hodges for his assistance with this material.

Appendix J:
Sorting Out Responsibilities*

A Plan for Promoting Unity in Marriage and Overcoming Marital Conflicts

Many times conflicts arise in marriage because there has been no clear delineation of responsibilities. Sometimes, when everything is *everybody's* responsibility, everything becomes *nobody's* responsibility. Then again, there are times when everybody is trying to do the same thing, and confusion, frustration, bitterness, and competitiveness are the result. One person has one view of how or when something should be done; the other person has another; and neither is willing to yield. Or, one person always seems to do all of the yielding. This provides the soil in which sinful resentment and bitterness may develop.

Much of this conflict can be eliminated if clear lines of responsibility are delineated. The husband under God is the head or manager of the home (Eph. 5:22-27; 1 Tim. 3:4-5). He is the one who is financially responsible to lovingly and biblically guide the home. The buck stops with him.

However, he may decide to let his wife (his chief helper according to Gen. 2:18; Prov. 31: 10-31) take the leadership responsibility in certain areas. Indeed, he will be wise to do this because she most certainly has more gifts, abilities, insight and experience in some areas than he does. In other areas, he will be more gifted and capable than she, and there he should take the lead in making decisions.

The husband and wife should share insights and advice in every area, but someone ought to be given the responsibility of seeing that things get done. Look over the following list and decide who'll have the responsibility to plan and implement the different areas. Remember, some things are not right or wrong—just different ways of doing things, or different ways of looking at something. In areas which are not vitally important or clearly spelled out by the Scriptures, be willing to defer to the other person. Don't make mountains out of molehills! Don't make everything a major issue! Talk matters over, assign responsibilities, make decisions, support each other, and help carry out decisions.

This sorting out of responsibilities does not mean that a given area is one person's exclusive responsibility. It means that when a difference of opinion arises, one person has the authority to make the choice. Certainly, in most areas, a full and frank discussion will be conducted, all options and alternatives, pros and cons considered. However, when a conflict of opinion arises, someone must be allowed to make the decision, even if that decision is to wait until God brings the two of you into agreement: *"If a house is divided against itself, that house will not be able to stand"* (Mk 3:25, NASB).

In making a decision, make sure that you do not violate a biblical principle, seek the insight and opinion of your mate, ask God in prayer to guide you, believe that He will, consider and evaluate all options, and then, if you are the person who is responsible, make the decision. The other person should support the decision wholeheartedly and seek to make the decision a success unless it clearly violates biblical principle. Unity in marriage (Gen. 2:24) is tremendously important, and should be maintained carefully. Following this plan is one way of promoting this unity. However, it will only work if both people agree to abide by it.

This "sorting out of responsibilities" does not mean the husband relinquishes his biblical responsibility to be the loving leader of the family. It does mean that he recognizes that God has given his wife certain abilities and capacities which make her more competent in some areas than he is. Therefore, he delegates to her certain responsibilities which are in keeping with her resources.

All the while, he maintains veto power, but he'll not use it unless his wife's decisions clearly violate biblical principles. Notice the following relevant passages:

> *[Love] is not rude; it is not self seeking* (1Cor. 13:5, NIV).

> *Make my joy complete by being like-minded, having the same love, being one in spirit and purpose. Do nothing out of selfish ambition or vain conceit, but in humility consider others better than yourselves. Each of you should look not only to your own interests, but also to the interests of others* (Phil. 2:2-4, NIV).

> *Be devoted to one another in brotherly love. Honor one another above yourselves* (Rom. 12:10, NIV).

> *Live in harmony with one another. Don't be proud, but be willing to associate with people of low position. Do not be conceited (Rom. 12:16).*

> *You, my brothers, were called to be free. But do not use your freedom to indulge your sinful nature; rather serve one another in love* (Gal. 5:13, NIV).

> *If you keep on biting and devouring each other...you will be destroyed by each other"* (Gal. 5:15, NIV).

The following "Sorting Out Responsibilities" plan is offered as a means of actualizing these Bible admonitions. On the blank space following the descriptive phrase, indicate who will be mainly responsible for the area described:

1. Children:
Neatness_____ Rules and Regulations_____
Bedtimes_____ Activities_____
Discipline_____ Social Life (friends, dating)_____
Clothing_____ Allowances (money management)_____
Chores_____ Manners_____

School work_____ TV watching_____
Hygiene_____ Spiritual life_____
Other (   )_____ Other (   )_____
2. Money Management (establishing a budget)_____
3. Financing and Bookkeeping (bills, keeping records)_____
4. Money Raising_____
5. Purchasing Food and Household Goods_____
6. Menu Planning and Cooking (dietitian and chef)_____
7. Housecleaning_____
8. Spiritual Oversight (church selection, attendance, family goals, family devotions, etc.)_____
9. Family Activities (fun times, recreation, family projects, supervision of family nights)_____
10. Vacation Plans_____
11. Clothing Purchasing_____
12. Clothing Maintenance_____
13. Automobile (selection, maintenance, etc.)_____
14. Savings Account_____
15. Hospitality (friends in for dinner, etc.)_____
16. Investment_____
17. Real Estate Purchases (home selection, etc.)_____
18. Gift Planning and Purchasing_____
19. Memorabilia Keeping (family records, pictures, newspaper clippings, letters, etc.)_____
20. Family Photography_____
21. Special Events (birthdays, anniversaries, etc.)_____
22. Furniture (selection, purchases, and maintaining)_____
23. Time and Schedule Organizing_____
24. Travel (motels, maps, directions, etc.)_____
25. Retirement (plans and provisions)_____
26. Yard Work_____
27. Gardening_____
28. Family Health Services_____
29. Occupation and Career_____
Add any other responsibilities you can think of ...

Notes

*Mack, Wayne, *A Homework Manual for Biblical Living, Vol. #2*, (P & R Publishing, Co., Phillipsburg, New Jersey), pp. 29-32

About the Author

Lou Priolo is the Director of the Eastwood Counseling Ministry in Montgomery, Alabama. He is a graduate of Calvary Bible College and Liberty University. Lou has been a full-time biblical counselor and instructor for over fourteen years, and is a Fellow of the National Association of Nouthetic Counselors. He lives in Wetumpka, Alabama with his wife Kim and his daughter Sophia.